The First Grace

To Dad, Christmas 2019

I hope you find this interesting,
enjoyable, or flammable kindling.
You have done more to teach me
to think + to seek the truths of
what we are made, + to prize
the "first grace."

Love you +
merry christmas!

fr Pauly

The First Grace

Rediscovering the Natural Law in a Post-Christian World

Russell Hittinger

ISI BOOKS

WILMINGTON, DELAWARE

Hittinger, Russell, 1947–

    The first grace : rediscovering the natural law in a post-Christian
    world / Russell Hittinger. — Wilmington, Del. : ISI Books, 2007.

    p. ; cm.

    Originally published in 2003.
    Includes bibliographical references and index.
    ISBN-13: 978-1-933859-46-0 (alk. paper)

    1. Religion and law. 2. Natural law. 3. Natural theology. 4. Catholic
Church—Doctrines. 5. Natural law—Religious aspects—Catholic Church.

BL65.L33 H58 2007   2007930264
171/.2—dc22   0711

ISI Books
Intercollegiate Studies Institute
Post Office Box 4431
Wilmington, DE 19807-0431

Cover design by Sam Torode
Interior book design by Brooke D. Haas

Manufactured in the United States of America

This book is dedicated to MZH
and to FRH on the year of his graduation.

Contents

Acknowledgments

Thanks are due to my editor at ISI Books, Jeremy Beer, who discovered "the first grace" buried in the obscurity of a footnote and had the good sense to see that it is just the right title for the entire volume. I thank my colleagues in the Department of Philosophy and Religion at the University of Tulsa. It has been a privilege to hold a chair of Catholic Studies at a Presbyterian university teaching, for the most part, Baptist students. On another ecumenical note, I thank Richard John Neuhaus and the Institute for Religion and Public Life, which is the epitome of ecumenical and intra-religious dialogue in the United States. In the different colloquia and symposia sponsored by the institute, I learned how other faiths and denominations make sense of natural law. I am grateful to the Earhart Foundation and the William K. Warren Foundation, both of whom provided material and moral support over the several years that I labored on these essays.

Some of the chapters in this book have previously appeared, in revised form, in the *American Journal of Jurisprudence, Review of Politics, Revue Générale de Droit, Loyola Law Review, Crisis, First Things,* and the *George Washington University Law Review.* I thank these journals, as well as the American Maritain Association, the Wethersfield Institute, William B. Eerdmans Publishing

Company, Ignatius Press, and the Catholic University of America Press for granting me permission to reprint some of the material that appears here. The reader is directed to the Notes for full publication details.

Introduction

The title of this book is taken from the letter of a presbyter named Lucidus who recanted of certain doctrines condemned at the second Council of Arles (A.D. 473). Lucidus and others in southern Gaul taught that after the sin of Adam no work of human obedience could be united with divine grace, that human freedom was not weakened or distorted but totally extinguished, and that Christ did not incur death for all human beings. In the letter of retraction, the natural law is mentioned twice. The natural law is said to be the "first grace of God" *(per primam Dei gratiam)* before the coming of Christ *(in adventum Christi).*[1] Lucidus also affirmed that, according to Romans 2:15, the natural law is "written in every human heart."[2]

The point at issue for the thirty bishops at Arles was how the human creature is located in an order of divine providence. On the one hand, the bishops wanted to avoid the heresy of Pelagius, who held that man's natural gifts are sufficient for salvation—a position that makes the economy of divine law and revelation superfluous.

---

1. Denzinger-Hünermann, *Symboles et définitions de la foi catholique* (Paris: Les Éditions du Cerf, 1997), §336.
2. Ibid., §341.

Thus, Lucidus confessed that humans "were not set free from the original slavery except by the intercession of the sacred blood."[3] On the other hand, the bishops worried that an overly severe doctrine of predestination would imply that God removes some creatures from the gifts of providence, leaving the human race, as Rousseau would later say of the state of nature, as "if it had been left to itself."[4]

The quote from Rousseau indicates the theme of the subtitle of this collection. For, beginning with the state-of-nature scenarios imagined by Enlightenment philosophers, natural law came to mean the position of the human mind just insofar as it is left to itself, prior to authority and law. Natural law constitutes an authority-free zone. The influential jurisprudent H. L. A. Hart accurately summarized the post-Christian estate of natural law discourse:

> Natural Law has . . . not always been associated with belief in a Divine Governor or Lawgiver of the universe, and even where it has been, its characteristic tenets have not been logically dependent on that belief. Both the relevant sense of the word "natural," which enters into Natural Law, and its general outlook minimizing the difference . . . between prescriptive and descriptive laws, have their roots in Greek thought which was, for this purpose, quite secular. Indeed, the continued reassertion of some form of Natural Law doctrine is due in part to the fact that its appeal is independent of both divine and human authority, and to the fact that despite a terminology, and much metaphysics, which few could now accept, it contains certain elementary truths of importance for the understanding of both morality and law.[5]

3. Ibid.

4. Jean-Jacques Rousseau, *Discourse on the Origin of Inequality* (Indianapolis: Hackett, 1992), preface, 15.

5. H. L. A. Hart, *The Concept of Law* (Oxford: Oxford University Press, 1961), 183*f*.

For Hart, the "core of good sense in the doctrine of Natural Law" need not be entangled in "theocratic" premises. Rather, it is reducible to certain "truisms concerning human nature and the world in which men live, [and] as long as these hold good, there are certain rules of conduct which any social organization must contain if it is to be viable."[6] Reminiscent of Hobbes, Hart's natural law is neither a higher law nor a lower law. It represents those contingent but pervasive aspects of the human predicament which provide the background problems and motivations for positive law.

Hart's assertion that natural law has an "appeal" that is separable from the premises of either natural or revealed theology has its own appeal to many, if not most, contemporary proponents of natural law.[7] The leading American critic of legal positivism, Lon Fuller, who maintained a long-standing debate with Hart over the moral bases of law, certainly did not disagree with his foe on the need to avoid or suppress theological and metaphysical referents in understanding natural law. Fuller insisted that natural law is not a "higher law," but one "entirely terrestrial," and therefore ought not to be brought into the precincts of propositions about "God's commandments."[8] In his famous tract on the "higher law" background of American constitutional law, Edward S. Corwin presents as a "a quaint argument" Sir Edward Coke's oft-cited dictum in Calvin's Case: "The law of nature is that which God at the time of creation of the nature of man infused into his heart, for his preservation and direction; and this is *Lex aeterna*, the moral law, called also the law of nature. And by this law, written with the finger of God in the heart of man, were the

---

6. Ibid., 187–94.
7. Natural theology is the study of what can be affirmed or denied philosophically of a superior cause. This inquiry was traditionally distinguished not only from revealed theology, but also from the mythical theology of poets and the civil theology celebrated by municipal priests.
8. Lon L. Fuller, *The Morality of Law*, rev. ed. (New Haven, Conn.: Yale University Press, 1969), 96.

people of God a long time governed before the law was written by Moses. . . ."[9] Perhaps this would be of mere antiquarian interest were it not for the fact that Coke was trying to make the point that the legal universe neither begins nor ends with the command of the human sovereign. When he referred to the eternal law—to the same law that taught the Jewish people prior to Sinai—Coke did not think of himself as making an argument to authority, but clarifying and concentrating the minds of his colleagues about an authority already recognized by a legal culture tutored by common sense and the Scriptures. Such claims today are usually regarded as rhetoric that the moralist or jurisprudent need not, ought not, or cannot make in advancing an argument about the natural law.

The essays in this volume investigate problems that arise once natural law is understood as free-floating with regard to authority, whether human or divine. The first two chapters treat theoretical issues related to the definition of natural law, particularly in the area of theology, which is the historical matrix of natural law doctrines. In these chapters I point out that even contemporary Catholic thinkers who have no aversion to theology as such are reluctant to predicate "law" properly of natural law. For Mortimer Adler and Joseph Fuchs, to mention two examples, natural law is related to a superior cause, but not in the manner of legality. Natural law is neither a higher law nor, strictly speaking, any law at all. I test this position against the older tradition, chiefly (but not only) that of St. Thomas Aquinas, and then draw out some of the consequences for theology once one derogates from the idea that natural law is authentically a higher law. In chapters 3 through 8 I examine theoretical and practical problems that emerge when appeals are made to natural law for or against laws made by civil authority. Given the widespread demand today for

9. Edward S. Corwin, *The "Higher Law" Background of American Constitutional Law* (Ithaca, N.Y.: Cornell University Press, 1955), 45*f*.

justiciable natural or human rights—which is to say, their recognition by courts—the issue of authority often becomes an acute question. At one level, the questions are institutional in nature. Why, for example, should we believe that natural law is best discerned by courts in the context of litigation?

At another level, which is the deeper one, we find functional appeals to a higher law that turns out to be no higher law at all. While retaining the nimbus and residue of an older tradition that really did affirm an order of obligation prior to the positive law, contemporary appeals to natural law often subvert that order. In its most extreme (but not uncommon) form, political institutions are required to recognize and protect the immunity of individuals from *any* known source of obligation and authority. In the name of authority—the authority of some "higher law"—the individual comes to occupy an authority-free zone in the very midst of civil society.

Although the ecclesiastical and civil spheres are quite different, we should not be surprised that problems in the one look very much like problems in the other. Until recently, the "higher law" doctrine, as divinely grounded, has been accepted by both spheres. This surely was Sir Edward Coke's point. Unless we suppose that there is more than one natural law—one for magistrates and one for churchmen— there will be a strong supposition that what is good for the goose is good for the gander. There are no theological claims completely separate from propositions about what is good for human beings and about the moral norms regulating the choice of these goods. And though sometimes camouflaged, there are no secular claims completely separate from propositions about the ultimate ground of authority. Therefore, while we must respect the differences between church and state, between revealed theology and philosophy, and between the authority of sacred Scripture and that of a human constitution, we cannot fail to recognize that natural law discourse inexorably migrates back and forth. Each of these contrasting pairs is relational, and it is hardly possible to know very much about one without knowing something about the other. Even in our own time this has proved true on issues of human rights, religious liberty, abortion, marriage, and euthanasia.

How can we begin to situate such a protean family of doctrines as "natural law"? Yves Simon has usefully proposed that the theories and ideologies of natural law seek to discover or assert the "prior premises" of human law.[10] Simon further suggests that the answers to "what is prior" to human law tend to coalesce around three foci: order in nature, order in the human mind, and order in the divine mind. Thinkers who defined natural law in light of metaphysical premises much disparaged today—Augustine, Thomas Aquinas, Richard Hooker, even John Austin—also believed that natural law encompasses what is prior in things and what is prior in the human mind. St. Thomas, for example, argued that the human soul receives a knowledge of divine providence in a "general sort of way" by starting "from the things themselves in which the order of divine providence has already been established in detail."[11] From what is first in nature or first in the mind we can infer what is absolutely prior in the order of being. The great tradition of natural law allowed each of these foci to have its own salience, depending on the problem at hand.

We can appreciate why the first two foci have such appeal in our time. Unlike premodern thinkers, we find ourselves immersed in state-made law. The nation-states that emerged after the Napoleonic Wars have proved to have a prodigious capacity and enthusiasm for lawmaking, including constitutional, statutory, and, increasingly, ad-

10. Yves R. Simon, *Tradition of Natural Law*, ed. Vukan Kuic, intro. Russell Hittinger (New York: Fordham University Press, 1992 reprint; orig. 1965), 129.
11. *Summa contra gentiles*, III.81 [1].

ministrative law. As state law becomes more expansive and intricate, and as customary law gives way to legal artifice, the relation of law to a prior moral order becomes an issue of some importance. Generally, the thinkers of late antiquity and the Middle Ages took it for granted that jurisprudence falls under the genus of morals. They thus set out to understand how moral reasoning is set within a cosmological order that has legal properties. Where jurisprudence, however, is by default a positivist account of the powers of the state it becomes all the more necessary to focus narrowly on how to render state law permeable to moral premises. Cosmological inquiry will strike most thinkers, as Hart said, as "grandiose." Paradoxically, at the same time that moral argument is used to limit the law of the state, usually in favor of natural or human rights, the legal culture has the general expectation of what Laurence Friedman has called "total justice."[12] Private complaints and moral desiderata are not regarded as merely private but as things (torts, entitlements) about which the state must take an interest and provide remedies. The simultaneous quest for zones of immunity from law and for the removal of barriers to works of justice on the part of the state creates a potent environment for the moral evaluation and critique of positive law.

Although unhappiness with positive law is favorable to various species of natural law thinking, argument about what is "prior" in morals often proves frustrating, especially when the moral premises are no less disputed than the estate of the black-letter law. Academic and legal professionals, it must be admitted, are of the class least likely to achieve consensus about the morality prior to law. Typically, arguments are expected to obey the (self-imposed) norm of refraining from appeal to controversial conceptions of the human good. Premises or conclusions even remotely theological (natural or re-

12. Laurence Friedman, *Total Justice* (New York: Russell Sage Foundation, 1985).

vealed) are unacceptable for public purposes. On the assumption
that ordinary law ought to be guided by moral theory, the principle
of "equal protection" must apply not only to the positive law but also
to the moral theory that informs it. Moral theory then must pass the
test of being equally facilitative of the life plans and beliefs of everyone subject to the law. While this norm of public reason does not
necessarily reduce morality to convention, it does deploy a convention to limit and filter what can count as morals for public purposes.
In this political and cultural environment, natural law thinking slips
into formalisms that are not entirely false, but not entirely true. In
Ethics after Babel, Jeffrey Stout appends a lexicon of terminology used
by moral philosophers. Under "natural law," which includes "the
moral law" and "realm of values," the entry reads: "fancy names for
all the moral truths, known and unknown, that can be formulated
in all the possible moral vocabularies."[13] Stout's peevish entry has a
point. Almost everyone believes that there is order prior to human
law, and that therefore human law ought to be made, criticized, and
emended on the basis of morality.[14]

One may doubt that the narrowing of natural law inquiry to the
first two foci has made it easier to reach consensus about what is prior
to human law. What should not be in doubt is that the term "natural
law" historically arose in reference to the third of Simon's foci—
order in the divine mind. It is well known that for the ancient
Greeks *physis* and *nomos* are opposites. In a remarkable essay,
"The Concept of Natural Law in Greek Thought," Helmut Koester
has shown that the term "law of nature" occurs fewer than six times

---

13. Jeffrey Stout, *Ethics after Babel* (Boston: Beacon Press, 1988), 300*f*.
14. Ronald Dworkin can say that if "any theory which makes the content of law
    sometimes depend on the correct answer to some moral question is a natural
    law theory, then I am guilty of natural law." "Natural Law Revisited," 34
    University of Florida Law Review 165 (1982), 165.

in the Greek literature of the pre-Christian era. In the work of the Jewish philosopher and exegete Philo of Alexandria (c. 20 B.C.–A.D. 50), however, more than thirty occurrences of the term can be found.[15] As a term that meant something more than a comical union of opposites, or a merely metaphorical extension of concepts that properly reside elsewhere, natural law emerged as part of the repertoire of moral and legal thought once the Greek *logos*-metaphysics was appropriated by the biblical theology of a creating and lawgiving God. Order in things and in the human mind are not laws, but the effect of a law that is not a positive law.

Before the Council of Arles defined natural law as the "first grace," Augustine had spoken of the eternal law impressed in the soul *(lex aeterna, impressa nobis est)*.[16] The human soul is induced to share in the divine law, he explained, not by "locomotion but by a kind of impression...."[17] The human mind can rule and measure action insofar as it is first ruled and measured. Thomas's work diverged significantly from Augustine's account of illumination and created nature,[18] but it did not differ from Augustine's in its neo-Platonic motif of participation allowing natural law to be placed in the genus of law.

> [A]s rule and measure, law can be in a person in two ways: in one way, as in him that rules and measures; in another way, as in that which is ruled and measured, since a thing is ruled and measured insofar as it partakes of the rule or measure. Since all things subject to divine providence are ruled and measured by the eternal law ... it is evident that all things partake somewhat of the eternal law, insofar as from

---

15. Helmut Koester, "The Concept of Natural Law in Greek Thought" in *Religions in Antiquity,* ed. Jacob Neusner (Leiden: E. J. Brill, 1968), 534–35.
16. *De Lib Arbit*. 16.
17. *De Trin*. XIV.21.
18. Matthew Cuddeback, *Light and Form in St. Thomas Aquinas's Metaphysics of the Knower,* dissertation (Washington, D.C.: The Catholic University of America Press, 1998).

its being imprinted on them they derive their respective inclinations to their proper acts and ends. Now among all others the rational creature is subject to divine providence in the most excellent way, insofar as it partakes of a share of providence by being provident both for itself and for others. It has a share of the eternal reason because it has a natural inclination to its proper act and end, and this participation of the eternal law *[participatio legis aeternae]* in the rational creature is called the natural law. Hence, the Psalmist after saying, "Offer up the sacrifice of justice," as though someone asked what the works of justice are, adds: "Many say, Who showeth us good things?"[19] In answer to which question he says: "The light of Thy countenance, O Lord, is signed upon us," thus implying that the light of natural reason whereby we discern what is good and what is evil and which pertains to the natural law, is nothing else than an imprint on us of the divine light *[impressio luminis divini in nobis]*. It is evident that the natural law is nothing else than the rational creature's participation of the eternal law.[20]

On what basis does Thomas reach this definition? Given our ability to know at least some rudiments of the moral measures of action, we can reason from the effect in us to a superior cause. While the tutoring of divine revelation makes that inference easier and clearer, Thomas does not insist that it depends in principle on religious faith. For even religious faith cannot disclose, from the inside out, as it were, how God imparts the first rules and measures of conduct via his creative act. "We cannot know the things that are of God as they are in themselves," Thomas writes, but "according to Romans 1, they are made known to us in their effects: 'The invisible things of God are clearly seen, being understood by the things that are

---

19. Psalms 4:6.
20. *Summa theologiae* I-II, 91.2.

made.'"[21] By the same token, Thomas shows no interest in making this inference depend on a formal demonstration. To be sure, he argued that the existence of God can be affirmed by such a demonstration. Yet to my knowledge, he never argued that knowledge of a superior cause is exclusively the work of demonstration. That the moral order bespeaks a higher cause is derived, by most people, from philosophically untutored inferences from the things that are,[22] from tradition, and also, for Christians, from infused faith.

In answer to the objection that it is an unnecessary repetition to have two laws, one eternal the other natural, Thomas responds that "this argument would hold if the natural law were something diverse from the eternal law, whereas it is nothing but a participation thereof."[23] Law is denominated chiefly by the active principle, by what mind actually rules and measures. Here, Thomas closely follows Augustine. There are not four or five kinds of law, but only two.[24] Law that proceeds from the divine mind and law that proceeds from the human mind; as Augustine said, one is eternal and the other is temporal.[25] The natural law is called natural, first, because it is by

---

21. *S.t.* I-II, 93.2 ad 1, citing Rom 1:20.
22. *Scg* III.38.
23. He argues that natural law "endures without change owing to the unchangeableness of the divine reason, the author of nature." q. 97.1 ad 1.
24. For this careful, and indeed correct, reading of the enumeration of laws in S.t. I-II 91–93, I am indebted to Stephen Louis Brock, *The Legal Character of Natural Law According to St. Thomas Aquinas,* dissertation (Toronto: University of Toronto Press, 1988), ch. 2-C.
25. "[L]aw denotes a kind of plan *[ratio]* directing acts towards an end. Now wherever there are movers ordained to one another, the power of the second mover must be derived from the power of the first mover, since the second mover does not move except in so far as it is moved by the first. We observe the same in all those who govern, so that the plan of government is derived by secondary governors from the governor in chief. Thus, the plan of what is to be done in a state flows from the governor's command to his inferior administrators; and again in things of art the plan of whatever is to be done by art flows from the chief craftsman to the under-craftsmen who work with their hands. Since, then, the eternal law is the *ratio* of government in the supreme governor,

the natural power of reason that we partake of the law; second, by mode of promulgation the law is instilled or indicted in us "so as to be known naturally [*naturaliter*]."[26]

If we ask whether natural law is first in things or in the human mind, Thomas gives the surprising answer that, properly speaking, it is neither. The order of nature and the order of the mind are law abiding but are not laws. It is true that modern philosophy abandoned the metaphysics of participation, and thus wrestled with the problem of whether law belongs properly to physical states of affairs or mental constructs,[27] but it is entirely anachronistic to impose this dilemma on the older tradition. For his part, Thomas denies that natural law can be reduced to what is prior as order constituted in the human species.

> [J]ust as the acts of irrational creatures are directed by God, inasmuch as they belong to the species, so are man's actions directed by God, inasmuch as they belong to the individual [*ad individuum*]. Now, in so far as they are actions belonging to the species, actions of irrational creatures are directed by God by a certain natural inclination, which is consequent to the specific nature. Therefore in addition to this something must be given to man whereby he is directed in his personal actions [*in suis personalibus actibus*]. And this is what we call law.[28]

---

all the plans of government in the inferior governors must be derived from the eternal law. But these plans of inferior governors are laws other than the eternal law [*aliae leges praeter aeternam*]. Therefore, all laws, in so far as they participate in right reason are derived from the eternal law. On account of this, Augustine states in I *De Lib. Arbit.*: 'in temporal law there is nothing just and lawful, but what man has drawn from the eternal law.'" *S.t.* I-II, 93.3. See also, 91.3 sed contra.

26. *S.t.* I-II, 90.4 ad 1.

27. On the emergence of natural law as laws of nature, see Jane E. Ruby, "The Origins of Scientific 'Law,'" *Journal of the History of Ideas* 47 (1986): 341–59.

28. *Scg*, III.114 [1].

Natural law is not Rousseau's *la voix de la nature*,[29] nor Hobbes's "Lawes of Nature" that conserve "men in multitudes."[30] For Thomas, law is the directive of reason promulgated by a competent authority for the common good, and he held that natural law preeminently satisfies these criteria. But natural law is not order embedded in the species as though individuals are moved by a kind of physical necessity. Rather, it is the communication of moral necessities to a created intellect. In this respect, among others, Thomas differs from modern philosophers who speak of inclination as mere physical appetition that provides the material for instrumental reason—reason as the slave of the passions.

The Christian tradition, in which the concept of natural law flourished for more than a millennium, expressed its understanding of "prior law" in more than one philosophical and theological vocabulary. Prior to the Reformation, scholastic opinion differed not only on the principle of divine illumination of the created intellect (whether the natural law is a create or an increate light), but also on the question of whether law is chiefly the act of intellect or will. Protestant reformers continued these debates, but with somewhat less commitment to overarching metaphysical schemes. Though Protestants of the sixteenth century questioned more deeply than the scholastics the efficacy of natural law in the human mind, as well as its place in the economy of salvation, the definition of natural law as a higher law retained its vigor in Protestant thought. As Hooker maintained, the "voice of nature is but God's instrument." It is "by her from Him we receive whatsoever in such sort we learn."[31] The anthropocentric turn of Hobbes (order in the species), Grotius (order in moral powers), and later Rousseau (order in a hypothetical state

29. Rousseau, *Discourse on the Origin of Inequality*, preface, 13.
30. Thomas Hobbes, *Leviathan*, I.xv.
31. Richard Hooker, *Of the Laws of Ecclesiastical Polity*, I.8 [3].

of nature), did not convince many Christians that the first two foci of natural law should be detached from the legislative source of obligation.

The prominence of higher law thinking at the time of the American founding is too well known to warrant more than a brief comment. Whatever may have been Thomas Jefferson's theological convictions, he understood well enough that the "Laws of Nature" needed to be situated in reference to "Nature's God." Similarly, Alexander Hamilton asserted that the "Sacred Rights of Mankind are . . . written, as with a sunbeam, in the whole volume of human nature, by the hand of the Divinity itself, and can never be erased or obscured by mortal power."[32] From every American pulpit, and in every legislative assembly, the higher law was a familiar coin of discourse. Within a generation of the American founding, the higher law doctrine was prominent in the debate over slavery, especially after the Fugitive Slave Act (1850). Interestingly, most of the federal judges who believed that slavery violates natural law did not use the higher law doctrine as an excuse for usurping constitutional authority.[33]

In his dissenting opinion in *Scott v. Sandford* (1857), Justice McLean reminded the majority that the much-vexed jurisdictional question of congressional authority over the territories did not entitle the Court to claim interpretive authority over the natural law. Chief Justice Taney had contended in the majority opinion that the appeal of the Declaration of Independence to "Nature's God" should be interpreted in light of public opinion, thereby rendering the natural law inferior to human judgment. To the contrary, McLean responded, the slave "bears the impress of his Maker, and is amenable to the laws

32. *The Works of Alexander Hamilton,* H. Lodge edition (1904), 1 at 113.
33. Robert M. Cover, *Justice Accused: Antislavery and the Judicial Process* (New Haven, Conn.: Yale University Press, 1975).

of God and man; and he is destined to an endless existence."[34] Although the Constitution gives the Court no authority to change the positive law of the Constitution, by the same token it does not hand over the higher law to the Court's estimation of public opinion.

Writing shortly after the Civil War, Orestes Brownson could say that it was a remarkable achievement of the American polity to bring into existence a modern state that recognizes a "higher law" above itself. "This is our American boast"—one that is especially justified in contrast to the European states of that era. These states followed the Rousseauvian principle that society is *un droit sacré,* a holy right.[35] Americans, Brownson argued, refused to submit higher principles to lower powers. They resisted, then, the one extreme of making government an instrument of private interests, as well as the other extreme of making the state the exemplar and judge of moral and spiritual order. He was convinced that Americans had properly located the position of ruling powers because natural law had not been reduced either to order in nature or order in the mind. The natural law "is not a law founded or prescribed by nature, but the law for the moral government of nature, under which all moral natures are placed by the Author of nature as supreme law-giver. The law of nature is God's law; and whatever rights it founds or are held from it are his rights, and ours only because they are his."[36]

As we have seen, H. L. A. Hart maintained that the "appeal" of natural law derives from the fact that it is "independent of both divine and human authority." The position that we have briefly sketched here takes the opposite point of view. Without denying

---

34. *Scott v Sandford* (1857), 60 U.S. 393, 550. Justice McLean, dissenting.
35. Jean-Jacques Rousseau, *Social Contract,* I.1.
36. Orestes Brownson, "Church and State" (May 1870), in *The Works of Orestes Brownson,* XIII (Detroit: Thorndike Bourse, 1884), 274*f.*

the importance of order in nature and in human cognition, the doctrine of natural law has located those two orders under a higher authority. It is precisely from this perspective that the very phrase natural law has meant something more than a metaphorical circumlocution for "nature." In *Veritatis Splendor,* Pope John Paul II calls it "participated theonomy." This is not the same thing as what Hart dismisses as "theocracy." For the usual, pejorative meaning of that term suggests an unmediated and undistributed exercise of sacral power. But when the Council of Arles spoke of natural law as the *prima gratia,* it meant an original gift, not the raw and unilateral projection of divine power in the fashion of a modern state.

At the beginning of Memorial and Remonstrance (1785), before he undertakes any public policy arguments about religion, government, and the rule of law, James Madison maintained:

> It is the duty of every man to render to the Creator such homage and such only as he believes to be acceptable to him. This duty is precedent, both in order of time and in degree of obligation, to the claims of Civil Society. Before any man can be considered as a member of Civil Society, he must be considered as a subject of the Governour of the Universe: And if a member of Civil Society, do it with a saving of his allegiance to the Universal Sovereign. We maintain therefore that in matters of Religion, no man's right is abridged by the institution of Civil Society and that Religion is wholly exempt from its cognizance. True it is, that no other rule exists, by which any question which may divide a Society, can be ultimately determined, but the will of the majority; but it is also true that the majority may trespass on the rights of the minority. Because Religion be exempt from the authority of the Society at large, still less can it be subject to that of the Legislative Body. The latter are but the creatures and vicegerents of the former. Their jurisdiction is both derivative and limited: it is

limited with regard to the co-ordinate departments, more necessarily is it limited with regard to the constituents.[37]

Madison's circular letter was a polemic meant to sharpen a legislative debate rather than an exercise in philosophy or theology. Even so, it summarizes an important insight about the rule of law. We notice first that he makes no appeal to a state of nature bereft of authority. Men are under an order of law and duty distinct from that of civil society. The priority of this order does not imply a historical priority nor a hypothetical condition of what men might look like if left to themselves. In the second place, what is prior is not simply the innate natural power of human reason and its acts of conscience. This is not a Hobbesian picture of human nature in which human powers generate pre-moral or amoral claims of rights. Neither is it an anticipation of a Kantian notion of autonomy, of practical reason binding itself to unconditioned laws that have no ground in an extrinsic authority. The claim that society lacks by nature a jurisdiction over the higher law does not suggest that the jurisdiction falls by default to the individual. Quite the opposite. The individual's rightful liberty vis-à-vis society derives from the proposition that the individual is already under another jurisdiction. Madison, of course, argued elsewhere (e.g., *Federalist* 10) that the art of human constitutions must consider the scheme of power checking power.

Yet here in Memorial and Remonstrance he is interested in presenting another order to which the power-checking-power artifice is subordinate. In other words, the rule of law, the artful assignment of ruling powers, is not a freestanding art. We must first understand the order of things that does not fall under human political authority, and, for that reason, is not a matter of human prudence and

---

37. James Madison, "Memorial and Remonstrance against Religious Assessments" (1785), reprinted in *Church and State in the Modern Age: A Documentary History*, ed. J. F. Maclear (New York: Oxford University Press, 1995), 60.

art. In chapter 9 of the present volume, I point out a potential problem with Madison's phrase "wholly exempt from its cognizance." The Supreme Court's post-*Everson* (1947) jurisprudence of the establishment clause appealed to Madison's Memorial for evidence of original intent on the part of the framers and ratifiers. In opinion after opinion, justices of the Court either suppressed or denied the full import of the passage we quoted above. The phrase "wholly exempt" was interpreted to be an independent proposition rather than the conclusion of an argument. It came to mean that human government is prohibited from taking any position on theological ideas as such. This construal makes no sense of Madison's own argument, which was meant to persuade the legislature of Virginia on the basis of an argument about divine jurisdiction vis-à-vis human conscience. It is one thing to say that human government cannot stand in judgment of the higher law, but it is quite another thing to prohibit government from recognizing the ground of its own inferior authority.

It is in light of this problem that the admittedly polemical essay in chapter 7, which deals with the Supreme Court's rather demeaning characterization of the religious liberty it is supposed to protect, can be read. First written nearly ten years ago, my report of the case law is not completely up to date. However, on the basis of more recent Court decisions and obiter dicta, I have no reason to change my characterization of the coy, and usually comical, endeavor of the Court to uphold higher law against higher law. In chapter 9, I discuss in a somewhat more serious vein how the Second Vatican Council articulated a right of religious liberty that managed *not* to suggest that governments are so theologically blind (in fact, or by norm) that they are released from obligation to act in accord with the higher law. While Madison would have agreed with most everything except the "Catholic" part, even the part objectionable to his mind better represents his argument than the Court's post-*Everson* jurisprudence.

From Madison we should not expect a refined metaphysics of natural law. Indeed, his penchant for the power-checking-power scheme of politics notably departs from the understanding of human polity avowed by classical and medieval thinkers. It is enough for us to see that, despite this, Madison retained a common sense tutored by the old tradition of higher law. At the Constitutional Convention, he understood that compromise on the question of slavery had a limit beyond the immediate institutional issue of allocating powers. Though a slaveholder himself, he argued that it would be "wrong to admit in the Constitution the idea that there could be property in men."[38] His point in this regard was similar to the one he made in Memorial and Remonstrance. Government has no natural right to bind or loose from the natural law, for such a right would engender not a plurality of jurisdictions but a contradiction between those rights and duties immediately derived from higher law and those affirmed in the Constitution.

In his debates with Stephen A. Douglas, Abraham Lincoln conceded that it was permissible to view the problem of slavery very narrowly, as "a mere negative declaration of a want of power in Congress to do anything in relation to this matter in the territories."[39] He continued: "I know the opinion of the Judges states that there is a total absence of power; but that is, unfortunately, not all it states. . . . Its language is equivalent to saying that it is embodied and so woven into that instrument that it cannot be detached without breaking the constitution itself."[40] In the order that belongs to human law, a constitution is a kind of "higher" law, for it establishes the

---

38. Max Farrand, ed., *The Records of the Federal Convention of 1787*, rev. ed. 4 vols. (New Haven, Conn.: Yale University Press, 1937), II, 417.

39. Speech at Columbus, Ohio (16 September 1859), in *Lincoln: Speeches and Writings 1859–1865* (New York: The Library of America, 1989), 53.

40. Speech at Columbus, 53.

rules and measures for the making, administering, and adjudicating of law by particular authorities embraced within that constitution. Lincoln was correct to see the gravity of perverting a constitution, which is all the more dangerous when undertaken in the name of natural rights.

The reader will see that several of the essays in this collection wrestle with issues raised by the Supreme Court's decision in *Planned Parenthood v. Casey* (1992) and by Pope John Paul II's encyclical *Veritatis Splendor* (1993). Coming within a year of one another, these two documents are striking when read in tandem not only because of their different positions on abortion (in these essays I spend relatively little time commenting upon or arguing about the morality of abortion) but also because of what they say respectively about the situation of authority.

The authors of the joint opinion in *Casey* (Justices Souter, O'Connor, and Kennedy) proposed, reasonably enough, that it is "a promise of the Constitution that there is a realm of personal liberty which the government may not enter."[41] So far forth, without further detail or elaboration, the Court states nothing especially controversial. Even St. Thomas argued that natural law prescribes limits to the authority of one human being over the body of another:

> [M]an is bound to obey his fellow-man in things that have to be done externally by means of the body: and yet, since by nature all men are equal, he is not bound to obey another man in matters touching the nature of the body, for instance in those relating to the support of his body or the begetting of his children. Wherefore servants are not bound to obey their masters, nor children their parents, in the ques-

---

41. *Planned Parenthood v. Casey* (1992) 505 U.S. 833, 847.

tion of contracting marriage or of remaining in the state of virginity or the like.[42]

With respect to some matters, such as the choice to be married or not, the human person is "immediately under God, by Whom he is taught either by the natural or by the written law."[43] Thomas, of course, did not include in this list any rightful liberty to work some injustice contrary to the moral order. Nor did he think that the negative liberty from human authority cast one into a pre-moral condition of liberty from every authority. Even the Supreme Court, from time to time, is capable of understanding that an argument for liberty is not an argument against authority. As Justice Douglas once observed, albeit in a dissenting opinion, the "institutions of our society are founded on the belief that there is an authority higher than the authority of the State; that there is a moral law which the State is powerless to alter; that the individual possesses rights, conferred by the Creator, which government must respect."[44]

The authors of the joint opinion in *Casey*, however, say more. "At the heart of liberty is the right to define one's own concept of existence, of meaning, of the universe, and of the mystery of human life. Beliefs about these matters could not define the attributes of personhood were they formed under compulsion of the State."[45] This is not a straightforward proposition about the absence of authority on the part of some institution or sector of government. Apropos of Lincoln's characterization of the situation of positive law with respect to slavery in the territories—"a mere negative decla-

---

42. *S.t.* II–II, 104.5.
43. *S.t.* II–II, 104.5 ad 2.
44. *McGowan v. Maryland* (1961) 366 U.S. 420, 562.
45. *Planned Parenthood v. Casey*, 847. Of course, the Court's discovery of a right to abortion did not begin in *Casey* but in *Roe v Wade* (1973). I spend more effort criticizing *Casey* for the good reason that it displays the philosophical and jurisprudential issues much more fully than *Roe*.

ration of a want of power in Congress"—the Casey Court folds the positive law into the principle of a natural right. The absence of legislative power is established by the right of the individual to be self-norming. The measures of justice regarding the killing or preserving of the unborn are not drawn from the order of nature, the common law, the positive laws of the several states, or the absence of power on the part of some sector of government, much less, need it be said, from the revealed law. The individual in this matter is under neither a higher nor a lower law, but is a law unto himself. It takes only a little historical imagination to consider the problems Madison might have encountered in late-eighteenth-century Virginia had he attempted to mount a higher law argument for religious liberty on the basis of a lawless conscience.

What makes the joint opinion especially reminiscent of the Dred Scott case is the purported authority of the Court to assert natural justice as a summary of public opinion. "The root of American governmental power," the Court maintains, "is revealed most clearly in the instance of the power conferred by the Constitution upon the Judiciary of the United States and specifically upon this Court. . . . The Court's power lies, rather, in its legitimacy, a product of substance and perception that shows itself in the people's acceptance of the Judiciary as fit to determine what the Nation's law means and to declare what it demands."[46] This notion of the Court as the basal or "root" power, functioning as a vicar of public opinion, tallies almost exactly with what Justice McLean attributed to Justice Taney. The Court claims a special mandate to decide issues of higher law, even while reducing that law to public opinion vicariously represented by the Court.

---

46. Ibid., 865. And, on p. 866: "Thus, the Court's legitimacy depends on making legally principled decisions under circumstances in which their principled character is *sufficiently plausible* to be accepted by the Nation." [emphasis added]

As I point out in some of the essays in this volume, this perversion of the rule of law is not easily contained. In 1996, the issue of physician-assisted suicide reached the Supreme Court from two circuit courts that deployed the *Casey* opinion to uphold a natural right of private parties to use lethal force to vindicate justice in dying. If the individual has a right to use lethal force against the unborn, it would seem that such a right implicitly contains the liberty to employ a third party to kill oneself. In *Washington v. Glucksberg* (1997), the Court refused to take this step. According to Justice Rehnquist, physician-assisted suicide is not so "deeply rooted in our history and traditions." How and why the personal autonomy doctrine of *Casey* is more deeply rooted in the matter of abortion than in physician-assisted suicide is neither explained nor justified. Nor is it explained how the Court has authority to give or deny remedies based on natural justice. Once the principle that the individual has a rightful dominion over life and death is admitted at constitutional law, it is difficult to see how such a principle can be contained. The options are threefold: (1) claim that for contingent reasons of history and precedent individual dominion over life and death is a fundamental value when one wishes to kill an unborn child, but not in the contract with a third party to kill oneself; (2) claim that the state has a compelling interest to override a fundamental value; (3) deny the rightfulness of the principle itself. The Supreme Court has hovered between the first two on the issue of physician-assisted suicide.

In chapters 3 and 4, I examine one of the most important but convoluted disputes about natural law, namely, its justiciability in courts. The issue is not only hampered by the vehement and often ugly politics of nominations to the federal bench; it is also beclouded by a very simplistic framing of the problem. For example, in *Democracy and Distrust* John Hart Ely lays out two alternative views of judicial review. According to the doctrine of interpretivism, it is the sole business of judges to interpret the positive law received from a competent legislative authority. According to the doctrine of noninterpretivism, judges may introduce moral values in deciding cases. Ely then proposes that "[t]he interpretivism-noninterpretivism dichotomy stirs a long-standing debate that pervades all of law, that between 'positivism' and 'natural law.' Interpretivism is about the same thing as positivism, and natural law approaches are surely one form of noninterpretivism."[47]

This confuses two quite distinct questions: (1) whether jurisprudence presupposes something prior in the order of morals, and (2) whether a particular system of positive law authorizes judges to render verdicts immediately on the basis of the morality prior to law. All natural law theorists affirm the first proposition, but not necessarily the second.[48]

I show in some detail in these chapters that a natural law theorist like St. Thomas would look more like an interpretivist than a noninterpretivist. But these terms are so misleading that they ought to be abandoned. For to put the issue in this way leads us into the cul-de-sac of choosing between two unacceptable options. If natural law permits or requires judges willy-nilly to appeal to moral norms or fundamental values outside the positive law, then natural law underwrites private judgment parading as public authority. If, on the other hand, judicial restraint means obedience to written law because that law is the only measure of justice, then we fall into positivism. This is the Hobbesian option, to be sure. But from the

---

47. John Hart Ely, *Democracy and Distrust: A Theory of Judicial Review* (Cambridge, Mass.: Harvard University Press, 1980), 1.

48. My position on natural law and judicial review is virtually the same as that of Robert P. George, with whom I have sometimes differed on other aspects of natural law theory. See Robert P. George, "Natural Law, the Constitution, and the Theory and Practice of Judicial Review," in *The Clash of Orthodoxies* (Wilmington, Del.: ISI Books, 2001), 168–209.

standpoint of the traditional concept of natural law, each of these options, in its own way, introduces a kind of lawlessness.

On the assumption that natural law signifies a participation in a higher law, all human judgment about the measures of action are set within a broader legal order. This was Madison's point in Memorial and Remonstrance. Individual judgments of conscience are personal but are not merely "private." That an individual, association, or church enjoys an immunity from the jurisdiction of the state is a real, but nonetheless restricted, notion of privacy. Parents are private agents with respect to the state, but in possessing authority to render judgment according to the natural law in matters affecting their domestic societies they are public agents. When Martin Luther King Jr. appealed to the eternal law in his famous Letter from Birmingham Jail he did not think of himself as making a merely private judgment.[49] Rather, he appealed to an order more public than the positive law, a supra-public law. At the same time, he did not suggest that he was vested with power to displace the order of authority allocated by the positive law. His understanding of civil disobedience recognizes both principles: While the state should not pervert the higher law, the individual ought not to usurp the authority of the state.

For his part, St. Thomas argues that participation in the eternal law includes individual judgment, social judgment, and political judgment. In each sphere, the human mind receives a rule and measure of acts and goes on to form judgments about action. In each sphere, the judgment enjoys, analogously, a kind of legality. According to the traditional perspective, the parent who uses prudence to make the natural law effective in the domestic society does so by a God-given right; he or she does not merely proceed from a moral

---

49. Martin Luther King Jr., *Why We Can't Wait* (New York: Harper and Row, 1963), 77–100.

power, but from a jurisdictional title higher than that of the state. Political authority draws from the same source, but participation at this level involves making new law for the entire community, and, in so doing, renders the natural law effective in something more than individual or domestic life. Natural law is not an authority-free zone. Typically, natural law is invoked on issues of parental rights not merely to clarify the moral norms of parenting, but rather, indeed primarily, to locate the origin of the jurisdiction of parents.

In any relatively well-developed polity, the human political authority participates in the natural law not only by issuing legal precepts, but also by fashioning different forms of order that we would call constitutional. This is nothing other than the prudential distribution of lawmaking, law-enforcing, and law-adjudicating powers. In a surprisingly direct and sophisticated way, Thomas contended that, constitutionally, the judgment of judges ought to be regulated by the written law. For as it bears upon the entire political community, natural law is best made effective if human law is not generated on a case-by-case basis. As I show in chapter 4, his position on judges exercising *iustum animatum* (animated justice, judgment unregulated by written law) seems to fit rather nicely with contemporary criticisms of "living constitutionalism."

But this has nothing to do with legal positivism. Rather, it is in respect of the entire system of positive law as a participation in natural law, including the proximate measures of legal authority that govern and mark the bounds of different offices, that Thomas favored the legislative office. For reasons that I discuss in chapter 4, obedience to the natural law might require a judge to render no judgment according to an unjust positive law, but he may never subvert the order of authority by imposing a law *ultra vires*. Usurpation of positive law is a violation of the natural law. This idea was not unfamiliar to Lincoln, who held that while the *Dred Scott* decision was a perversion of both the higher law and the Constitution, the positive law gives the president no judicial power to retry the case or unilaterally to impose upon the polity a new positive law. The tradition of higher law doctrine has been the great matrix rather than the dissolvent of the rule of law.

Chapter 8—which contains two essays—originated in the much-publicized, and much-criticized, *First Things* "End of Democracy?" symposium. On my last count, the symposium had generated more than 175 reviews and comments in periodicals and books. Some of our most determined critics were on the political Right; these men and women were dismayed that anyone should suggest that the Court's assertions about natural justice could raise genuine philosophical and theological questions. Speaking here only for myself, and not for the other contributors to the symposium, my quarrel with the Court's imposition of a perverse higher law doctrine should be read in tandem with the first seven chapters in this volume, which defend a natural law ground for the rule of law and judicial restraint. The default positivism of the political Right is at odds with its commitments on many other issues. At the time of the American founding, during the crisis leading to the Civil War, and once again during the crises brought about by the Court's uncritical adoption of a "fundamental values" jurisprudence after World War II, the best friends of judicial restraint in obedience to the rule of law were those who had a very substantive understanding of natural law. The reason is clear: Obedience to properly constituted authority is not a mere side-piece of the higher law tradition. Positive law tells us who has authority under specific institutional constraints. Therefore, whether any branch or officer of government has usurped authority is a question of positive law. But usurpation is forbidden by the natural law. Presumably, this is why the Constitution does not have to include a precept forbidding its officers from transgressing the positive law.

Veritatis Splendor (1993) is the first papal encyclical devoted exclusively to moral theology. Unlike other recent encyclicals that treat particular issues of human conduct—e.g., *Humanae Vitae* (contraception), *Sollicitudo rei Socialis* (distribution of wealth), and *Evangelium Vitae* (abortion and euthanasia)—*Veritatis* has relatively little to say about the application of moral norms to disputed problems, the situation of positive law, or the agenda of public policy. The subtitle alerts us that the encyclical intends to turn us back to the sources of moral theology: *De Fundamentis Doctrinae Moralis Ecclesiae,* "On the Fundaments of the Church's Moral Teaching."[50] Natural law figures prominently among the "fundaments."

The encyclical is an authoritative teaching about moral theology and therefore ought not to be confused with the quotidian investigations and arguments of secular philosophers who do not recognize this authority. Yet it would be a mistake to read the encyclical as asserting propositions grounded merely in the teaching authority of the Church. To be sure, the encyclical maintains that human practical reason should be understood within the setting of divine wisdom. However we distinguish the objects of faith or reason, the "fundaments" of which the encyclical speaks are not the work of the Church. The Church has no more power to change the natural law than does the state, public opinion, or the professional guild of moral philosophers.

---

50. The English translation renders it "Regarding Certain Fundamental Questions of the Church's Moral Teaching," which is not only a bad translation, but introduces a perspective that the encyclicals sets out to refute. Even more curious was the advertisement of the National Conference of Catholic Bishops summarizing the encyclical as follows: "It reverses pre-Vatican II legalism by speaking of the good and the bad rather than the forbidden and permitted, and by speaking about the invitation to live a moral life in God rather than the enforcing of laws or norms." Since the encyclical wishes to overcome the dichotomy of the good and law, obedience and freedom, the NCCB advertisement typifies the very problem treated by the encyclical.

In its discussion of natural law, *Veritatis* introduces some interesting terminological changes. The first is the "natural moral law" *(lex moralis naturalis)*.[51] This was used once in the encyclical *Humanae Vitae* (1968) and once a few years later in the instruction *Donum Vitae* issued by the Congregation for the Doctrine of the Faith (1987).[52] In the *Catechism of the Catholic Church* (1994), written at the same time as *Veritatis Splendor*, the section on natural law is titled the "natural moral law."[53] Why alter the traditional rubric by inserting "moral" between "natural" and "law"? Apparently, Rome wished to make it clearer that natural law is not to be reduced either to order in things or to order in the human mind. In *Donum Vitae*, for example, we read that: "The natural moral law expresses and lays down the purposes, rights and duties which are based upon the bodily and spiritual nature of the human person. This law cannot be thought of as simply a set of norms on the biological level; rather it must be defined as the rational order whereby man is called by the Creator to direct and regulate his life and actions and in particular to make use of his own body." Here, the insertion of *moralis* is clearly intended to obviate the depiction of natural law as a lower law that bears no legal or moral predicates whatsoever.

In *Veritatis Splendor* the "natural moral law" cuts in the other direction, reminding the reader that the natural law is something more than order in the human mind:

> Some people, . . . disregarding the dependence of human reason on Divine Wisdom and the need, given the present state of fallen nature, for Divine Revelation as an effective means for knowing moral truths, even those of the natural order, have actually posited a "complete

---

51. *Veritatis Splendor* (1993), §36.
52. *Humanae Vitae* (1968), §4; *Donum Vitae* (1987), III.
53. *CCC* (1994), §§1954–60.

sovereignty of reason" in the domain of moral norms regarding the right ordering of life in this world. Such norms would constitute the boundaries for a merely "human" morality; they would be the expression of a law which man in an autonomous manner lays down for himself and which has its source exclusively in human reason. In no way could God be considered the Author of this law, except in the sense that human reason exercises its autonomy in setting down laws by virtue of a primordial and total mandate given to man by God. These trends of thought have led to a denial, in opposition to Sacred Scripture (cf. Mt 15:3–6) and the Church's constant teaching, of the fact that the *natural moral law* has God as its author, and that man, by the use of reason, participates in the eternal law, which it is not for him to establish. (§36)

If we turn to the *Catechism,* issued just a few months after *Veritatis,* the natural moral law *(lex moralis naturalis),* the old law *(lex vetus)* and the new law *(lex nova seu evangelica)* are organized under the genus "moral law" *(Lex Moralis).* The purpose here is the integration of all three foci in the ancient doctrine of participation. The "moral" is not bereft of law, nor law of morals, though the modes of promulgation and reception, as well as the precepts, differ according to the economy of divine providence. As I see it, the rubric "natural moral law" highlights issues that are at once theological and anthropological. Whether we speak of the order of nature, the Covenant, or the Gospel, the creature is not in a condition in which morals and law have to be brought together *ab initio* by the human mind—*fiat lex.* The terminology of *Veritatis* and the *Catechism* is somewhat novel, but the definitional scheme is virtually the same as that of St. Thomas, who, relying on St. Augustine, distinguished all law proceeding from the divine mind from laws promulgated by the human mind. The moral order remains within the setting of divine wisdom, though our

location in, and participation in, this order differs in each case.
The second novel term in *Veritatis* is "participated theonomy."

> Others speak, and rightly so, of "theonomy," or "participated
> theonomy" *[de theonomia participata]*, since man's free obedience to
> God's law effectively implies that human reason and human will
> participate in God's wisdom and providence. By forbidding man to
> "eat of the tree of the knowledge of good and evil," God makes it
> clear that man does not originally possess such "knowledge" as some-
> thing properly his own, but only participates in it by the light of
> natural reason and of Divine Revelation, which manifest to him the
> requirements and the promptings of eternal wisdom. Law must
> therefore be considered an expression of divine wisdom: by submit-
> ting to the law, freedom submits to the truth of creation. (§41)

The phrase "participated theonomy" is borrowed perhaps from
the Swiss thinker Martin Rhonheimer.[54] But the term "theonomy"
seems to have been coined originally by nineteenth-century Protestant theologians (mostly Lutheran) who wanted to overcome Kant's
dichotomy of autonomy and heteronomy.[55] That dichotomy, of
course, expressed a completely anthropocentric setting of ethics.
Either human practical reason acts according to a merely conditional
maxim drawn from instinct, or practical reason acts according to an
unconditional maxim grasped *a priori* by the mind. Protestant theologians of the era well understood that, on this view, obedience to
divine law of any kind would prove heteronomous. Hence, they
proposed a third term, *theonomie,* to make clear that the human drama

---

54. For the phrase, "participated autonomy," see Martin Rhonheimer, *Natural Law
and Practical Reason: A Thomistic View of Moral Autonomy,* trans. Gerald Malsbary
(New York: Fordham University Press, 2000).
55. For the Protestant antecedents, I am indebted to the unpublished M.A. thesis by
Stefan Reuffurth, OMV, "Theonomy: The Historical Origins and Development of a Theological Term and Its Use by John Paul II in *Veritatis Splendor,*"
St. Johns Seminary, Boston, 1998.

of autonomy versus heteronomy is relative to God's law as revealed in Scripture. *Veritatis Splendor* adds the traditional term "participated," which brings the idea back around to the patristic tradition and the speculative language of the medieval schools.

The idea of "participated theonomy" is also similar to the neo-Calvinist understanding of "sphere sovereignty," propounded by Abraham Kuyper, Prime Minister of a Dutch Protestant-Catholic coalition from 1901 to 1905.[56] Kuyper's social theory was developed at the same time that Pope Leo XIII (for whom Kuyper expressed admiration) adopted a high concept of natural law in order to defend a structured plurality of human authorities, each participating in its own way in the natural law.[57] Like Leo XIII, whose pontificate lasted from 1878 to 1903, Kuyper insisted that authority does not arise originally through a social contract or the state. "[H]igher authority," he wrote, "is of necessity involved" if we are to make sense of plural spheres of society that have real authority not reducible one to the other.[58] "In a Calvinistic sense we understand hereby, that the family, the business, science, art and so forth are all social spheres, which do not owe their existence to the state, and which do not derive the law of their life from the superiority of the state, but obey a high authority within their bosom; and authority which rules, by the grace of God, just as the sovereignty of the State does."[59]

---

56. For my understanding of the concept of sphere sovereignty, I am indebted to Jonathan Chaplin, James Skillen, and Keith J. Pavlischek. For an introduction to Kuyper, see Peter Heslam, *Creating a Christian Worldview: Abraham Kuyper's Lectures on Calvinism* (Grand Rapids, Mich.: Eerdmans, 1998), and James D. Bratt, ed., *Abraham Kuyper: A Centennial Reader* (Grand Rapids, Mich.: Eerdmans, 1998). Kuyper's most widely read English work is published as *Lectures on Calvinism* (Grand Rapids, Mich.: Eerdmans, 1931).

57. Leo XIII almost always uses natural law in relation to the origin of authority. See for example *Immortale Dei* (1885), §§4, 18, 24; *Libertas* (1888), §§3, 7–9, 13; *Tametsi futura* (1900), §7; *Sapientiae Christianae* (1890), §8; *Arcanum* (1880), §32; *Diuturnum* (1881), §11.

58. Kuyper, *Lectures on Calvinism*, 91.

59. *Ibid.*, 90.

Kuyper and his disciples spoke of higher law, but kept the phrase natural law at arm's length. This was due in part to the fact that Kuyper was alarmed that the orders of nature and mind had been reduced to what he called "pantheism"—a spontaneous order unstructured with regard to authority. The Catholic doctrine of "participation" and the Reformed position on "sphere sovereignty" differ in important ways. The model of "participation" emphasizes mediation, whereas "sphere sovereignty" emphasizes a more direct constitution of authority. Both, however, account for a structured pluralism of authority in a theonomic principle.

Until recently, natural law as a "fundament" of moral theology has not been an issue much disputed in the Catholic tradition. Leo XIII, Pius XI, Pius XII, and John XXIII were careful to orient the discourse of natural law in terms of a higher law.[60] That Pope John Paul II felt it necessary to write an encyclical clarifying the matter indicates that the situation has changed. The change is due in part to the intra-ecclesial dispute sparked by the magisterial teaching on contraception promulgated in *Humanae Vitae*, which appeared in 1968. Since that time, many theologians have complained that the "official" concept of natural law is based on an outmoded understanding

---

60. If we take, for example, Pope John XXIII's *Pacem in Terris* (1963), we find some twenty-five discrete rights listed in §§11–27. It would be a mistake, however, to think that this "liberal" pope jettisoned the theory of participation in higher law. "Hence, representatives of the State have no power to bind men in conscience, unless their own authority is tied to God's authority, and is a participation in it," §49. "But such an order—universal, absolute and immutable in its principles—finds its source in the true, personal and transcendent God. He is the first truth, the sovereign good, and as such the deepest source from which human society, if it is to be properly constituted, creative, and worthy of man's dignity, draws its genuine vitality. This is what St. Thomas means when he says: 'Human reason is the standard which measures the degree of goodness of the human will, and as such it derives from the eternal law, which is divine reason. . . . Hence it is clear that the goodness of the human will depends much more on the eternal law than on human reason.'"

of nature. Obedience to natural law, it is said, requires human liberty and prudence to submit to something lower than itself. Without here rehearsing the details of this dispute, the charge of "biologism" was the least important challenge to the tradition, among other reasons because it was the one most easily answered. The more interesting issue is whether natural law includes an order of obligation, whether natural law is an authority-free zone.

The report submitted to Pope Paul VI by a special commission instituted to study the question of contraception strongly criticized what it understood to be the older tradition of natural law. "[T]he concept of the natural law, as it is found in the traditional discussion of this question, is insufficient: for the gifts of nature are considered to be immediately the expression of the will of God, preventing man, also a creature of God, from being understood as called to receive material nature and to perfect its potentiality. Churchmen have been slower than the rest of the world in clearly seeing that this is man's vocation."[61] This characterization misrepresents the Catholic tradition by making the natural law an expression of divine voluntarism. Putting that problem to one side, the important thing is that the authors of the report set up a dichotomy between what we have been calling the first two foci of natural law, order in nature and order in the mind. If the natural law is order in nature, then man is prevented from exercising his own natural gift of prudence. Given this opposition— nature or prudence—the latter would seem higher than the former, for as the report notes, even Genesis considers man "as the prudent administrator and steward of the gifts of nature."[62] But then the central question comes clearly into view: What is the norm of prudence?

Classically understood, the virtue of prudence requires a situation in which there is a gap between a precept and an end. Whenever there is more than one legitimate way to achieve an end pru-

61. "The Argument for Reform," *The Tablet* (May 6, 1967), 511.
62. Ibid., 510.

dence must be exercised. There can be no prudence, however, concerning an action already forbidden by a precept. While there might be a range of options about how to murder, for example, there is no prudence about such means. The authors of the report mean by prudence the liberty of intelligent choice about the so-called gifts of nature without a prior precept. The concrete norms are entirely the work of the human mind. The authors concede that there is something "sacred in nature," for God is the creator of the "totality of created nature."[63] But there is no law, no precept. Prudence in this respect is indistinguishable from what modern philosophers understand as instrumental reason—the human mind at work on pre-moral measures of nature.

Hence, the traditional concept of participation in a higher order is not so subtly transposed into a deism in which God supplies the material but man supplies the concrete norms. From this perspective, it follows that binding law can emerge only after the fact of human dominion. As in various state-of-nature scenarios of the Enlightenment, we have here a depiction of Genesis 2 without a norm. Undoubtedly, this is not the *prima gratia* affirmed by the Council of Arles. Pope Paul VI must have found it odd that a commission of his own moral theologians was asking him to authoritatively declare a human dominion free of higher law, or, for that matter, of any law. The Pope refused on grounds of faith and reason to admit the existence of a zone of absolute human dominion. Regrettably, the secular polity with the greatest tradition of higher law thinking allowed its Court in *Casey* to transfer dominion over life and death to self-norming persons.

The problem of natural law cannot be understood adequately as an argumentative exercise pointing to, or issuing from, moral premises. Such an exercise is important, but it does not touch and

---

63. Ibid., 511.

therefore cannot resolve the deeper issue of the original situation of human practical reason. When the Pope's commission of moral theologians argued for the priority of a human dominion in which human practical reason supplies the concrete norms, or when the Supreme Court declared in *Casey* that the individual has natural immunity from positive law in the matter of abortion, it is important to understand that these are not moral arguments but claims about what is prior to arguments. The answer to this question is entirely relevant to morals, but nothing in the logic of moral argument *per se* can win the case. The question turns upon considerations of anthropology and theology. To attempt to rediscover the natural law in a post-Christian world we must pick up the discussion precisely at this point.

Section One

Rediscovering the Natural Law

CHAPTER ONE

Natural Law and Catholic Moral Theology

I n his 1958 lectures at the University of Chicago, later published under the title *The Tradition of Natural Law: A Philosopher's Reflections,* Yves R. Simon remarks that the subject of natural law is difficult "because it is engaged in an overwhelming diversity of doctrinal contexts and of historical accidents. It is doubtful that this double diversity, doctrinal and historical, can so be mastered as to make possible a completely orderly exposition of the subject of natural law."[1]

My intention in this opening chapter will be to examine the problem of natural law only *ad intra,* within Catholic moral theology.[2] In this chapter I will have almost nothing to say about any particular issue of justice in the public sphere. I will proffer no "natural law" answers as to what judges ought to do, or how the budget deficit ought to be resolved, or what moral perspective should guide welfare funding. Furthermore, while hoping to persuade Protestants that the idea of natural law in the Catholic tradition has only recently, and as an aberration, been developed as a concept completely detached from theology, I shall not attempt to reconcile the Catholic tradition with any particular species of Protestant thought.

Rather, I will endeavor to show how the concept of natural law became a serious problem in modern Catholic moral theology and how the papal encyclical *Veritatis Splendor* responds to that problem. My account will be very imperfect indeed, for it will be necessary both to tell a story and to make a number of distinctions along the way, allowing each to illuminate the other. To do both these things at once, and in a brief space, is a difficult task.

Three Foci of Natural Law Discourse

But first, what is a theory of natural law a theory *of?* The question can be approached in three ways. In the first place, natural law can be regarded as a matter of propositions or precepts that are first in the order of practical cognition. Thus, when a theorist reconnects debate about justice back to first principles, from which the mind can lay out properly considered and argued conclusions, he can be said to have (or practice) a theory of natural law. In the second place, natural law can be regarded as an issue of nature or human nature, in which case it is a problem not only of epistemology and logic but also of how practical reason is situated in a broader order of causality. Third, natural law can be approached not only as order in the mind or order in nature but also as the ordinance of a divine lawgiver.

Discourse about natural law can gravitate toward any one or a combination of these three foci: law in the human mind, in nature, and in the mind of God. Contemporary literature on the subject shows there is little or no agreement as to how the three foci ought to be integrated. For there is no general agreement about what should count as a proper problem, much less about what philosophical instruments to apply to it.

Rather than engage in an interminable survey of the methodological problems, I shall begin with an assertion. The theologian is (or ought to be) chiefly concerned with the third of these foci: namely, natural law as an expression of divine providence. As Karl Barth said in *Church Dogmatics,* "Ethics [is] a Task of the Doctrine of God."[3] Whatever else Barth said or thought about natural law, the proposition that moral theology is a task of the doctrine of God is incontestable. The Christian theologian is interested in who God is, and what God does.

Who we are and what we do are questions that can be asked outside of theology, to be sure, and the theologian will be interested in how persons outside the faith pursue such questions. Catholic and Protestant theologians have different attitudes toward these strands (Balthasar says "fragments") of moral inquiry and behavior separated from the living Word of God. While Catholic theologians have perhaps been tempted to overestimation, Protestants have been inclined to underestimation. But the main focus for the theologian *qua* theologian is, as Barth said, the doctrine of God.

Until recently, the proposition that natural law is chiefly a theological issue was uncontroversial in Catholic moral theology. Natural law in the human mind and natural law in nature were regarded as distinct but not architectonic foci. Let us first consider two passages from the Church Fathers.

In the second century, Tertullian took up the problem of divine governance prior to the written law. Like so many other of the patristic theologians of both East and West, Tertullian argued that the law given to Adam (Gn 2:17) was the natural law: "For in this law given to Adam we recognize in embryo all the precepts which afterwards sprouted forth when given through Moses." After reciting the ten precepts of the Decalogue, Tertullian concludes that the first law is "the womb of all the precepts of God"—a "law unwritten, which was habitually understood naturally, and which the fathers kept."[4] Which of the patriarchs? Tertullian mentions Noah, Melchizedek, Enoch, and Abraham.

This teaching is simple and familiar. Our first parents were given an unwritten law, expressing the rule of law itself: men govern only by

sharing in divine governance. Adam and Eve, who understood the law
naturaliter (naturally), did not keep it. But the patriarchs before Moses
adhered to the unwritten law. In this brief passage Tertullian alludes to
natural law in the mind and in nature. His principal interest, however,
is the economy of divine laws. As to what men knew or did after sin
(*post peccatum*) Tertullian commits himself only to saying that the patriarchs were counted "righteous, on the observance of a natural law."[5]

> In the fourth century, Gregory of Nyssa proposed that human nature
> at its beginning was unbroken and immortal. Since human nature
> was fashioned by the divine hands and beautified with the unwritten
> characters of the Law, the intention of the Law lay in our nature in
> turning us away from evil and in honoring the divine. When the
> sound of sin struck our ears, that sound which the first book of Scrip-
> ture calls "the voice of the serpent," but the history concerning the
> tables calls the "voice of drunken singing," the tables fell to the earth
> and were broken. But again the true Lawgiver, of whom Moses was
> a type, cut the tables of human nature for himself from our earth. It
> was not marriage which produced for him his "God-receiving" flesh,
> but he became the stonecutter of his own flesh, which was carved by
> the divine finger, for *the Holy Spirit came upon the virgin and the power*
> *of the Most High overshadowed her.* When this took place, our nature
> regained its unbroken character, becoming immortal through the
> letters written by his finger.[6]

Like Tertullian, Gregory of Nyssa alludes to natural law in the mind.
The "intention of the Law," he writes, "lay in our nature in turning us
away from evil and in honoring the divine." This is the traditional
notion of a *lex indita,* a law instilled in the mind, which later patristic
and medieval theologians would call *synderesis.*[7] Gregory also speaks of
the order of human nature. Yet it is clear that Gregory's focus is set
upon what God does: first in ordering man by nature, second in dis-

ciplining men through the written law, and finally in recreating men through the mystery of the Incarnation and Redemption.

These two passages are fairly typical of the patristic thinking on natural law. Issues of epistemology and human nature are distinct but not architectonic foci. Not even moral theology (in our modern sense) is the main focus. Rather, theology proper, the doctrine of revelation, organizes the Fathers' perspective. Chief among the theological themes are (1) the economy of divine laws, (2) the manner in which Christ recapitulates not just Moses but Adam, and (3) generally, getting the story right, which is to say, thinking rightly about Scripture.[8]

As early as the Second Council of Arles (A.D. 473), the "law of nature" (*lex naturalis*) was defined as "the first grace of God."[9] Beginning in late antiquity, theologians transformed the nomenclature of the lawyers to bring it in line with Christian theology. The *Corpus Iuris Civilis* divided law generally into *ius naturale, ius gentium,* and *ius civile.*[10] The word *lex* was not reserved for written law (according to the *Institutes of Justinian, scriptum ius est lex,* "law is the written *ius*") but was especially associated with imperial pronouncements.[11] The Lex Julia, for example, was the Julian Act.[12] This usage was also adopted by the canonists. *Lex,* Gratian states in the *Decretum,* is a written statute, a *constitutio scripta;* and a *constitutio,* he goes on to explain, is "what a king or emperor has decided or declared."[13] In St. Thomas's *Summa Theologiae,* the *iura* are classified as *leges.* So, rather than the *ius naturale,* we get not only *lex naturalis* but a classification of law according to diverse *leges,* such as *lex aeterna (the eternal law), lex nova (the new law), lex Mosaicae (the Mosaic law), lex membrorum (the law of the members), lex humana (the human law),* and *lex vetus (the old law).*[14] The term *lex,* which the lawyers reserved for a written edict issued by an imperial lawgiver, had become for theologians a usage emphasizing the divine origin of all law, whether it be instilled in the heart or imparted by written or oral arts.

As regards the being and cause of the natural law, the theological tradition moved steadily away from any anthropocentric or merely naturalistic conception of the *ius naturale*.[15] Theologians did not, of course, deny the existence of natural norms of justice; in late antiquity, this was not a disputed issue. Rather, they brought the two foci of norms in nature and in the human mind under the doctrine of divine providence. Natural justice bespoke a lawgiving God. This point is important, because some contemporary critics of the Catholic tradition allege that natural law is a mistaken biologism, a reduction of human moral freedom to order inherent in nature. From late antiquity, however, Catholic thought moved in precisely the opposite direction. Evidence for the "law" is gathered from order inherent in nature and in the human mind, but law is predicated not merely of the effects but rather chiefly of the divine mind. Once the theme of divine providence is dropped, natural law will become the problem of whether norms of conduct are principally "in nature" or "in the (human) mind." This is a post-Kantian problem that can be attributed to the older tradition only at the price of anachronism.

Misperceptions of Thomas

The thought of Thomas Aquinas has, of course, become nearly synonymous with "Catholic" doctrine of natural law. It would take volumes to dispel the modern misperceptions and misrepresentations of his natural law theory. Many misperceptions are due to the fact that Thomas, more than the patristic theologians, articulated the epistemological and natural foci with some philosophical precision. Those discussions in Thomas are often lifted out of context and debated as if they were completely independent of theology, natural or revealed.

I have no intention of trying to dispel all these misperceptions at their proper level of detail and complexity. Two general points, however, need to be made. First, nowhere does Thomas *define* natural law in anything but theological terms. Indeed, in answer to the objection that for there to be both an eternal law and a natural law was needless duplication, Thomas responds: "this argument would hold if the natural law were something diverse from the eternal law, whereas it is nothing but a participation thereof."[16] Natural law is never (and I must emphasize *never*) defined in terms of what is first in the (human) mind or first in nature.[17]

Although his modern readers have little inclination to discriminate among the three foci—natural law in the mind, in nature, in the mind of God—or to reflect upon their order of priority, Thomas understood what is at stake in arriving at a proper definition. The fact that we first perceive ourselves discovering or grasping a rule of action does not mean that the human mind is first in the causal order, or in the ultimate order of being. For example, the judge who discovers a rule does not equate the cause of discovery with the cause of the rule—unless, perchance, they are one and the same. In the case of natural law, Thomas defines the law from the standpoint of its causal origin (that is, what makes it a law), not in terms of a secondary order of causality through which it is discovered (the human intellect).

Without the order of priority, we have either nature or the human mind as the cause of the law—not the cause of knowing or discovering, but the cause of the law itself. This would destroy the metaphysical continuity between the various dispensations of divine providence. For if God is to govern, he will have to supersede, if not destroy, the jurisdiction constituted (allegedly) by human causality. Insofar as the natural law is regarded as the foundation of the moral order, and insofar as that is thought to be caused (and not merely discovered) in some proper and primary way by human cognition, God will have to unseat the natural law. Almost all the modern theories of natural law seek to relieve that conflict in favor of what is first in the human mind. Thomas understood what is at stake in giving definitions, and was exceed-

ingly careful not to confuse what is first in human cognition with
what is first in being.[18]

In the second place, as we saw earlier, Tertullian used the adverb
naturaliter (naturally) not to characterize the law but rather to describe
how it is known. Nature is not the law but the mode of knowing it.
This Latin adverb would eventually find its way into the Vulgate translation of Romans 2:14–15 to characterize what the gentiles know or
do without benefit of divine positive law. Thomas Aquinas frequently
uses the same term in order to emphasize the mode of divine promulgation.[19] Natural law is *lex indita,* instilled in the human mind by God,
moving the creature to its proper acts and ends. As for his estimation
of the efficacy of natural law in the human mind, Thomas never wa-
vered from the judgment that only the rudiments (or the *seminalia,* the
seeds) are known by the untutored mind. With regard to the gentiles
mentioned in Romans 2:14, those "who having not the Law, did naturally [*naturaliter . . . faciunt*] things of the Law," St. Thomas points out
that the words *naturaliter* and *faciunt* indicate that St. Paul was referring
to gentiles whose "nature had been reformed by grace [*per naturam
gratia reformatam*]." Any other interpretation, Thomas warns, would be
Pelagian.[20]

Thomas is well known for having insisted upon the *de jure* possibility of demonstrating the existence of God by natural reason. His
estimation of the *de facto* condition of the human mind led him to
make the cautious statement "known by a few, and that after a long
time, and with the admixture of many errors."[21] More to the point,
however, Thomas explicitly and emphatically denied that the philosophers were able to translate such scraps of theology into virtuous acts
of religion. None of the pagan theologies satisfied the natural, not to
mention supernatural, virtue of religion.[22]

In his last recorded remarks on the subject of natural law, made
during a series of Lenten conferences in 1273, Thomas's judgment is

even more stern: "Now although God in creating man gave him this law of nature, the devil oversowed another law in man, namely, the law of concupiscence. . . . Since then the law of nature was destroyed by concupiscence, man needed to be brought back to works of virtue, and to be drawn away from vice: for which purpose he needed the written law." As the critical Leonine edition of 1985 confirms, the words are *destructa erat*—"was destroyed."[23]

How can he say that natural law is destroyed in us? First, he certainly does not mean that it is destroyed in the mind of the lawgiver. As a law, natural law is not "in" nature or the human mind, but is rather in the mind of God. The immutability of natural law, he insists, is due to the "immutability and perfection of the divine reason that institutes it."[24] Insofar as natural law can be said to be "in" things or nature, it is an order of inclinations of reason and will by which men are moved to a common good. While the created order continues to move men, the effect of that law (in the creature) is bent by sin—not so bent that God fails to move the finite mind, for the fallen man is still a spiritual creature, possessed of the God-given light of moral understanding, but bent enough that this movement requires the remediation of divine positive law and a new law of grace.[25] In fact, Thomas held that God left men in such a condition—between the time of the Fall and the Mosaic law—in order to chastise them.[26] The so-called "time of natural law," which refers, of course, to the historical and moral condition of man, not the precepts of the natural law itself, is not normative for Thomas's ethics. And it is the effort to *make* that condition normative that marks the modern project.

By Thomas's day, natural law theory was being used in debates over jurisdiction between civilians and canonists; it was also being used on at least a partial basis for trying to get right answers about disputed matters of personal conduct. But in Thomas there is little of this. There is only one sustained discussion, extending over several articles, in which

Thomas subjects a disputed issue of personal conduct to what could be called a natural law analysis. It is from the very beginning of his career, when he was still a graduate student, in his exposition of the *Sentences of Peter Lombard*. This exposition, which is now appended to the *Summa* and called the "Supplement," contains an extended natural law argument on the problem of polygamy.

Interestingly, the problem was one he could not resolve by using natural law. Thomas ends up saying that polygamy violates no first precept of the natural law. With the ordering of sex to procreation, the polygamist does not violate the natural law. The remainder of Thomas's argument was a tentative one, namely, that polygamy made social life inconvenient, and that it would be difficult for the society of husband and wife to maintain itself properly intact in that kind of an arrangement. His only decisive argument against polygamy is sacramental— Jesus cannot have plural churches, man cannot have plural wives. And so the one serious effort he made to resolve the kind of issue we talk about today—a disputed moral issue—ended somewhat inconclusively on the natural law note. Once he reached that stalemate, he quickly reverted to sacramental theology as a way of resolving the issue.

Eclipse of the Theology

In the modern era, the theology of natural law was moved to the periphery, and was usually eclipsed altogether. The epistemological and natural foci become architectonic. The new sciences adopted the method of resolutive analysis and compositive synthesis. Under this method, the appearances of nature are analytically reduced to the most "certain," which is to say, the most predictable, elements: namely, modes of quantity, such as size, shape, and velocity. Then, through compositive synthesis, the quantities can be rebuilt as mathematical objects. This method was applied beyond physics to humane matters. In *De Homine,* for example, Hobbes takes man as he is, a thing of "meer nature," and reduces the appearances to stable and predictable modes of quantity. Once we have done this, we do not find Presbyterians and Catholics; rather, we find a stimulus–response mechanism that endeavors to augment its power. What is first, then, is natural laws as "lower" laws rendering men amenable to the law of the sovereign. In *De Cive,* man is rebuilt according to rules that are true laws. Hobbes explains: "Politics and ethics (that is, the sciences of just and unjust, of equity and inequity) can be demonstrated *a priori;* because we ourselves make the principles—that is, the causes of justice (namely, laws and covenants)—whereby it is known what justice and equity, and their opposites injustice and inequity, are."[27]

Hobbes, of course, was a materialist. But this method of reduction and recomposition was not tied to materialist doctrines. Continental rationalism and idealism also deployed methods of reduction to what is first in the mind, from which reality can be constructed, modeled, predicted. In the reduction, Hobbes could find only "lower" laws; other Enlightenment thinkers purported to find first principles of justice and equity. Whatever the differences, the trademarks are certainty and predictability, gauged according to what is first in cognition.

Yet the main reason for the eclipse of the theology of natural law was the theologico-political problem. What better way to solve such a problem than to imagine men's appealing to no authority other than what is first in the mind? Virtually all of the Enlightenment "state of nature" scenarios make this move. In Hobbes, Locke, Rousseau, and Kant, man is considered in an "original" position, under the authority of no pope, prince, or scripture. If there is a God, he governs through no mundane authority. Authority will have to make its first appearance in the covenants of individuals constrained to reach a consensus on the basis of what is (or seems) self-evident. The twelfth-century summist Johannes Faventinus declared: "The streams of natural rectitude flow into the sea of natural law, such that what was lost in the first man is regained in the Mosaic law, perfected in the Gospels, and decorated in human customs."[28] The modern myth of the "state of nature" rejects this scheme of divine pedagogy—not directly, but indirectly, by rendering it superfluous to the quest for first principles of the political order. Indeed, the "state of nature" was meant to be a secular substitute for the story of Genesis. Never a pure science of morality, it was rather a merely useful one, designed for the political purpose of unseating the traditional doctrine of natural law.

The fact that a proposition is pellucid, knowable without logical need of a middle term (e.g., "life is good," which can be grasped without a set of theological inferences or authorities), is supposed reason enough to conclude that logical independence means ontological independence; and the "state of nature" mythology had the aim of representing that independence. Since no orthodox Christian theology holds that God and his orders of providence and of salvation crop up as what is first in untutored cognition, to force natural law into that one understanding is bound to destroy moral theology on the reefs of half-truth. The half-truth is that there are principles of practical cognition that are proximate to the natural functioning of the intellect. But they are only the beginning (the *seminalia*) of practical reason. When the starting points are made autonomous, the human mind declares independence not only from the deeper order of divine tutoring but also from the tutoring afforded by human culture, including human law.

This is why natural rights, for so many modern advocates, turn out to be nothing other than immunities against the order of law. Thus, what began for the Christian theologians as a doctrine explaining how the human mind participates in a higher order of law is turned into its opposite. The natural law becomes "temporal," the temporal becomes "secular," and the secular becomes the sphere in which human agents enjoy immunity from any laws other than those they impose upon themselves.

For a time, Catholics were not confused by the new ideologies of natural law, for these conceptions were expressed by political movements vehemently hostile to the Church. But once political modernity became the "normal" state of affairs, and once the Church found a way to respond to modernity in something more than a purely reactive mode, it was almost inevitable that the new conceptions of natural law would begin to color moral theology.

There is a superficial congruity between the tradition of Catholic moral theology and modernity. Both (in various ways) hold that there is a moral order first in the mind, and that some problems can be reasoned without immediate introduction of premises drawn from revelation or from a fully worked-out cosmology of nature. The overlap of traditions on this specific point is apt to be misleading. Thomist, Cartesian, and Kantian conceptions of what it means to be "first" in the mind express very different understandings of practical reason, and how practical reason is situated with regard to what is "first" in nature and in the ultimate order of being.

But when the focus on what is first in the mind is conjoined with the desperate modern need for consensus, it becomes easy for Catholic uses of natural law theory to cross over into something new. The use of natural law by moral theologians has always been Janus-faced. Natural law can be used to express specifically theological propositions about divine providence, or it can be used to ground or mount arguments about particular disputed issues of conduct.

In modern times, we observe a steady drift toward the latter use, and with it a gradually diminishing sense of the sapiential context afforded by theology proper. Nowhere can this be seen more clearly than in the tradition of modern social encyclicals. As to things that have been declared contrary to nature and/or reason, a short list includes dueling, communism, divorce, contraception, Freemasonry, *in vitro* fertilization, and contract theories of the origin of political authority. And this is not to mention the bevy of rights and entitlements that have been declared to be owed to persons under the rubric of justice *ex ipsa natura rei,* by the very nature of the thing. Read carefully, the encyclicals assume that all three foci (law in the mind, in things, and decreed by divine providence) are legitimate and in principle are integrated in moral theology. Compared with his successors, Leo XIII was especially careful to make the distinctions that kept divine providence in the picture.[29]

Natural Law as a Persuasive Tool

It is not my intention to cast doubt on any particular assertion about natural law or natural rights in these official documents. The problem (for our purposes here) is not particular judgments about the morality of dueling or contraception, but the tendency of contemporary readers to interpret magisterial discourse about natural law without the doctrine of providence—that is, without the principles that would allow us to think of natural law as "law." From this follows the impression that talk about natural law is a rhetoric designed to achieve consensus about matters of public policy, or, worse still, conclusions grounded in Church authority.

Humanae Vitae (1968) suffered especially in this regard. The encyclical does not fail to note that natural norms are expressions of a real order of divine providence, and that the natural law is not reduced to its created effects, biological or otherwise (§4, 18, 23). But if *Humanae Vitae* is compared with Pius XI's *Casti connubii* (1930), which is the first modern magisterial treatment of contraception, one is struck how Pius XI repeatedly locates marital norms in the overall scheme of divine providence. The beginning of all the errors about the issue is the reduction of divine providence to the "mind of man" (§49), which must then impose an order upon nonmoral structures of the natural world. Indeed, almost all the references to natural law in *Casti Connubii* concern the jurisdictional location of the human mind under divine providence (§§49, 80, 94–95, 103, 105). In *Humanae Vitae*, this theme, while not entirely absent, was muted. Not surprisingly, Pope John Paul II has devoted much of his pontificate to filling out the picture, beginning with a book-length set of allocutions on the proper exegesis of Genesis.

In any case, the teaching method of trimming arguments to fit what is first in cognition, buttressed perhaps with appeals to what is first in the chain of legal command (the papal office), would eventually yield diminishing and disappointing results, not only for the gentiles but also for the faithful—especially the moral theologians. By almost imperceptible steps, it was easy to fall into the habit of regarding discourse about natural law as an instrument of persuasion, the truth of which becomes measured by its success in garnering assent.

Take, for example, Roy's 1973 remarks the "Occasion of the Tenth Anniversary of the Encyclical '*Pacem in Terris*.'" Addressing himself to Pope Paul VI, Cardinal Roy has this to say about the encyclical's references to natural law:

> Although the term "nature" does in fact lend itself to serious misunderstandings, the reality intended has lost nothing of its forcefulness when it is replaced by modern synonyms. . . . Such synonyms are: man, human being, human person, dignity, the rights of man or the rights of peoples, conscience, humaneness (in conduct), the struggle for justice, and more recently, "the duty of being," the "quality of life." Could they not all be summarized in the concept of "values," which is very much used today?[30]

Interestingly, on John XXIII's remark that peace is "absolute respect for the order laid down by God,"[31] Roy observes: "But here again, this word jars the modern mentality, as does, even more, the idea that it summons up: a sort of complicated organic scheme or gigantic genealogical tree, in which each being and group has its predetermined place." Eager to reinforce truths proximate to the human mind (or, perhaps, those least proximate to the chain of church authority), Roy seemed to find even the phrase "order laid down by God" too theologically strong. Whereas earlier generations of theologians addressed the gentiles by emphasizing the relationship between moral order and divine providence, a new generation of Catholic theologians was being taught (inadvertently) that the rudiments of moral order ought to be discussed without any reference to divine governance, or, for that matter, to created nature.

To give credit where it is due, it must be said that the Church was thrust into the position of having to teach, *ad extra,* about precepts of the moral order that are in principle proximate to the human mind. That nations or individuals must not murder, must not rape, and must not plunder are not uniquely theological propositions. Many of the precepts advanced in papal encyclicals have been held by men of good will who do not explicitly assent to Christian doctrines. The Catholic Church has always regarded itself as a consensus-builder among the peoples and nations.

Seizing the Postwar Moment

The high tide of the overestimation of natural law discourse was the post–World War II era, when the Church was eager to reinforce the right lessons of the war. Western modernity found itself recoiling from legal positivism, and moving honestly (if temporarily) to reform its polities on the basis of ideas about human dignity and natural rights. Catholic philosophers and theologians like Jacques Maritain and John Courtney Murray did remarkable work trying to show how the Catholic tradition should seize the moment: notwithstanding the gentiles' disordered theories *about* the moral order, the experience of the war and its aftermath rendered them teachable.[32] In retrospect, we see that there was an overestimation, not only of what the gentiles knew, but also of what they were willing to do with their knowledge. (Perhaps the most bizarre overestimation of common ground came in 1989 with Cardinal Bernardin's recommendation that Catholic lawyers ought to adopt the natural law theory of Ronald Dworkin.)[33] From another point of view, we could say that there was a drastic underestimation of the Church's teaching mission. In the literature and discourse of that period, it is often difficult to say who was teaching whom.

Fifty years after World War II, in *Evangelium Vitae,* Pope John Paul II laments the fact that the children of Locke and Rousseau have decided to reject the natural law foundations of civil government. He writes: "A long historical process is reaching a turning-point. The process which once led to discovering the idea of 'human rights'—rights inherent in every person and prior to any Constitution and State legislation—is today marked by a surprising contradiction. Precisely in an age when the inviolable rights of the person are solemnly proclaimed and the value of life is publicly affirmed, the very right to life is being denied or trampled upon, especially at the more significant moments of existence: the moment of birth and the moment of death."[34]

"[P]aradoxically," John Paul continues, what were once crimes now "assume the nature of 'rights,' to the point that the State is called upon to give them legal recognition." It is "sinister," the Pope says, that states are "departing from the basic principles of their Constitutions." For when they recognize as moral rights the rights to kill the weak and infirm, the "entire culture of human rights" is threatened. "It is a threat capable, in the end, of jeopardizing the very meaning of democratic coexistence."[35]

Thinking it had seized upon a moment favorable to making common cause with the modern notions of human dignity and rights, the Church finds that the culture has retreated from the few things that seemed right about its modernity. In any case, it is surely significant that most of the encyclical *Evangelium Vitae* involves a detailed exegesis of the first four chapters of Genesis. The Pope takes his audience back to the Scriptures.

Piecemeal Theology

If the papacy overestimated the efficacy of the instruction *ad extra,* it underestimated the problems *ad intra.* Not only was natural law disembedded from moral theology, but moral theology was disembedded from the rest of theology. In his encyclical *Aeterni Patris* (1879), Leo XIII anticipated the problem of theology's being done piecemeal, with a lurching from issue to issue, and with the chief means of resolution being the application of authority. He wrote: "For in this, the most noble of studies, it is of the greatest necessity to bind together, as it were, in one body the many and various parts of the heavenly doctrines, that, each being allotted to its own proper place and derived from its own proper principles, the whole may join together in a complete union" (§5).

Unfortunately, this ideal was not successfully realized prior to Vatican II. Perhaps the best account of the dwindling estate of moral theology before the Council is the recent book by Servais Pinckaers, O.P., *The Sources of Christian Ethics.* Regarding the typical presentation of moral theology in the manuals used in seminaries, Pinckaers notes: "Moral theology was divided into fundamental and particular sections. Fundamental moral theology included four chapters, covering human acts, laws, conscience, and sins. Particular moral theology, after a chapter on the theological virtues and their obligations, was generally divided according to the Ten Commandments, to which were added the precepts of the Church and certain canonical prescriptions. The sacraments were studied in the light of the obligations required for their administration."[36]

If, *ad extra,* doctrines of natural law were being used to produce conclusions to vexed moral issues among the gentiles, the opposite tendency prevailed *ad intra.* The task of moral theology was to lay out premises from reason and church authority for the purpose of directing the legal dimension of marital and sacramental actions. Not only in the seminaries but also in the universities, the thought of St. Thomas was accorded great respect; yet it was extracted from the *Summa Theologiae* in a way that favored the rationalistic elements of law. Almost everyone who teaches Thomas today would agree with Pinckaers that Thomas's thought was deeply misrepresented when the first seven questions of the so-called Treatise on Law (*S.t.* I-II, qq. 90–97) were isolated from the questions on beatitude and virtue, and ultimately from the questions on the Old Law and the New Law.

The subject of natural law was placed in the most unfortunate position of being organized around two extreme poles. On the one end, it represented the conclusions of church authority; on the other, it represented what every agent is supposed to know according to what is first in cognition. We have Cartesian minds somehow under church discipline.

The response was inevitable. In our time, there is a deep and ultimately irrational reaction against any depiction, much less any organizing, of the moral life in terms of law. We cannot here sort through all the species of this reaction in contemporary moral theology. Earlier we saw Cardinal Roy trying to construe "order laid down by God" in any way that might avoid the notion of a legal order. As we will see in due course, *Veritatis Splendor* tries to moderate this reaction against the notion of conduct regulated by law. Yet the National Conference of Catholic Bishops's advertising of the encyclical exemplified the very sort of reaction that *Veritatis Splendor* tries to moderate: "It reverses pre–Vatican II legalism by speaking of the good and the bad rather than the forbidden and permitted, and by speaking about the invitation to live a moral life in God rather than the enforcing of laws or norms." This is precisely the simplistic attitude that the encyclical tries to overcome.

Natural Law as Individual Autonomy

Before moving to *Veritatis,* let us look at one particular reaction against law, the reaction that the encyclical takes the most pains to refute. I have said that once natural law was disembedded from moral theology, and moral theology from theology, the concept was precariously stranded between two poles of authority: a chain of command somehow terminating in the authority of the Church, and a chain of propositions somehow terminating in the individual mind. Rather than fundamentally reconsidering this picture, casuists and confessors valiantly endeavored to relieve the burden of conscience. So, in the case of *Humanae Vitae,* the conclusions of the natural law deriving the official chain of command seemed (to many) to conflict with what individual "reason" pronounced.

We should not be surprised that casuistry would not have the last word. Natural law itself would have to be reformulated to side with individual conscience. Through the sluice-gates of this problem, the distinctively modern notions of natural law as individual autonomy would flow into Catholic moral theology. If this response went no further than to claim the individual's competence to respond to divine providence (with the Church as a non-authoritative support), then the story would have ended with a surprising "Protestant moment" for Catholic moral theology. But that is not where it ended. At least in contemporary moral theology, it ends with the claim of autonomy in the face of providence: the creator God exists, perhaps, but he does not govern.

For example, in a recent book, Father Joseph Fuchs contends: "When in fact, nature-creation does speak to us, it tells us only what it is and how it functions on its own. In other words, the Creator shows us what is divinely willed to exist, and how it functions, but not how the Creator wills the human being qua person to use this existing reality."[37] Fuchs goes on to assert: "Neither the Hebrew Bible nor the New Testament produces statements that are independent of culture and thus universal and valid for all time; nor can these statements be given by the church or its magisterium. Rather, it is the task of human beings—of the various persons who have been given the requisite intellectual capacity—to investigate what can and must count as a conviction about these responsibilities."[38] In other words, God creates, but he gives no operating instructions.[39]

Father Fuchs further asserts: "One cannot . . . deduce, from God's relationship to creation, what the obligation of the human person is in these areas or in the realm of creation as a whole."[40] Regarding *Gaudium et Spes,* where the human conscience is spoken of as a *sacrarium* in which we find ourselves responsibly before God—*solus cum solo*[41]—Fuchs states that the notion that the human person "is illuminated by a light that comes, not from one's own reason . . . but from the wisdom of God in whom everything is created . . . cannot stand up to an objective analysis nor prove helpful in the vocabulary of Christian believers."[42]

Father Fuchs's rejection of the Council's teaching on the nature of conscience at least has the virtue of consistency. It follows from his own doctrine that while God creates, he does not govern the human mind. The human mind is a merely natural light, to which there corresponds a merely natural jurisdiction over ethics. In its work of discovering moral norms, the mind discovers the contextual proportions of good and evil, case by case as it were. Although Fuchs struggles to avoid the implication, it would seem that a general statute of positive law could never concretely bind human conscience, because it could never adequately measure the proportions of good and evil across cases and contexts. At best, law would be a summary of previous findings, which then functions as an indicator (rather than a norm) of present or future choices.

Hence, specifically on the issue of natural law, Fuchs insists that "[a] classical understanding of natural law is basically a 'positivist' understanding of natural law (a static law 'written on nature'), and precisely does not offer genuine natural law as the living and active creaturely participation in God's eternal wisdom."[43] The traditional words are still present: e.g., "written on the heart," "participation in God's eternal wisdom." But they now mean something different, and in fact the opposite of the tradition in Augustine and Aquinas. For the older tradition, there is a clear distinction between the mind's *discovering* or discerning a norm and the being or *cause* of the norm. The human mind can go on to make new rules because it is first ruled. This, in essence, is the doctrine of participation as applied to natural law. Natural law designates for Fuchs, however, the human power to make moral judgments, not any moral norm regulating that power—at least no norm extrinsic to the operations of the mind. This is not a subtle departure from the tradition; it is no more subtle than the difference between giving a teenager the keys to the car with a set of instructions, and just giving him the keys to the car.

Veritatis Splendor: **Reaffirming Foundations**

The encyclicals usually have pastoral purposes. Fundamental principles are cited only insofar as they are needed to address the problem at hand, or perhaps to remind the faithful of what every one believes. *Veritatis Splendor* takes a different approach. Noting that the Church has proposed moral teaching on "many different spheres of human life," Pope John Paul goes on to declare: "Today, however, it seems necessary to reflect on the *whole* of the Church's moral teaching, with the precise goal of recalling certain fundamental truths of Catholic doctrine which, in the present circumstances, risk being distorted or denied."[44]

Veritatis Splendor is not aimed at consensus-building among the gentiles. It is addressed to the episcopacy. And it is chiefly concerned not with applied ethics but with the foundations of moral theology.[45]

The first statement about the crisis over foundations concerns the authority of the Church: "The Magisterium itself is considered capable of intervening in matters of morality only in order to 'exhort consciences' and to 'propose values,' in the light of which each individual will independently make his or her decisions and life choices."[46]

If the crisis concerned only the authority of the Church, the Pope would be putting moral theology into precisely the corner where the modern mind wants it: for it would look like the assertion of a this-worldly power to command an assertion that is immediately answered by a counter-assertion of the authority of individual conscience. The Pope needs to show that being commanded by another is not merely a device of ecclesiastical powers and offices; it is not created by papal authority or by tradition.

The Pope therefore reformulates the issue:

[C]ertain moral theologians have introduced a sharp distinction, contrary to Catholic doctrine, between an "ethical order," which would be human in origin and of value for "this world" alone, and an "order of salvation" for which only certain intentions and interior attitudes regarding God and neighbor would be significant. This has then led to an actual denial that there exists, in Divine Revelation, a specific and determined moral content, universally valid and permanent. The word of God would be limited to proposing an exhortation ... which the autonomous reason alone would then have the task of completing with normative directives which are truly "objective," that is, adapted to the concrete historical situation.[47]

Here, at last, we reach something fundamental for moral theology. Is the moral order a creature of divine providence, or does divine governance have to be added on to an already complete and autonomous human jurisdiction over morals? Here we are not worrying about the morality of gambling or contraception. Rather, the problem is the condition(s) of the possibility of moral theology. If God provides only the "natural" conditions for human practical reason, giving the human mind a kind of plenary authority over all the material norms, then God does not govern—except perhaps in the metaphorical fashion suggested by some of the deists. The Pope goes on to say: "Were this autonomy to imply a denial of the participation of the practical reason in the wisdom of the divine Creator and Lawgiver, or were it to suggest a freedom which creates moral norms, on the basis of historical contingencies or the diversity of societies and cultures, this sort of alleged autonomy would contradict the Church's teaching on the truth about man. It would be the death of true freedom: 'But of the tree of the knowledge of good and evil you shall not eat, for in the day that you eat of it you shall die' (Gn 2:17)."[48]

Throughout *Veritatis,* the Pope tries to give all three foci of natural law their due: (1) an order of nature (the "truth about man"), (2) the rudiments of which are "in principle accessible to human reason,"[49] and (3) are expressions of divine providence. At least in passing, he notes the relevance of the first two of these to the "demands of dialogue and cooperation with non-Catholics and nonbelievers, especially in pluralistic societies."[50] Reflection on the good and evil of human acts and of the person who performs them is "accessible to all peoples."[51] However, there can be no mistaking the main emphasis of the encyclical, which concerns number three.

The Strategy: Dialogue with God

The question is how to give all three foci their due, while still showing their proper organization in theology. In the *Institutes,* John Calvin quotes St. Bernard of Clairvaux: "With propriety, therefore, Bernard teaches that the gate of salvation is opened to us, when in the present day we receive the Gospel with our ears, as death was once admitted at the same doors when they lay open to Satan. For Adam had never dared to resist the authority of God, if he had not discredited his word."[52]

The Pope adopts a similar strategy of exposition, one that is dialogical from the very beginning. While never denying the fact that man enjoys natural starting points for grasping moral good and evil, the Pope puts man into conversation with God; he interrupts the soliloquy. Notice how the major chapters of *Veritatis Splendor* are arranged:

- In the first, the reader is situated along the road where the rich young man encounters Christ (Matthew 19). The Pope contends that questions about the good are essentially religious questions.
- In the second, the reader is re-situated in the light of the original conversation between God and man in Genesis 2. Most of the discussion of natural law takes place in this context.
- In the third, the reader is turned toward the world, according to the theme of martyrdom and witness.
- In the conclusion, the reader stands with Mary at the foot of the cross.

The Pope explains in the first chapter that the first and ultimate question of morality is not a lawyerly question. Unlike the Pharisees, the rich young man does not ask what the bottom line is, from a legal standpoint. Rather, he asks what must be done in order to achieve the unconditional good, which is communion with God. Christ takes the sting out of law, not by annulling it, but by revealing the Good to which it directs us. Remove or forget the Good and law inevitably becomes legalism.

The Scripture relates that the young man went away sad, for he had many possessions. But the modern audience is more apt to turn away sad when faced with the teaching that there is a moral law that is indispensable, and that indeed binds authority itself. The Pope points out that all issues of circumstance, culture, place, and time notwithstanding, certain actions can never be made right; no human "law" can make them right. Just as from the scales and axiomatic measures of music there can come a Beethoven sonata or a Schoenberg twelve-tone composition, so obedience to the commandments opens the possibility of a creative, fluid, and completely realized human liberty. The point of learning the musical scales is not to engage in mindless repetition; the point is to prepare to make beautiful music. A piano teacher who taught only the scales would be a legalistic simpleton. But a piano teacher who *neglected* to teach these rudiments would be unworthy of the name teacher. Musical order cannot begin solely with human spontaneity and creative improvisation. And the same is true in the domain of moral action. Anyone who sets up an opposition between law and freedom, and then takes the side of freedom, not only underestimates the need for law but also misrepresents the nature of freedom.

The story of the rich young man shows the essential unity of the law and the Gospel, and in *Veritatis* the Pope spends considerable effort on a related theme: the unity of the two tables of the Decalogue. "Acknowledging the Lord as God," he says, "is the very core, the heart of the law, from which the particular precepts flow and toward which they are ordered."[53] Each precept, he continues, "is the interpretation of what the words 'I am the Lord your God' mean for man."[54]

"To ask about the good," in fact, "ultimately means to turn towards God," the fullness of goodness. Jesus shows that the young man's question is really a "religious question, and that the goodness that attracts and at the same time obliges man has its source in God, and indeed is God himself."[55] Georges Cottier, the Dominican theologian of the papal household, has underscored the importance of this point in the encyclical: "awareness of the self as an image of God is at the root of moral judgments, beginning with the norms of the moral law. . . . The image is turned toward its Archetype and is the origin of a desire for union with it and assimilation to it. The natural law makes known to our reason the essential goods to which we must tend in order to reach God, who is the supreme Good."[56]

Back to Genesis

In the second chapter, the Pope takes the discussion of the foundations of the moral order back to the original situation in Genesis 2. This is the patristic common place for the discussion of natural law. Ever since his catechesis on Genesis, given during his weekly audiences in 1979–80 (published under the title "Original Unity of Man and Woman"), the Pope has returned over and over to the first four chapters of that book.[57]

> Some people . . . disregarding the dependence of human reason on Divine Wisdom . . . have actually posited a "complete sovereignty of reason" in the domain of moral norms regarding the right ordering of life in this world. Such norms would constitute the boundaries for a merely "human" morality; they would be the expression of a law which man in an autonomous manner lays down for himself and which has its source exclusively in human reason. In no way could God be considered the Author of this law, except in the sense that human reason exercises its autonomy in setting down laws by virtue of a primordial and total mandate given to man by God. These trends

of thought have led to a denial, in opposition to Sacred Scripture (cf. Mt 15:3–6) and the Church's constant teaching, of the fact that the natural moral law has God as its author, and that man, by the use of reason, participates in the eternal law, which it is not for him to establish.[58]

Turning to the injunction in Genesis 2:17, the Pope writes: "By forbidding man to 'eat of the tree of the knowledge of good and evil,' God makes it clear that man does not originally possess such 'knowledge' as something properly his own, but only participates in it by the light of natural reason and of Divine Revelation, which manifest to him the requirements and promptings of eternal wisdom. Law must therefore be considered an expression of divine wisdom."[59] The natural condition of man is one of participation in a higher norm. Man has liberty to direct himself because he is first directed by another.[60]

The Pope makes use of a number of authorities to express the idea of natural law as "participated theonomy."[61] He refers to Psalm 4:6, "Let the light of your face shine upon us, O Lord," emphasizing that moral knowledge derives from a divine illumination;[62] using Romans 2:14, "The Gentiles who had not the Law, did naturally the things of the Law," he calls attention to the idea that it is not just by positive law that humans are directed in the moral order;[63] from Gregory of Nyssa he cites the passage that autonomy is predicated only of a king;[64] and from St. Bonaventure he cites the dictum that conscience does not bind on its own authority but is rather the "herald of a king."[65] The very existence of conscience, the Pope argues, indicates that we are under a law that we did not impose upon ourselves.[66] Conscience is not a witness to a human power; it is a witness to the natural law. And this is only to say that the natural law is a real law that cannot be equated with our conscience. It was precisely this equation, the Pope notes, that beguiled our first parents, when the serpent in Genesis 3:5 said they could be as gods. What does it mean to be "as gods"? It means that the human mind is a measuring measure, having plenary authority to impart the measures of moral good and evil.

The Pope also notes that the topic of natural law has been too readily detached from the economy of divine laws and pedagogy:

> Even if moral-theological reflection usually distinguishes between the positive or revealed law of God and the natural law, and, within the economy of salvation, between the "old" and the "new" law, it must not be forgotten that these and other useful distinctions always refer to that law whose author is the one and the same God and which is always meant for man. The different ways in which God, acting in history, cares for the world and for mankind are not mutually exclusive; on the contrary, they support each other and intersect. They have their origin and goal in the eternal, wise and loving counsel whereby God predestines men and women "to be conformed to the image of his Son" (Rom 8:29). God's plan poses no threat to man's genuine freedom; on the contrary, the acceptance of God's plan is the only way to affirm that freedom.[67]

The Moral Theologians

It is surely a token of the disrepair of Catholic moral theology that the Bishop of Rome would have to remind the episcopacy, and through them the moral theologians, that natural law does not constitute a sphere of immunity (a kind of cosmic tenure for moral theologians) from the plan of divine laws.[68] But once again, what the Pope has to grapple with in this respect is not only decades of neglect *ad intra,* where the theme of natural law was detached from the fundamental principles of theology, but also the history *ad extra,* where natural law and natural rights betokened that ground of liberty in which men find themselves under no mundane authority. This secular myth, which was developed as a counter to Genesis, is contrary to the most fundamental principles of Christian theology.

However the Church might find a common ground of discourse with the gentiles, it cannot be done on the basis of that counter-myth. Of course, some truths about the nature of man and the structure of moral reasoning are, as the Pope says, "in principle accessible to human reason." He does not discredit the effort of modern polities to affirm human rights and to place moral limits upon the power of the state.

Having duly noted the existence of principles proximate to human reason, the Pope emphasizes two things that correspond to the two foci of natural law that he says less about: natural law in the mind, and natural law in nature. First, he reminds the reader of the wounded human condition that needs to be repaired by Christ: "What is more, within his errors and negative decisions, man glimpses the source of a deep rebellion, which leads him to reject the truth and the good in order to set himself up as an absolute principle unto himself: 'you will be like God' (Gn 3:5). Consequently, freedom itself needs to be set free. It is Christ who sets it free: He 'has set us free for freedom' (cf. Gal 5:1)."[69]

Second, he insists that human reason, endeavoring to construct the conditions for human fulfillment, needs revelation and grace: "Only in the mystery of Christ's Redemption do we discover the 'concrete' possibilities of man. It would be a very serious error to conclude . . . that the Church's teaching is essentially only an 'ideal' which must then be adapted, proportioned, graduated to the so-called concrete possibilities of man, according to a 'balancing of the goods in question.' But what are the 'concrete possibilities of man'? And of which man are we speaking? Of man dominated by lust or of man redeemed by Christ?"[70]

Some Implications for Protestants

What can evangelical Protestants learn from this story? They might conclude that Karl Barth was right in saying:

> It [moral theology] is in agreement with every other ethics adduced to the extent that the latter is obviously aware—explicitly or implicitly—of its origin and basis in God's command; to the extent that it does not seek authorization before any other court; to the extent that it actually attests the existence and validity of this principle. But it cannot and will not take it seriously to the extent that it tries to deny or obscure its derivation from God's command, to set up independent principles in face of autonomies and heteronomies which comprise the theonomy of human existence and action, to confront divine ethics with a human view of the world and of life which is supposed to have its own (if anything) superior value, and to undertake the replacement of the command of the grace of God by a sovereign humanism or even barbarism.[71]

It would be tendentious, of course, to suggest a meeting of the minds between Barth and *Veritatis Splendor*. But on this one point of theonomous ethics, there is more than a merely facile similarity. By way of negation, we can agree that the modern, secular construction of natural law is contrary to the Gospel. It is as destructive within the house of Catholic moral theology as it was in the Protestant denominations, which passed through the challenge of deism and liberalism a century before the Catholic Church.

In a certain respect, the degrading of Catholic moral theology is more cruel because Catholicism has staked more on this issue of natural law than Protestantism. The repair will also be more complicated for Catholics, because, among other reasons, the Catholic tradition has regarded the foci of natural law in the mind and natural law in things as having at least some intelligibility for those who know little or nothing of the revelation of Jesus Christ, and who have not given any effort to reconnecting these two foci back to the architectonic perspective of divine providence. The two cannot be brushed away under the rubric of the "epistemology of sin," as some Protestants are wont to do. Moreover, the Catholic Church has endeavored to address problems of justice in the temporal order according to principles immediately proximate to it.

The problem, for Catholics, is how to do all this without *ad extra* creating the misleading impression that these proximate principles are the end of the story, and also without *ad intra* reducing the Church's own moral theology to a habit of extroversion—to having a merely worldly opinion about disputed issues in the temporal order, which opinion is then configured to conform to the consensus (if any) among the gentiles.

Today, especially in the United States, evangelical Protestants find themselves reconsidering the issue of natural law. Their interest seems to be occasioned by two things. First, the political success of evangelical Protestantism has made it necessary to frame an appropriate language for addressing civil politics and law. Second, evangelicals find themselves in dialogue with Catholics, with whom they share many common interests in matters of culture and politics—interests that would seem amenable to natural law discussion. Even though it is true that many Protestants today are chiefly interested in the use of natural law *ad extra,* as a way to speak to the "world," the lesson they might learn from recent Catholic moral theology runs in the other direction. For assuming the legitimate and persistent need of the Christian churches to address worldly issues of justice and morality, it is easy to lose control of this discourse, so that natural law makes moral theology superfluous, and even impossible.

It seems to me that the expression "natural law" ought to be avoided whenever possible in the Christian address to the world about worldly things. I realize that this is practically impossible, but I shall give the reasons anyway.

Catholics, and most Protestants, will agree that there is a sphere of moral discourse about public matters that can be distinguished from sermonics and catechetics. The question is whether we should refer to the moral discourse in this sphere as "natural law." Of course, we believe it is the natural law that renders the gentiles amenable to the rudiments of moral discourse. In view of the traditional Catholic understanding of this matter (still put forth in the new Catechism of the Catholic Church),[72] we believe that what the gentiles know is an effect of divine pedagogy, whether the gentiles know that or not. Christians do not need to teach or to construct the first rudiments of the "natural law," for this much is not the effect of human pedagogy in the first place. God, not our discourse, constitutes human creatures as moral agents. The basis of moral order will not stand or fall on whether, or to what extent, we use the words "natural law."

The problem is not whether the gentiles are moral agents, but rather the meanings they assign to the rudiments they possess by virtue of the natural law. In modern times, the rudiments have been gathered into ideologies of natural law or natural rights that not only are false but are expressed in the form of a belligerent universalism. In our country, there is a long tradition of political rhetoric about natural rights. Sadly, today most uses of this rhetoric are degraded, signifying the expansion of individual liberty on terms that are either nonmoral or contrary to the moral order. Even John Courtney Murray insisted that the rhetoric was historically rooted in ideologies of the Enlightenment that ought to be corrected by a true account. Indeed, Murray's account of the American consensus includes explicit theological propositions about the relationship between moral order and divine providence. If there were a widespread dissent from these propositions, the basis for a public philosophy would collapse.[73]

"Good" and "Bad" Natural Law

Father Murray would have been mortified, but perhaps not completely surprised, by the spectacle of that collapse in our times. In 1991, on the eve of the Senate hearings on the nomination of Clarence Thomas to the Supreme Court, Senator Joseph Biden took the position that the Judiciary Committee should explore whether Judge Thomas held a "good" or "bad" theory of natural law. A bad theory of natural law, in Biden's view, would seek to expound a "code of behavior . . . suggesting that natural law dictates morality to us, instead of leaving matters to individual choice."[74] A good theory would support individual rights of immunity against morals legislation on matters of personal sexual conduct and abortion. The natural law teachings in recent papal encyclicals would therefore have to be regarded as "bad."

For public purposes, it is more prudent to ridicule than to argue with positions like Biden's. But the problem remains. Christians in search of a sphere of public moral discourse quickly realize that they no longer live in the age of Jefferson and Lincoln. The rhetoric of natural law is abundant in the moral discourse of the public sphere, to be sure; but it is terribly degraded. The most serious setbacks in our political and legal order have been done in the name of natural law, abortion rights being the most evident but by no means the only case in point. How then do Christians correct the ideologies in which natural law is ensconced without going on to discuss those very things which public discourse is supposed to avoid? How can they avoid the task of having actually to reconstitute the sphere of public moral discourse? *If* Christians wish to do so, I can see no alternative than to restore natural law rhetoric to its true and adequate premises. At the very least, we should return to the older American custom of speaking of "higher law." This usage, employed by Martin Luther King Jr., indicates the more than human ground for the public moral order.

The Church Fathers referred to pagan learning as the gold of Egypt, which can be melted down from the idols. But the modern ideologies of natural law and natural rights are quite different. For the moderns took the theological notion of natural law and reshaped idols. If it is necessary to take public discourse as it stands and by the arts of dialectic and rhetoric to move it away from the idols, this task must be done very cautiously. When the Christian theologian plays with the modern rhetoric of natural law, he is apt to underestimate the anti-theological meanings of modern natural law (essentially, man as a free agent without God), meanings that are easily reinforced if the rhetoric is not corrected; *ad intra,* he is liable to bring the idols back into the house of moral theology.

Both of these problems are addressed in recent encyclicals. To conclude, let us return to John Paul II's example. As I pointed out earlier, the Pope vigorously supports the modern experiment in constitutional democracy and human rights. But once he discerned that the rhetoric of natural rights was being used to justify killing the unborn and infirm, he took his readers in *Evangelium Vitae* back to the book of Genesis. The gentiles need and deserve the whole truth, even in order to preserve the rationality embedded in their own "secular" experiment. As for the use of natural law within moral theology, *Veritatis Splendor* reintegrates natural law into the dogmatic theology of revelation and Christology. It seems to me that these two encyclicals, one aimed *ad extra,* the other *ad intra,* get the problem of natural law situated just about right.

CHAPTER TWO

Natural Law as "Law"

As I suggested in the first chapter, Pope John Paul II's encyclical *Veritatis Splendor* raises a set of issues that tend to get short shrift in the contemporary literature on natural law. Ordinarily, the natural law is taken to mean a body of practical principles that are known independent of those duties sanctioned or determined by positive law. The encyclical does not reject this characterization of natural law. "The moral order, as established by the natural law, is in principle accessible to human reason" (§74). The encyclical, however, does not dwell on moral epistemology. Instead, it emphasizes a quite different line of inquiry regarding how natural law stands in the order of being. According to the encyclical, natural law is a real, and not a merely metaphorical, "law."

The shift of perspective, from what is first in the order of cognition to what is first in the order of being, makes questions of theology unavoidable. If natural law is to be defined as real law, a lawgiver will need to be brought into the picture. Of course, that natural law needs a lawgiver in order to be placed in the genus of law is not a point that has been overlooked by theologians and jurisprudents. For example, the well-known definition given by St. Thomas, "and this participation

in the eternal law by rational creatures is called the natural law," presupposes the existence of an eternal law in relation to which natural
law is defined.[1] Critics of natural law, from Hobbes to Austin, have
maintained that natural law can be included in the science of jurisprudence only insofar as the phrase denotes a nonmetaphorical "law," which
is to say, only insofar as it is regarded as a species of *lex divina*.[2] Whatever
kind of philosophical or revealed theology is required to secure the
definition, it should be clear that giving a real rather than merely nominal
definition of natural "law" is a task belonging to either natural or revealed theology.

Since theological argument is not regarded today as forming any
part of the philosophy of law, some of the most fundamental questions
that need to be asked about the natural law get moved to the side.
Veritatis Splendor provides us with an occasion to freshly reconsider the
theological themes that tend to be muted in the contemporary discussion of natural law. The encyclical's teaching about natural law is interesting not only for the amount that is said about where it stands in the
genus of law,[3] but also for its use of texts and authorities. The encyclical
gives only passing attention to the well-known proof text in Romans
2:14 ("The gentiles who had not the law, did naturally things of the
law"); but repeated reference is made to the second chapter of Genesis,
particularly Genesis 2:17 ("Of the tree of the knowledge of good and
evil, you shall not eat"). Rather than making the issue of natural law
rest principally on what people know (or do) independent of the divine positive law, the passage in Genesis raises the more basic theological issue of how to characterize divine governance prior to Torah, and
indeed prior to the Fall, as recounted in Genesis 3. Framing the issue
of natural law in terms of Genesis, the encyclical reconnects with the
patristic theologians, who argued that humankind were (1) under a
law from the very outset, which (2) was never superseded by divine
positive law. Tertullian, for example, characterized the injunction in

Genesis 2:17 "as the womb of all the precepts of God"—a "law un-written, which was habitually understood naturally."[4] There never was a sphere or a state of lawless ethics; that is to say, a sphere in which the created mind posits moral norms without any antecedent rule of law.

Turning to the injunction in Genesis 2:17, the Pope writes in *Veritatis:* "By forbidding man to 'eat of the tree of the knowledge of good and evil,' God makes it clear that man does not originally possess such 'knowledge' as something properly his own, but only partici-pates in it by the light of natural reason and of Divine Revelation, which manifest to him the requirements and promptings of eternal wisdom. Law must therefore be considered an expression of divine wisdom. . . ."[5]

Right away, we see that the injunction in Genesis 2:17 is being used as a scriptural warrant for the well-known definition of natural law given by St. Thomas, "the natural law is nothing other than a par-ticipation of the eternal law in the rational creature."[6] The notion of participation is restated in the context of Genesis 2:17 in order to emphasize that the human mind is a measured measure, and that the first principle of its practical activity is its participation in a divinely given law.[7] On the Pope's interpretation, the scriptural injunction means that the finite, created intellect is not the first measure of the *bonum* and *malum*. In other words, theologically considered, there is not morality and then law. Rather, there is a relationship between the creature and the creator that includes a principle of governance. This principle is that creatures share in, but do not constitute the measure of, moral good and evil. As we shall see later, the injunction carries a double meaning. For the prohibition against usurping divine sovereignty is also a prohibition against violating the natural principles by which humankind are ordered.

As we saw in chapter 1, the encyclical makes use of a number of authorities to express the idea of natural law as "participated theonomy,"[8] including Psalm 4:6 ("Let the light of your face shine upon us, O Lord"),[9] Romans 2:14 ("The Gentiles who had not the Law, did naturally the things of the Law"),[10] Gregory of Nyssa's insight that autonomy is predicated only of a king,[11] and St. Bonaventure's dictum that conscience is the "herald of a king"—that is, it does not bind on its own authority.[12] We also saw in the first chapter that the theological characterization of natural law as "law" is one with a long history; for example, as early as A.D. 473, at the Second Council of Arles, the *lex naturalis* was defined as "the first grace of God."[13] Indeed, the term *lex* became for medieval theologians like St. Thomas a useful theological concept for emphasizing the law's divine origin. As regards the being and cause of the natural law, the theological tradition moved steadily away from any anthropocentric conception of the *ius naturale*. The theological upgrading of the idea of natural justice can be detected in Justinian's *Institutes,* where it is proposed that the *ius naturale* is "sanctioned by divine providence."[14] This formulation has no textual parallel in the *Digest* or elsewhere in the *Code,* and can be inferred to be the Christian emperor Justinian's own interpolation.[15]

It is impossible here to survey the vast patristic literature on the idea of natural justice; just now it will suffice to mention two theological controversies that deeply influenced the application of *nomos/lex* to natural justice. The first was the polemic against the Gnostics. Some Gnostics held that the injunction in Genesis 2:17 was, like the Law, a positive (dietary) law of the Demiurge contrary to human nature. The law not only could be disobeyed, but indeed must be disobeyed. Therefore, in *De Genesi contra Manichaeos,* St. Augustine stressed that the tree of life mentioned in Genesis 2:9 represented the integrity of human nature under God. It was of the natural law that the human soul held a middle rank between spirit and corporeality. The other tree mentioned in Genesis 2:17 symbolizes the prohibition against violating this natural order of the soul. St. Augustine writes:

> Thus they refused to obey his law as if, by his prohibition, he jealously begrudged them an autonomy that had no need of his interior light, but used only their own providence, like their own eyes, to distinguish good and evil. This is what they were persuaded to do; to love to excess their own power. And, since they wanted to be equal to God, they used wrongly, that is, against the law of God, that middle rank by which they were subject to God and held their bodies in subjection. This middle rank was like the fruit of the tree placed in the middle of paradise. Thus they lost what they had received in wanting to seize what they had not received. For the nature of man did not receive the capability of being happy by its own power without God ruling it. Only God can be happy by his own power with no one ruling.[16]

Of course, the point that St. Augustine was particularly eager to make was that the destruction of the "ordered integrity of [our human] nature" was due to the violation of the natural law.[17] The fact that human beings find themselves handed over to an inferior order of the flesh is a punishment, not the original order of nature.[18]

In *De Paradiso*, St. Ambrose contended that the violation of the injunction in Genesis 2:17 required Adam to know "by nature" the legislative point of origin of the law.[19] Against the Gnostics, he argued that the misery of the human condition stems from a treason within the natural commonwealth. So in Genesis we find not merely a *culpa*, but a kind of *contemptus legis;* that is, a denial of the sovereign. St. Ambrose insists that part of the punishment for that denial was a gradually diminishing sense of the lawgiver of the natural law.[20]

The patristic explication of Genesis 2:17 as a regime of natural "law" also figured prominently in polemics against the rabbinical es-

tablishment. For example, on the text of Romans 7:11 ("For sin taking
occasion by the commandment . . ."), Chrysostom commented that
when St. Paul argued that the law was an occasion of sin, and that
Christians are no longer subject to the law, he cannot have meant the
"natural law," for this would suggest that humankind were without a
law in the absence of the Mosaic law, which is tantamount to saying
that there is (or was) a time when God does not govern.[21] "Neither
Adam, nor anybody else, can be shown ever to have lived without the
law of nature."[22] Divine positive law enters the picture as correction
for violation of the natural law. According to Chrysostom, the natural
law is superior to positive law in every way but one: clarity.[23] As to the
perfection in the mode of promulgation, the natural law is more like
the New Law than the Mosaic Law. Both are instilled, unwritten laws,
requiring perfection of the agent.[24]

In any case, in their effort to distinguish the New from the Old
Law, theologians like Chrysostom emphasized that moral norms naturally known do not constitute a lawless ethics, but represent a commonwealth under law that is antecedent to Torah and the Jewish state.
Although the natural law given to Adam is transfigured by Christ, it is
not superseded in the fashion of the Mosaic Law.[25] In short, the idea
of a natural law gave Christian theologians a ready way to express the
doctrine that God governs universally, first in Adam and then in Christ.

St. Thomas, of course, had much to say about natural law, including its specifically legal character. Nowhere is this brought out more
clearly than in his treatment of the moral precepts (*moralia*) of the
Decalogue. In I-II, q. 100.8, the question is posed whether the precepts of the Decalogue are dispensable. St. Thomas answers that the
ceremonial and judicial precepts of the Law are *determinationes,* positive laws of the Jewish state. Given all of the factors that would make
any other kind of positive law dispensable, these precepts, too, are dispensable. The moral precepts, however, are nothing other than

conclusiones of the natural law. Each one, St. Thomas argues, represents the "intention of the lawgiver" with respect to actions that have a per se order to the end, which is God himself. The natural law precepts of justice to neighbor contained in the second table are set within a full-fledged context of law. For instance, the fifth commandment (in the Vulgate) bears a double meaning characteristic of law. First, it proscribes killing the innocent. The healthy part cannot be ordered to the whole by cutting it off.[26] Second, the precept proscribes killing on one's own authority. In this respect, killing is not a double-effect issue. It is unlike self-defense, for self-defense is the anomalous case where someone who has no authority to kill takes action to protect his life, and in doing so kills another. This kind of action is not intentional killing. The deadly effect is *praeter intentionem*—outside the intention. In cases of intentional killing, the key issue is whether someone has been delegated the authority to use lethal force in defense of the commonwealth.[27] To kill the guilty is to exact a punishment, which only a competent legal authority can do.[28]

While we might routinely treat the proscription of murder as an ethical norm that regulates positive law, St. Thomas regards the precept as having a political and legal meaning from the outset. The Decalogue contains the natural law given in Genesis 2:17. Precepts of the second table (e.g., *non occides*) bear reference to the sovereign, whose care and governance of the common good cannot be usurped. Hence, too, in *Veritatis* the Pope maintains that "[a]cknowledging the Lord as God is the very core, the heart of the law, from which the particular precepts flow and toward which they are ordered."[29] Each precept, he continues, "is the interpretation of what the words 'I am the Lord your God' mean for man."[30] The negative precepts of the second table have a double intelligibility, with one arrow pointing toward neighbor, and the other pointing to the authority of the *princeps* of the commonwealth.

To summarize, although the doctrine of natural law in *Veritatis Splendor* acknowledges that the law is "in principle" accessible to human reason, the emphasis is not on moral epistemology but on the definitional question. This emphasis is guided by the effort to keep the natural law properly situated in the economy of divine laws. Hence, "[e]ven if moral-theological reflection usually distinguishes between the positive or revealed law of God and the natural law, and within the economy of salvation, between the 'old' and the 'new' law, it must not be forgotten that these and other useful distinctions always refer to that law whose author is the one and the same God and which is always meant for man."[31]

Whenever we find someone laboring to get a definition right, we know that there is a problem. Encyclicals of the recent past have not shown much interest in the definition of natural law.[32] The phrase natural law is used unproblematically, often as a prelude to the articulation of human rights. *Veritatis,* however, makes the definition a principal issue. We now turn to the problem behind the definition. The theological formulation of natural law figures so prominently in the encyclical because the definition itself has become a disputed issue in contemporary moral theology.

It is important to understand that the problem is not simply the application of natural law to this or that issue in moral conduct (e.g., contraception), but what the natural law is in the first place. Whereas the classical theological position situated natural law within the economy of divine laws, some contemporary theologians hold that natural law denotes the human practical reason. Once the natural law is equated with the human power to make practical judgments, its specifically legal character as a received (or participated) law is muted, if not abandoned.[33]

The theological problem underneath the effort to define natural law is the positing of a sphere of "ethics" immune from divine governance. In *Veritatis,* the Pope observes that an autonomous natural law will split the two tables of the Decalogue. The question, then, is whether the precepts of the second table represent an ethics of reason, functionally autonomous with respect to the ordering principles of the first table.

As we saw in the previous chapter, the Pope recognizes that "certain moral theologians" have alleged the existence of an autonomous natural law. This conception of natural law commits moral theology to an intolerable crisis with respect to natural law. On the one hand, the theologian is bound to recognize the revelation of divine sovereignty in the first table of the Decalogue; on the other hand, he is bound to recognize the claim of autonomy on the part of human reason with respect to "ethics." In which of these does natural law belong, if not the latter? Given this crisis, we should not be surprised that the moral theologian will try to split the difference by arguing that the Church only has authority to pastorally exhort the human conscience to do what it must do on grounds completely independent of God—which is to say that the Church, if not God himself, only has authority over matters directly pertaining to the first table. And even this jurisdiction will, in a sense, have to be justified in reference to the "natural" sphere of human practical reason and its rights.

The Pope does not mention any particular moral theologians by name. But we have already seen that such a prominent theologian as Joseph Fuchs certainly seems to hold the position that "natural law" designates the human capacity for practical reasoning, not a law given as a norm for the exercise of reason. Fuchs writes: "When in fact, nature-creation does speak to us, it tells us only what it is and how it functions on its own. In other words, the Creator shows us what is divinely willed to exist, and how it functions, but not how the Creator wills the human being qua person to use this existing reality."[34] The classical conception of natural law, Fuchs contends, is "positivist,"[35] for it implies that moral action is handcuffed to law, all the way down, as it were. If all law is positive law (an assumption that is made, but never clearly spelled out by Fuchs), it certainly would be odd, at least for the Pope, to suggest that moral norms are, *ab initio,* positive laws. One of the major themes of the encyclical is that some moral norms are binding from the very nature of the case, and not merely by a *determinatio* of positive law.

Actually, Fuchs presents his own view more accurately when he accuses the older theological tradition of "fundamentalism." To look in the scriptures for a categorical and determinate moral norm is, he says, a kind of "fundamentalism."[36] So, too, is looking for such a norm in nature, even when nature is described from the theological perspective of creation. The one thing upon which Fuchs and the Pope agree is that once the idea of natural law as "law" is removed, the different, but related, idea of natural law as prelegal moral norms must also be removed. They have different reasons for their respective positions. Relying chiefly on St. Thomas, the Pope contends that practical reason is not, *ab initio,* its own norm. The human agent orders himself (or others) to justice by virtue of participating in a received norm. Therefore, if it is the very idea of a received norm that constitutes the reason for rejecting natural "law," both the legal and moral meanings of natural law fall together. For his part, Fuchs argues that human participation in the divine plan does not begin with a reception of a moral law, much less with absolute moral norms; rather, moral reasoning creatively uses the gift of nature, ordering it according to practical judgments. Practical judgments do not proceed from pre-existing law, but from the practical reason's interpretation of what action requires in the light of the totality of concrete circumstances.[37]

Thus we can appreciate why the dispute between the Pope and

moral theologians like Fuchs will not be easily resolved, for disputes over particular vexed issues of conduct are being framed in terms of very different theological suppositions about the origin of moral norms. Whereas the classical theological tradition regarded the fifth and sixth Decalogue precepts concerning life and death as matters over which God retains sovereignty (and only partially delegated to human agents), Fuchs contends that although it is true that God is sovereign, he is a transcendent sovereign—a fact from which follows no determinate moral norms.[38] In other words, there is no norm prior to reason's consideration of the concretely situated action. At least as a question of moral theology, Fuchs's case proceeds from the premise that, at creation, God gave humankind a plenary jurisdiction over natural goods. Natural law is nothing more nor less than the competence of human reason to render moral judgment (see ch. 4).

Our intention at this juncture is not to rehearse the dispute between the Pope and any particular moral theologian. Instead, we are trying to draw into view how the phrase "natural law" can become a theological problem. If the finite practical reason relates to a nature that is given (in the factive sense), but not normed by God (in the moral sense), then norms can arise in only two ways: either from the human practical reason itself, or from divine positive law. This then leaves the moral precepts of the Decalogue in a precarious situation. Either these precepts merely reiterate the norms reached by human practical reason, or they represent the imposition of divine positive law. The first option renders the Decalogue superfluous; the second option renders it an exercise in divine positivism. The traditional formulation holds that God creates the first norm(s) as a natural law, which can be further determined (either by divine or human positive law); the other position holds that humans working upon nature create the first norms, which are then further determined (either by divine or human positive law).

The difference between the two positions cannot be settled by substituting the language of "moral norms" for what the tradition meant by natural "law." For by natural "law" the tradition understood a divinely given norm(s) of conduct for the common good. This is to say that the moral norms are law. Of course, the tradition can also say "moral norm(s)." But the problem is not essentially semantic in nature. The traditional position calls natural law "law" because it has the requisite properties for something being a law, while the second position refuses to call it law at all, and focuses instead upon the material of nature that still awaits the introduction of a moral norm or a moral point of view. Finally, it should be observed that the difference of perspective is not immediately solved by characterizing the first as theological and the second as philosophical. The second position is a kind of theology, too, albeit one that looks very much like deism.

To summarize thus far, the meta-ethical issue of natural law is not essentially semantic. The problem is not the words, but their theological context. The encyclical attends not merely to the words but to their definition. The purpose for doing so seems clear. At least for moral theology, particular disputed issues about moral conduct depend on whether there is a specifically theological principle in the first place. If, in fact, natural law only designates the human reason, operating within a sphere of "ethics" (encompassing the material of the second table of the Decalogue), then it would seem to follow that natural law is not a divinely given law, and indeed is no law at all. "Ethics" (or at least a part of it) has no necessary and specific theological principle. The problem here is ignited by quite different claims about the origin of moral norms. Do they have their origin in a divinely given law, one that in principle can be understood "naturally," or do they have their origin in the human practical reason, which "naturally" produces for itself rules of conduct?

The question to which we can now turn is whether the problem of the definition of natural law is amenable to clarification if we move it out of the immediate context of the encyclical. We shall examine two quite different ways to handle the problem of predicating "law" of natural moral norms. In this section, we will consider Francisco Suarez's position. In the next, we will look at Mortimer Adler's. Both Suarez and Adler try to resolve the definition by detecting the presence or absence of the legal property in our first grasp of moral norms. Both, I shall argue, fail. But their failure can teach us about the problem of the legality of natural law.

For ordinary legal purposes, it would seem sufficient to recognize that positive laws (human or divine) make moral norms effective, or more fully effective, in the political community by way of determination (*determinatio*). These *determinationes* simply sanction at (positive) law what is morally binding by nature (e.g., proscriptions against murder); in other cases the *determinationes* render more determinate what natural norms of justice leave indeterminate (e.g., by laying down specific penalties, times, and places); in still other cases, the positive law provides *determinationes* for how additional rules are to be made, enforced, or adjudicated. Provided that we have moral norms and a human lawgiver, there would not seem to be any need to be moving from one law to another. It is quite enough to understand how "law" in its ordinary sense, which is positive law, makes (moral) norms of practical reason determinate in the political community.

Perhaps we can retrace the steps of the problem of whether law can be predicated of natural moral norms by briefly considering Suarez's approach to this issue. Of all the modern scholastic theologians, Suarez was perhaps most alert to the problem of the legality of natural law. For Suarez, the problem can be stated as follows: Any rigorous definition of law requires that the obligating norm be known in reference to its point of legislative origin.[39] A rigorous definition of law must include not only the command, but also, to borrow a phrase from H. L. A. Hart, a rule of recognition whereby we can identify the authority under which a command is issued.[40] While this rule of recognition, as it were, is usually clear in the case of positive laws, it can be argued that it is not so clear in the case of natural moral norms—unless, of course, God as legislator is somehow already in the picture. For this to be the case, Suarez reasoned, there must reside in the concept of a moral precept a certain *signum,* or sign, that bespeaks a divine lawgiver.[41]

Suarez insisted that this was the "opinion held by St. Thomas and common to the theologians."[42] So put, this opinion can contain two quite different positions. On one hand, we might emphasize the *legislated deed* regardless of what the recipient of the law knows about the legislative point of origin. Hence, natural law is real law because basic moral norms are actually made-to-be-known (promulgated) to the rational creature who grasps the divine law "naturally" (*naturaliter*).[43] In this case, the promulgation is effective even if the creature has only the foggiest idea of law's origin in the divine mind. The recipient of the law might go on to reason from the *signum* (as an effect) to the legislative point of origin in order to confirm the divine pedigree. For St. Thomas, the definition of natural law requires such inferences. On the other hand, it could be argued that the naturally known moral norms also—and in some sense simultaneously—require knowledge of the deed of the legislator in order to be grasped as norms of conduct. On this view, natural law is recognized as law more or less in the same way we understand that a traffic law is both a norm of conduct and a norm legislated by the political community.

Which of these did Suarez hold? It seems that he held the latter. "Hence, this natural light is of itself a sufficient promulgation of the natural law, not only because it makes clearly manifest the intrinsic conformity or nonconformity of actions [with respect to that law], a conformity and nonconformity which are indicated by the increate light of God; but also because it makes known to man the fact that actions contrary [to the law so revealed] are displeasing to the Author of nature, as Supreme Lord, Guardian and Governor of that same nature."[44] In short, Suarez held that there are two conditions for natural law being "law": (1) in the order of being, a God who legislates by instilling a knowledge of the moral measures of action; (2) in the order of knowledge, a recognition that God so legislates and binds the creature to act according to his will.

This is not, however, the position of St. Thomas. When St. Thomas said that proper authority and promulgation are two essential traits of law, he did not stipulate that the recipient of the law necessarily has to know the ultimate legislative point of origin.[45] The sovereign's intention to coerce or impose a sanction does not enter into the definition of law sketched in *Summa Theologiae* I-II, q. 90. This is important, because if the lawgiver's will to impose a sanction is of the very essence of law, then the recipient of the law must immediately know the norm in conjunction with the legislator's will. Of course, in the order of being, it is true that there is a legislative command backed by sanctions. The question, however, is whether the recipient of a law needs to know all of this in order to grasp, in the case of natural law, that there are moral terms of good and evil at stake in human action.

Interestingly, in his exposition on the text of Romans 2:15, where St. Paul says that "it is conscience itself that renders testimony of good and evil, [and] is an evident sign [*est evidens signum*] that the work of the law is inscribed on the heart of man,"[46] St. Thomas contends that the *signum* means that their knowledge of moral right and wrong testifies to the fact of a legislated law, by which they knew the terms of good and evil—not that the Gentiles themselves knew the law in reference to the lawgiver. St. Thomas writes: "Although they have no written law, yet they have the natural law, whereby each one knows, and is conscious of, what is good and what is evil [*quid sit bonum et quid malum*]."[47] The *quid* of which they are conscious is moral good and evil, not necessarily the legislator. For those who are tutored in revelation, the *signum* does indeed testify to the legislated deed. St. Paul invites *us* to see that God governs all men, including those who know nothing of Torah.

As to the gentiles mentioned in Romans 2:14 ("who having not the Law, did naturally [*naturaliter . . . faciunt*] things of the Law"), St. Thomas points out that the words *naturaliter* and *faciunt* indicate that St. Paul was referring to gentiles whose "nature had been reformed by grace" [*per naturam gratia reformatam*].[48] It is one thing to speak of what some gentile converts *did* (fulfilling the law under grace, which required knowledge of the sovereign and reform of the will) and what the gentiles in general seemed to *know* (viz. rudiments of moral good and evil, but not necessarily what this knowledge testified to).

Make no mistake—St. Thomas thinks that a human agent ought to know, not just by argument, but by simple inference, that moral norms bind by virtue of something other than our own mind. There is a kind of blameworthy stupidity when the image fails to know itself turning toward its archetype.[49] Not everything is captured by such a simple inference, for man is ordered to an end that exceeds his comprehension; moreover, he is ordered in ways that exceed his comprehension (the role played by natural law in the total economy of divine laws is an issue of theological wisdom drawn from Scripture). But the movement of the mind from the effect (moral truth) to the cause (God) is something that, in principle, falls to human reason.[50] And it was because of this stupidity and idolatry that the Old Law had to begin the correction of the human mind through faith in the sovereign, to whom *latria* is owed.[51]

In this regard, St. Thomas followed the opinion of patristic theologians. Upon the violation of the injunction in Genesis 2:17, the increasingly dim knowledge of natural law as "law" is a punishment for sin. As St. Ambrose remarked, it was the "authority of natural law" that was obscured as a punishment for sin.[52] St. Augustine, commenting on Genesis 3:18, put it this way:

> Toward evening God was walking in paradise [Gn. 3:8], that is, he was coming to judge them. He was still walking in paradise before their punishment, that is, the presence of God still moved among them, when they no longer stood firm in his command. It is fitting [that he comes] toward evening, that is, when the sun was already setting for them, that is, when the interior light of the truth was being taken from them. They heard his voice and hid from his sight. Who hides from the sight of God but he who has abandoned him and is now beginning to love what is his own? ... For the human soul can be a partaker in the truth, but the truth is the immutable God above it. Hence, whoever turns away from that truth and turns toward himself and does not rejoice in God who rules and enlightens him, but rather in his own seemingly free movements, becomes dark by reason of the lie.[53]

The fact that many, if not most, people do not immediately recognize the rudimentary moral norms as law is not evidence for the existence of an independent sphere of ethics; rather, it is evidence of the moral reasoning in a diminished state. And for Augustine this diminished condition signified a disordered politics of men separated from the sovereign. But not men who know nothing of the natural measures of good and evil.

Suarez did not accurately represent the tradition "held by St. Thomas and common to the theologians." In his effort to keep the *lex naturalis* within the science of jurisprudence, Suarez insisted that the *signum* represents the rudimentary knowledge of both the moral norm *and* its point of origin. Like our first parents, who knew the command, the sovereign, and the threat of punishment ("when you eat of it, in that day you will die"), Suarez reasoned that all human knowers must know the legal *bona fides* of the moral order: "the natural law, as existing in man, points out a given thing not only as it is in itself, but also as being forbidden or prescribed by some superior."[54]

Why did Suarez make things more complicated for himself? He thought that it was necessary to refute a position that looks very much like that of Joseph Fuchs. Suarez characterized the position as follows:

> [I]t is clear that natural reason and its dictates are a divine gift, descending from the Father of Light. It is one thing, however, to say that this natural law is from God, as from an efficient primary cause; and it is quite another thing to say that the same law is derived from Him as from a lawgiver who commands and imposes obligations. For the former statement is most certain, and a matter of faith, both because God is the primary cause of all good and the illumination which it affords constitutes a great good.... Therefore, without doubt, God is the efficient cause and the teacher (as it were) of the natural law; but it does not follow from this, that He is its legislator, for the natural law does not reveal God issuing commands, but [simply] indicates what is in itself good or evil, just as the sight of a certain object reveals it as being white or black, and just as an effect produced by God, reveals Him as its Author, but not as Lawgiver. It is in this way, then, that we must think of [God in relation to] the natural law.[55]

Again, Suarez restates the objection that he wants to refute: "However, some one may object that these arguments have weight only with respect to 'law' in the strict sense of the term [*dici lege in eo rigore*], and may therefore easily be rendered inefficacious by the declaration that the natural law is not termed law in the rigorous sense in which law is said to be a universal precept imposed by a superior, but is so termed for the more general reason that it is a measure of moral good and evil [*regula boni* and *mali moralis*], such as law is wont to be."[56] At this time, no one denied that God providentially creates, or that everything in the created order can be referred to God as author.

Suarez was perceptive in seeing that modern schemes of natural law were en route to making a counterclaim that does indeed conflict with the tradition. For it is one thing to remain silent on the larger metaphysical picture, but it is quite another thing to suggest or argue that moral norms are grounded *only* in human reason. The latter position allows God to be a creative "author" but not a "legislator" of nature. If God should choose to legislate it can only be in the mode of positive law. Yet, in attempting to rescue the tradition, Suarez looked to the epistemic order for immediate evidence of the divine pedigree of moral law. In this sense, Suarez's response was characteristically modern. Indeed, the older tradition, which distinguished more sharply than did Suarez between what is first in the order of cognition and what is first in the order of being, is much weakened when it is forced to defend the intelligibility of natural "law" on the basis of immediate cognitive evidence of the lawgiver. From a theological standpoint, Suarez perhaps picked the right battle, but he transposed the terms of the older tradition in a way that made it less credible. The Suarezian theory certainly appears to make the natural law look like a positive law.

Yet if Suarez misstates his case in one direction, it is possible for the opponent to overstate the case in the other direction. If natural law is not properly a law, then the tradition running from the patristic theologians through St. Thomas, and through them to *Veritatis Splendor,* is mistaken—not perhaps about natural moral norms and their relation to positive law, nor even about the notion that all creatures, including moral norms, have God as their ultimate efficient cause; rather, the encyclical would be mistaken in how it places the moral norms in the genus of law.

The position that natural law is law only by analogy to positive law has been developed in an especially clear way by Mortimer Adler.[57] Adler bases his case on a reading of St. Thomas's definition of law in *Summa Theologiae* I-II, q. 90, which, according to Adler, rules out placing natural law in the genus of law by anything but analogy. Adler misrepresents St. Thomas, but even so, his position is interesting.[58]

Adler proposes that "modern misunderstandings of natural law arise from the supposition that what is signified by the phrase 'natural law' is law in exactly the same sense as what is signified by the word 'law' when it is used to refer to positive enactments of human legislators."[59] Adler contends that law cannot be said univocally of both natural law and positive law, "in the sense of expressing the same definition when imposed on both."[60] He concludes that the word law "is said univocally of the latter, and equivocally of the former, the type of intentional equivocation here being what is traditionally called 'analogy of attribution.'"[61]

Regarding the analogy of attribution, Aristotle said that health is predicated properly of a living body, but is attributed to diet (as a cause) or to urine (as a sign).[62] In scholastic jargon, this is called analogy of extrinsic attribution. When the definition (or *ratio propria*) applies properly to one class of things, the perfection or property (e.g., *sanitas*) can be analogically predicated of other things that do not intrinsically possess the property, provided that there is some real relation or order that obtains between these things and the primary analogate. Applied to the definition of law, the moral norms to which (positive) law is related can be regarded as elements or partial causes of law (as diet stands to bodily health), but are not laws in the strict sense of the term.

Thus, for example, for a positive law to have proper order to an end, it must incorporate moral principles of justice. Without such principles, the positive law would be deformed, and perhaps so deformed as to be no law at all. Moral norms are causally related to laws, as diet stands to health. Moral norms, however, are necessary rather than sufficient conditions for laws. The fact that something is a cause of a law being morally right is not, for Adler, evidence that it is itself a law. In the absence of a positive law, agents would still be bound to do justice according to these moral dictates. Seeing as how the moral norms guide the creation of positive law, they certainly have a law-like look and function. Adler would say that this is precisely the point. They are law-*like*.

The first point to be made is that analogical extension does not tell us whether the other analogate(s) possesses the properties or elements intrinsically or extrinsically. According to the classical example, we predicate *sanitas* of a body, but not properly of inert medicine. Notice, however, that it is not the analogical signification itself, but our knowledge of the being of the thing that tells us that inert medicine is not "healthy." The analogy signifies something we already know about the members of the analogical set. To belabor the point: if we did not already know that medicine cannot properly possess the perfection of health, then analogy of extrinsic attribution would be merely provisional.

We should note that two questions are apt to be confused: (1) Whether by analogy we can predicate "law" of precepts other than those of positive law; and (2) Whether there really exist non-positive law(s). Adler addresses the first question, but it is the second question that needs to be asked and answered if we are to settle the problem of natural law being a real "law." Adler assumes that positive law is law in the strict sense of the term; thus it is always the primary analogate.[63] Yet it could turn out that positive law is *not* the first analogate in the order of being.[64]

When St. Thomas mentions the analogy of health in *Summa Theologiae* I, 13.6, he remarks that "when anything is predicated of many things analogically, it is found in only one of them according to its proper nature, and from this one the rest are denominated." But in this very article, Thomas also insists that "as regards what the name signifies, these names are applied primarily to God rather than to creatures, because these perfections [wisdom and goodness] flow from God to creatures; but as regards the imposition of the names, they are primarily applied by us to creatures which we know first." Using the example of health, he makes precisely the same point about "truth" in *Summa Theologiae* I, 16.6. In other words, the same example can be used to signify different analogies, depending on whether we work from the imposition of the names, or whether we work from what is first in being. So, when St. Thomas gives the definition of natural law as our participation in the eternal law (I-II, 91.2), he certainly seems to be giving a real rather than a nominal or provisional definition. From this perspective, human positive law is not the prime analogate. The human ordinance "has" legality insofar as it stands in relationship to the eternal law, which contains the property/perfection of law most excellently.[65]

All that can be concluded from Adler's argument is that natural law is not a positive law. Without further knowledge obtained independently of the logical signification expressed by the analogy of extrinsic attribution, we cannot (yet) determine whether non-positive law(s) exists. In fact, we cannot conclude that we have framed the right analogy.[66]

In summary, the point we made earlier in connection with Suarez will have to be made once again to Adler. At least in the case of natural law, the predicate "law" is not yielded in immediate experience; nor can it be yielded analytically merely by examining what belongs to positive law. From different directions, Suarez and Adler try to settle the issue by detecting the presence or absence of the predicate "law" in the immediate datum of moral norms. For Suarez, every apprehension of a fundamentalist moral norm contains both a judgment about the moral *honestum* and a recognition of the divine *imperium*. For Adler, moral norms are called law only by analogy to positive law, because the legal datum given to our experience is human positive law. Neither one of the approaches accurately represents the older theological tradition.

The papal position in *Veritatis Splendor,* drawn from St. Thomas, is that the natural moral norms are law, but this law differs from positive law in the following senses: (1) It is not made by a human legislator, but by God; (2) It is not imparted by written art, but is given interiorly; (3) It is not a determination of something left indeterminate, but the basic principles of the order of justice; (4) It is not legislated for this or that political community, but for the natural commonwealth. Natural law is law, but not a positive law.

No one who has followed the discussion this far can be in doubt about the missing piece of the puzzle. It is, of course, the legislator. St. Thomas himself makes it clear that the definition of natural law is not arrived at simply by examining the meaning or concept of law; it is defined in reference to what is absolutely first in the order of being. In *Summa Theologiae* I–II, 91.1, where he first outlines and defines the various laws, he notes that the existence of the eternal law (in reference to which the natural law is defined in 91.2) follows from the supposition that divine providence rules the entire community of the world" "law is nothing but a dictate of practical reason issued by a sovereign who governs a complete community. Granted that the world is regulated by divine providence . . . it is evident that the entire community of the universe is governed by the divine mind." St. Thomas refers the reader to the *prima pars,* where he undertook that investigation.[67] In the absence of infused faith, inferences will have to be made from moral norms to the eternal law in order to arrive at a definition of natural law. Again, we are dealing here with the definition of natural law, not with the epistemological issue of knowing something *about* the natural law in the course of experience.

The categories and usages of philosophers and lawyers today take their bearing from the question of how positive law is to be placed in the genus of morals. Understandably, natural law is discussed and debated almost entirely within the boundaries of that question. The premodern theological tradition, however, asked a related, but different, question: How are moral norms to be placed in the genus of law? What complicates our perspective is that the phrase "natural law" is inherited from a tradition that asked the question about law(s) in the economy of divine providence.[68] When natural law thinkers began to fashion answers to a different kind of question (the morality of law rather than the legality of morals) is a complicated issue that goes beyond the bounds of the chapter. Among secular philosophers and jurisprudents, the theological question became burdensome, especially in political, legal, and professional discourse that has no stake in, or even rejects, the possibility of consensus about matters theological. On this view, it is quite enough to tackle the problem of whether human laws should be placed under the genus of morals. While this kind of inquiry truncates the older tradition, and often misinterprets it altogether, it can remain open to being reconciled with the tradition; for the older tradition likewise insisted that jurisprudence is a moral art. When Catholic moral theologians, however, evacuate the theological premises allowing morals to be placed under the genus of law, a different problem emerges. Once divine providence is stripped of the predicates of law (a command of reason, on the part of a proper authority, moving a multitude toward a common good), moral theology is reduced, at best, to deism (which posits a creating but not a commanding God). In that case, moral theology has but two options: (1) Law as exclusively the work of human practical reason; (2) Law as the positive law of the Church.

CHAPTER THREE

Natural Law
in the Positive Laws

Debates over natural law routinely confuse three quite different sets of issues. First, there are the properly philosophical questions of whether a natural law exists, and whether positive laws are valid completely apart from their moral specifications. Second, there are questions that properly belong to political theory. These include how a constitution ought to allocate responsibility to make natural justice effective, and how a particular system of positive law handles this issue. Third, assuming that a judiciary is limited by written law, it can still be asked whether this necessarily prohibits judicial uses of natural law theory. Questions at these different levels are sufficiently different that what it takes to solve a question at one level does not necessarily carry over to the others. It is vain, therefore, to search for a single method that brings closure on these issues.

In the only article of the *Summa* exclusively devoted to the issue of natural right (*ius naturale*), Aquinas observes that by analogy to medicine, which first signifies the remedy and then the remedial art, the word *ius* (the right) was first used to signify the "just thing itself," and then was understood to signify the "art whereby it is known what is just."[1] Aquinas explains that rules of art express the work of reason in matters of justice: "Just as there pre-exists in the mind of the craftsman an expression of the things to be made externally by his craft, which expression is called the rule of his craft, so too there pre-exists in the mind an expression of the particular just work which the reason determines, and which is a kind of rule of prudence. If this rule be expressed in writing, it is called a law, which according to Isidore is 'a written decree'" [*constitutio scripta*].[2]

From the canonists and civilians of the medieval period, to the common lawyers and constitutional theorists of the eighteenth century, there was broad agreement that although the natural and positive laws can be distinguished from one another on more than a merely nominal basis, the human positive law expresses—or to use the favored medieval term, "contains"—the natural law.[3] To be sure, medieval schoolmen and canonists regarded St. Paul's opinion in Romans 2:14 as authoritative, that "[g]entiles who do not have the law keep it as by instinct." In the first instance, natural law is an unwritten *lex indita*— a law impressed upon the human mind.[4]

But they also revered the art of written law.[5] Indeed, on the issue of how this law is to be realized in the human community, they turned to the biblical example, which taught that God promulgated the precepts of natural law in the Decalogue as *lex scripta*. What better example could be found for how to assist the completion of the natural law than that set by the sovereign of the natural commonwealth, who taught men to conform to a natural law by obeying a written word?[6] Many centuries later, even such a secularized advocate of natural law as Thomas Jefferson called law, very simply, "written reason."[7]

In this chapter, I shall explore this teleological theme of the natural law as effective law—that is, the natural law as it is realized through the prudential insights and artful determinations of human law. I shall explore this theme in applied teleology, as it were, in terms of a disputed question of our own day. Who should have responsibility for making the natural law effective, and how should it be done? Should the matter be controlled primarily by the legislative enactment of written statutes, or perhaps left largely to the work of judges who develop a body of law on a case-by-case basis?

In our legal and political culture, the problem of natural law is almost always debated in terms of what judges do, or ought not to do, with respect to the moral argument of law. Rather than viewing natural justice in terms of the written reason of a legislative body, we tend to look toward the judge to speak the law according to an unwritten or trans-textual rule of reason. On this view, the natural law, particularly as it concerns individual rights and civil liberties, achieves its telos through adjudicative judgment.

As a token of this dispute, we can recall that during the summer of 1991, opponents of Clarence Thomas sought to discredit his nomination to the Supreme Court on several grounds, including his views on the subject of natural law. In a 1987 speech, he praised an essay by Lewis Lehrman on the subject of abortion. Thomas remarked that the Lehrman essay, which treated the right to life in the light of the Declaration of Independence, "is a splendid example of applying natural law."[8] In two other publications, Thomas addressed the "higher law" background of the privileges or immunities clause of the Fourteenth Amendment,[9] as well as the role of the Declaration of Independence in constitutional interpretation.[10] In neither article did Judge Thomas have anything to say about abortion. Rather, he made some very general points about the relation between natural law and the project of limited government, as well as about the importance of natural law in understanding issues of racial equality under section one of the Fourteenth Amendment. Because of the apparent link between his remarks on abortion and his willingness to use natural law in constitutional interpretation, these publications were regarded by both the Left[11] and the Right[12] as evidence for any number of different intellectual felonies.

On the eve of the Senate hearings, Senator Joseph Biden took the position that Judge Thomas should not be regarded with suspicion simply because he believed in natural law, or, for that matter, because he would use it in judging cases. But, as we saw in chapter 2, Senator Biden urged the Judiciary Committee to explore whether Judge Thomas held a good or bad theory of natural law. A bad theory of natural law, in Biden's view, would seek to expound a "code of behavior . . . suggesting that natural law dictates morality to us, instead of leaving matters to individual choice."[13] Members of the Senate committee, as well as scholars and pundits, expressed incredulity that Judge Thomas could hold, on the one hand, that the written Constitution embodies a natural law of rights, while insisting on the other hand that the appellate judge has no authority to adjudicate cases on the basis of his understanding of the natural law. These two notions were regarded not only as theoretically incompatible, but also as nothing short of deception on Judge Thomas's part. The supposition, of course, was that a jurisprudent who evinces enthusiasm for the natural law, especially for the natural law basis of the written Constitution, had to be an activist prepared to pronounce upon matters of natural justice from the bench.

In this chapter I shall challenge that assumption, not indeed regarding Judge Thomas's views, but rather the general assumption that a natural law understanding of jurisprudence requires judicial activism.

At least three different kinds of questions crop up when we debate the relationship between the natural law and human positive law. The first are properly philosophical, concerned broadly with (a) the existence and knowledge of natural law, and (b) the intelligibility and/or validity of human law in relation to moral principles. The second are properly constitutional, concerned with the issue of the creation and allocation of lawmaking and law-adjudicating powers. Here, questions about the validity of law(s) are apt to concern the issue of jurisdictional authority to make, adjudicate, or administrate the law. The third are concerned with what judges do, either with respect to procedural rules of prudence and art, or with respect to the arts of interpretation.

Here, I make no claim that these categories are exhaustive. Rather, I propose that anyone who carefully examines the issues will notice that there are at least these three clusters of questions that are interrelated, but nevertheless analytically quite distinct. Therefore, we must first try to sort them out.

(1) At the first level, we can ask whether there exists a law of nature, and whether it sets any specifically moral norms for human action. This, of course, is an ancient question. As early as Plato's *Gorgias,* we find it suggested that predicating "law" of "nature" is a contradiction in terms, since nature seemingly dictates the very opposite of what we institute as justice. That is, nature seems to dictate that the strong should rule and possess more than the weak, whereas human law does not regard this proposition as either true or just.[14] Whether or not the words "law" of "nature" represent an egregious equivocation, and whether or not something more than a merely metaphorical analogy can be found between natural and moral laws, are persistent questions of philosophy.

So, too, are the questions that stand closer to the concerns of the practical science of law. For example, in the Anglo-American world, the problem of natural law is usually joined once it is asked whether a system of positive law is valid apart from its moral specifications. In the literature of the Anglophone legal world, "positivists" and "naturalists" have carried on a steady and (sometimes) quite nuanced debate about this matter.[15] I do not intend here to even briefly summarize the history of this debate. Rather, I propose that such questions are theoretical in nature, and that the truth or falsity of the answers do not depend upon the answers we might give to questions that crop up at the next two levels. Although the answers tendered at this first level may set some general guidelines for answering the questions at the remaining levels, I contend that even were these properly philosophical problems settled in favor of natural lawyers, much is still left indeterminate by natural law.

(2) At the second level, if we accept that we have reason to believe that a natural moral law exists, and that some human agents can know it sufficiently to be guided by it in the formation of human laws, the question then emerges as to how the natural law is to be made effective.[16] Should it be done legislatively by written statute, or should the responsibility fall primarily upon a judiciary who announce the principle of law in the particular case? Or, should it entail some combination of the two? This question, in turn, can be further distinguished into two parts. First, if we adopt the standpoint of the framers of a constitution, we can ask how a constitutional order *ought* to parcel out the authority to make law and to resolve cases arising under laws. Second, if we take the view from within the positive law of a particular constitution, we can ask how this positive law *in fact* allocates authority. This question can only be answered descriptively, on the basis of an analysis of the legal texts, traditions, and practices of a particular polity.

In the context of American law, many of the disputed questions about natural law are ignited here. That is to say, the problem of natural law either begins, or quickly becomes, a jurisdictional issue of who has, or ought to have, authority to decide. In our polity the answer to this question will be complicated; in addition to the allocation and enumeration of the powers of the federal legislature and judiciary, there are fifty different state jurisdictions; and taken altogether, there are at least nine different sources of valid positive law.[17]

This problem of jurisdiction is often confused with philosophical debates between positivists and naturalists about the existence of a natural moral law, the substantive morality dictated by its precepts, and the obligation in conscience to obey a human law that contradicts natural law. This is a debilitating confusion, made all the more frustrating because it is so easily avoided. As Aquinas himself argued, a law can be invalid for two reasons: first, because of morally perverse content, as when a law contradicts either natural or divine law; second, because the human agent acts *ultra vires,* beyond the power of his office.[18] In short, the substantive moral properties of a legal enactment is a different issue than the morality of jurisdictional authority.

One might argue that laws made *ultra vires* are prohibited by the natural law itself. That is to say, it could be argued that even when the content of a human law is in conformity with the natural law, insofar as that law is made by someone lacking the authority to make it, the natural law is not made effective in the human community, but rather is perverted on account of failing to satisfy the criterion of rightful authority. While there is much good sense to this approach (I will revisit it later), it still fails to settle the problem of who has, or ought to have, the authority to make the natural law effective. Though it be true, for example, that much of Nazi law was substantively unjust, and that no one was under a moral obligation to obey it, the moral fact that the positive law was *malum in se* does not answer the question of who had authority to make, emend, or unmake German law. It simply won't do to say that the natural law itself prescribes that all positive laws must be made by a proper authority. For there is no way to move from that proposition, in itself, to the judgment that so and so has, or ought to have had, authority. My point is that there are questions that arise at this second level (who decides?) that cannot be answered simply by repairing to the first (what are the precepts of natural law?). Neither the most vehement natural lawyer, nor the unreconstructed positivist, can claim to have settled the jurisdictional issue simply by dint of their respective theories about what (in general) makes law valid.

(3) Finally, assuming, for the sake of argument, that a particular constitutional order prefers written statute to judicial determination of natural law, it can be further asked whether *all* judicial appeals to natural law in constitutional interpretation constitute judicial "activism" (in the pejorative sense of the term).[19] We can ask whether adjudication can ever completely avoid natural principles of justice, which are implicit in the act of judgment. A positivist like H. L. A. Hart, for example, concedes that adjudication of law must remain at least implicitly committed to standards of impartiality and fairness.[20] For example, the maxim "Like cases should be judged alike, and different cases differently" represents something more than a proverbial rule of thumb. It seems to bespeak a principle of procedural fairness, without which legal judgment would prove dystelic, as it were. Principles of procedural fairness do not arise merely from the texts of written law, nor from the arrangements of a particular legal culture; nor, finally, do they seem to depend upon what *theory* of law one happens to hold. Indeed, such a prominent positivist as Neil MacCormick has noted that "[l]egal reasoning should be permeable to moral reasoning; and, in particular, consideration of those aspects of justice to which law necessarily aspires should inform all legal reasoning."[21]

While we may doubt that the norms inherent in such procedures would retain their telic ordinacy if the substance of the laws is unjust, we should be cautious about concluding that this settles much of anything about the questions posed at the first two levels. The fact that a judge understands that like cases are to be treated alike and different cases differently certainly indicates that adjudicative acts are, as

MacCormick says, "permeable" to moral aspirations. But, as contemporary positivists correctly insist, this only tells us something that is not under dispute: namely, that fairness is a goal transparent in all authentic acts of adjudication. To resolve the ontological and epistemological questions about natural law—that is, to tackle the problem of whether laws are valid in terms of their moral substance—it will be necessary to introduce other premises and arguments than those which avail to the end of showing that procedural fairness is an inherent moral value in the law.

Furthermore, as to the problems that crop up at the second level, what MacCormick calls the permeability of legal reasoning to moral aspirations surely does not in itself tell us who has lawmaking or law-adjudicating authority, and hence whether a particular legal act is valid. In other words, the ineliminable standards of procedural justice cannot settle the quite different question of how and to whom legal powers are to be delegated.

Beyond the issues of procedural natural law, there stand other interesting hermeneutical questions. For example, the constitutions and bills of rights of both the United States government and the governments of the various states reflect a commitment to the idea of fundamental rights. Most everyone knows, or should know, that these rights were formulated in light of natural law theories of one sort or another. Yet constitutions are exercises in "written reason," to use Jefferson's expression. A polity, having a written constitution, of necessity requires judges to engage in interpretive acts in order to understand the intent of the law and to assist its application to the case. Assuming, then, that judges are duty-bound to "cognize" natural law only through the media of written positive laws, it would still seem impossible to prohibit judges from exercising some interpretive responsibility in the matter of natural law. Indeed, Judge Thomas, who has a very rigorous notion of judicial discipline, conceded to the Judiciary Committee that, insofar as the written law reflects the intent of the legislator to make the natural law effective, the judicial interpreter does not act *ultra vires* when he searches out the legislative intent in terms of its natural law concepts. Judge Robert Bork has made the same point.[22]

In summary, I have sketched out three clusters of questions that, although interrelated, are nevertheless quite distinct. Assuming that there exists a natural law, it leaves indeterminate whether a particular polity ought to make it effective primarily through written constitutions and statutes or through judicial sentences; and, assuming further that a particular polity decides to invest the legislature with the authority to make the natural law effective via written constitutions, codes, and statutes, there remains the question concerning the rules of prudence and art that pertain to judges when they play their role in making the natural law effective. As we will now see, this scheme roughly represents Aquinas's approach.

Aquinas's understanding of the guidelines that natural law sets for human positive laws are very general. First, no human positive law should contradict either the natural or divine laws.[23] Second, human positive law has no competence, and therefore no jurisdiction, over the interior movement of the human will. Although the natural law itself enjoins rectitude for both the external and interior acts, human law can enjoin only the exterior act. Because only God can discern competently the interior movement of the will, the sanctions at this level are to be let to the *lex divina,* the divine positive law.[24] Third, human law enjoins the outward acts of virtues only insofar as they concern matters of justice. Of course, the *finis* of human law is something more than justice.[25] Laws aim to make their subjects good.[26] The human good includes all of the natural virtues, set to the end of the love of friendship, and ultimately to such contemplative acts as are available to human nature. Nevertheless, Aquinas insists that in the matter of precepts, human law can only enjoin those outward acts which are necessary to the justice of the civil commonwealth.[27] In sum, the jurisdictions of natural law and human positive law overlap, but the latter can make effective only a part of the natural law.[28]

We can now move to the main question, which concerns how the natural law should be made effective, and by whom. In the first article of the first question of his treatment of the *lex humana,* Aquinas poses the following question: Shouldn't justice be left to the arbitration of judges?[29] The historical background of the question is Aristotle's distinction between animate and inanimate justice.[30] Animate justice denotes the justice brought about by the virtuous person, whose virtue (rather than any written, or inanimate law) permits a sure judgment about what justice requires. Given the option between administrating justice on the basis of written laws or on the basis of the virtuous discernment of a wise judge, why shouldn't we always prefer the latter to the former?

Aquinas, of course, agrees that (ideally speaking) we ought to prefer animate to inanimate justice. But the prudential answer to the question is that it is better that all things be regulated by (written) law than left to be decided by judges. He gives three reasons:

> First, because it is easier to find a few wise men competent to frame right laws, than to find the many who would be necessary to judge aright in each single case. Secondly, because those who make laws consider long beforehand what laws to make; whereas judgment on each single case has to be pronounced as soon as it arises: and it is easier for man to see what is right, by taking many instances into consideration, than by considering one solitary fact. Thirdly, because lawgivers judge in the abstract and of future events; whereas those

who sit in judgment judge of things present, towards which they are affected by love, hatred, or some kind of cupidity; wherefore their judgment is perverted.

He concludes on this note: "Since, then, the animate justice of the judge is not found in every man, and since it can be deflected, it was necessary, whenever possible, for the *law* to determine how to judge, and for very few matters to be left to the decision of men."

Assuming that there exists a natural law, the precepts of that law will be made effective in the community through the mediation of human reason. But what kind of reason? If I correctly understand Aquinas, his answer is twofold. First, natural law is best made effective, in either the life of an individual or in a society, by virtue. That is to say, the practically wise man is the best jurisprudent, since he can see what the natural law requires not only in general, but in particular. If we had authorities whose virtue could bespeak the natural law, then we would have an answer to the question of *how* natural law is best made effective in the human community. But this does not decisively settle the question of the office. There is no necessary reason why the practically wise person should be a judge rather than a legislator; nor, for that matter, why the "few" should be legislators rather than judges. Indeed, in a democracy where majorities carry the day in legislatures, there might be good reason to look for a few good judges to act as a moral check upon the willfulness of a majority.

Why does Aquinas identify animate justice with the judicial rather than the legislative office? No doubt, one reason is that Aquinas simply assumed that a legislator ordinarily directs the citizens by means of written or inanimate law. But it can also be argued that the judicial act appears more finally determinate in the order of practical reasoning. Whereas the legislator pronounces that "this shall be so" for the general run of cases, the judge pronounces "this is so," in which pronouncement the law reaches the concrete case. And perhaps for this reason, Aquinas remarks later in the *Summa* that judgment is "like a particular law regarding some particular fact."[31] We might imagine a situation in which laws reach all of the particular facts. This situation, of course, would not resemble what prevails under the codes of laws enacted by the human legislator. For the *leges* of the human legislator need to achieve adequate generality to direct the actions of a multitude. Rather, such perfectly realized animate justice would approximate divine providence.

Aquinas's second answer is that political prudence dictates that, wherever possible, we should prefer the inanimate justice of written laws. It is easier, he reckons, for legislators to take a broad, well-considered view of what justice requires of the positive laws than it is for a judge to ascertain what is required in the more immediate context of litigation. Here, Aquinas's position evinces the Aristotelian teaching that as practical reason moves from general notions to the singularities of action more and more is required of right reason. Because it is usually easier to determine what justice requires of the positive laws in general than on a case-by-case basis, he reasons that a polity is best governed by general, standing laws. By and large, laws that try to reach all the contingencies and singularities of action will prove deficient not only in the order of prudence, but also in the order of art. We can imagine what would ensue if we tried to write laws with the same degree of detail that a judge ordinarily considers in the context of litigation. Finally, Aquinas believes we ought to prefer written law in order to put some constraints upon the cupidity of the judge. At least in those polities which cannot rely upon having judges who are Solomonic in virtue, we do not want justice to depend solely upon whatever virtue or vice that soul of the judge might bespeak.

Aquinas's opinion that positive law (ordinarily written) ought to constrain the judge is a matter of prudence rather than a precept drawn from the order of moral necessity. However, later in the *Summa,* when he returns to the issue of constraints upon the office of judges, we find that he is somewhat more adamant about strict judicial discipline. In Q. 60 of the II–II, he treats the issue under the rubric of the virtues and vices of "judgment." Judgment, he says, is "the act of a judge insofar as he is a judge." Thus, judgment is not the act of a virtuous person acting in a merely private capacity. For this, the natural law would suffice. Rather, judgment (*iudicium*) implies the notion of justice rendered by one who has authority.[32]

According to Aquinas, the judge's principal act is *ius dicens,* speaking the law. But which law is he to speak? In article 5 of Question 60, Aquinas notes that something becomes just either because of the nature of the thing itself, that is, by virtue of the natural law, or because of human positive law. But again, of which does the human judge judge?

In the *sed contra,* Aquinas cites the authority of St. Augustine: "In these earthly laws, though men judge about them when they are making them, when once they are established and passed, the judges may judge no longer of them, but according to them."[33] Then, he writes, "Now laws are written for the purpose of manifesting [*declarationem*] both these rights, but in different ways. For the written law does indeed contain natural right, but it does not establish it, for the latter derives its force from nature: whereas the written law both contains positive right, and establishes it by giving it force of authority. Hence it is necessary to judge according to the written law, else judgment would fall short either of the natural or of the positive right." In order to interpret this passage correctly, we should first take note of an important difference between Aquinas and John Locke. Locke, it can be recalled, argued in the *Second Treatise of Government* that, in the state of nature, every individual is judge and executor of the natural law.[34] Aquinas, however, does not believe that anyone has the authority of judgment from the natural law itself.[35] Human judgment depends upon an office of authority conferred through custom, positive law, or perhaps by divine decree. Therefore, the human judgment about natural law, at least in matters of justice, depends upon the holding of an office. It will always be a mediated rather than an immediate authority concerning natural justice.

Once the natural law is made effective in the form of positive laws (ordinarily written), the judge, having no natural law jurisdiction to begin with, must judge according to the dictates of whoever has authority to make law. To depart from this discipline is to subvert not only justice as determined by positive law, but also the natural justice that the positive law sought to make effective. According to Aquinas, law has at least four essential traits. It is a work of reason, promulgated by he who has authority, for the sake of the common good.[36] The key here is the criterion of authority. Hence, he writes that "even as it would be unjust for one man to force another to observe a law that was not approved by public authority, so too it is unjust, if a man compels another to submit to a judgment that is pronounced by other than the public authority."[37] The fact that an individual having proper authority lacks the moral virtue of judgment does not invalidate a judgment; but should even a materially correct judgment be made by one who lacks the requisite authority, the judgment bespeaks usurpation (*usurpatio*) rather than law.[38]

Thus, turning his attention to the injustices of a judge, Aquinas once again cites Augustine: "A good judge does nothing according to his private opinion [*ex arbitrio suo facit*], but pronounces sentence according to the law and the right."[39] Sentence, Aquinas argues, must be given not according to private knowledge, but "from what he knows as a public person [*tanquam personae publicae*]."[40] And again, regarding judicial sentences: "In matters touching his own person, a man must form his conscience from his own knowledge, but in matters concerning the public authority, he must form his conscience in accordance with the knowledge attainable in the public judicial procedure."[41] Elsewhere, Aquinas maintains that a judge who knows that a man has been convicted by false witnesses may use the public procedures to expose the false testimony; he may remit the case to a higher tribunal; but the judge has no authority to rescind the conviction on the basis of his personal knowledge.[42]

To summarize, Aquinas held that the natural law provides very general guidelines for political prudence. The proximate telos of human law is to direct the multitude of a civil community in matters of justice. For Aquinas, the thread of moral precept connecting the first and second levels of questions we outlined earlier is that of authority to render justice. Whatever other moral issues that still need to be answered will consist of the application of the rules of prudence and art. His position does not rule out, in principle, that a particular polity could invest a judiciary with lawmaking powers.[43] Indeed, so long as the adjudicator has authority, we could imagine a situation in which the written laws are simply the sentences of the wise judge, committed to writing. But this is not what Aquinas recommends. Rather, he recommends that human prudence and art institute a judicial discipline that directs and constrains the public role of the judge.[44]

At the outset, I cautioned the reader that we would not read Aquinas for the purpose of engaging, much less settling, problems connected with the institution of judicial review in American constitutional law. Rather, our brief survey of Aquinas helps us to clarify the more abstract problem of whether the natural lawyer must be committed to judicial supremacy over natural law. We saw that there is nothing contradictory in arguing, on the one hand, for a natural law basis of government, and indeed of positive law itself, while at the same time holding that judges ought, whenever possible, to be bound by written law. To argue that judges are bound to interpret the written law, rather than speculate immediately about the natural law, in no way requires us to believe either that the written law is morally valid only by dint of the will of a legislature, or that the positive law is morally binding completely apart from its moral specifications. Whatever estimation one has of Aquinas's position on the ontological and epistemological aspects of the problem of natural law (at the first level), he has these things clearly distinguished from the problems of jurisdictional authority (at the second level). Moreover, he distinguishes between the invariable elements (e.g., the moral content of laws, and the criterion of authority) and the elements that need to be brought under prudence and art (e.g., the particular political and legal institutions).

Our polity has witnessed a judicialization of the Constitution and its rule of law.[45] Not surprisingly, this has led to a judicialization of the question of how natural standards of justice are made effective in the human community. The reasons behind the American preference for natural law theories tailored to judicial rather than legislative activity are complicated. No doubt, one reason is the legacy of English common law and courts of equity, in which the judge rather than codifier played such a prominent role in formulating the terms of justice. Moreover, the American Constitution created an independent judiciary as a co-equal branch of government. The judiciary acquired the power of judicial review. Over time, this power was exercised as a check upon legislative majorities at both the federal and state levels. Given the power of judicial review, which after the Civil War was exercised across all of the different legislative jurisdictions, it perhaps was predictable that debates about justice would be magnetized toward the judicial rather than the legislative power.

If theories can be said to vote with their feet, then we can understand why the paths of natural law theories have led to the branch of government that has the power to invalidate the positive laws. Why develop a theory to guide legislatures, when the theory that guides the judge will have the last word? The germ of the issue is already in Alexander Hamilton's *Federalist* 78: "It is far more rational to suppose that the courts were designed to be an intermediate body between the people and the legislature, in order, among other things, to keep the latter within the limits assigned to their authority. The interpretation of the laws is the proper and peculiar province of the courts. It therefore belongs to them to ascertain its [*sic*] meaning as well as the meaning of any particular act proceeding from the legislative body."[46]

But the key passage in *Federalist* 78 is Hamilton's dictum that the judiciary "may truly be said to have neither Force nor Will, but merely judgment."[47] It is the "least dangerous" branch, he argued, because it is deprived of the power of either the sword or the purse. Hamilton's dictum seems to suggest a limit upon the judiciary; yet inasmuch as the judicial power is contrasted with the legislative according to the metaphor of judgment in contrast to will, it is easy, by a short and almost insensible step of the mind, to construe the matter as a contrast between reason and willfulness. On that contrast, authority to render the natural law effective should be vested in the organ of reason rather than the will. Given a choice between the cognitive and the appetitive powers, the great Western tradition of natural law theory would not hesitate to align natural law with the cognitive part. Thus, we should not be surprised that it came to pass that the judiciary was expected to enforce natural principles of justice against "willful" legislatures.[48]

While there are many more interesting and complicated aspects to the history of this problem,[49] let us pause here to summarize why the American preoccupation with judicially determined natural law creates problems for one who would try to understand the theme of natural law in the positive laws.

First, it tends to reduce the more general, and properly philosophical, issue of whether there are natural law foundations for human positive law to the more narrow, and properly constitutional issue, of who has the power to make and/or interpret the law. As we have seen, these are two different issues. Once conflated, we can expect to find proponents of judicial discipline arguing against the relevance, and, in some cases, the very existence of natural law in order to secure the good of authority; and, correlatively, proponents of a natural law defending (or acquiescing in) judicial activism in order to secure the moral substance of law. Although this is put somewhat simplistically, it is not an inaccurate statement of how the problem of natural law is typically debated among lawyers and constitutional scholars.

As a token of this confusion, let us turn for a moment to Mortimer Adler's essay "Robert Bork: Lessons to Be Learned." As the title indicates, Adler uses Robert Bork as a foil in order to develop a sharp contrast between natural lawyers and positivists. This dichotomization is on display in the table on the following page, which is taken from his article.[50]

Adler fails to see that one can subscribe to every proposition in the naturalist column (indeed, one can remain a thoroughgoing Aristotelian or Thomist with regard to natural justice) without having to decide, for instance, either for or against Robert Bork's understanding of judicial discipline. Furthermore, that such a prominent positivist as Joseph Raz can also subscribe to the "naturalist" tenets outlined by Adler, indicates that there might be serious problems in Adler's characterization of what distinguishes "positivists" and "naturalists."

Once again, the argument that, in human law, written statute ought to take precedence over judicial sentence in matters of natural justice simply does not require us to believe that the written law is morally valid only by dint of the will of a legislature. Adler might have solid reasons against moral skepticism and/or legal positivism; he might have

Positivism	Naturalism
o that might is right	o that might is not right
o that there can be no such thing as the tyranny of the majority	o that majorities can be tyrannical and unjust
o that there are no criteria for judging laws or constitutions as unjust and in need of rectification or amendment	o that principles of justice and of natural right enable us to assess the justice or injustice of man-made laws and constitutions and to direct us in their rectification and amendment
o that justice is local and transient, not universal and immutable, but different in different places and at different times	o that justice is universal and immutable, always the same everywhere and at all times, whether or not recognized at a given time and place
o that positive laws have force only, and no authority, eliciting obedience only through the fear of punishment that accompanies getting caught in disobeying them	o that positive laws have authority as well as force, if caught disobeying them, but obeyed by just individuals by virtue of the authority they exercise when they prescribe just conduct
o that there is no distinction between *mala prohibita* and *mala in se*	o that there are *mala in se* as well as *mala prohibita,* that is, acts that are wrong in themselves whether or not they are prohibited by positive, man-made laws

good reasons why legislatures are under the obligation to make good on natural principles of justice; but these reasons do not necessarily defeat Judge Bork on the issue of what kind of moral argument is available to the judge when he exercises judicial review. Adler, however, is mistaken when he suggests that the moral basis and argument of law depends upon allowing judges directly to speak the natural law.[51]

Senator Biden, it can be recalled, voted against the confirmation of Robert Bork, among other reasons, because Bork expressly rejected judicial appeals to natural law. Biden declared: "I have certain inalienable rights because I exist."[52] Well he might. But this does not mean that someone else has the authority to impose a judgment about these rights. It is one thing for critics like Senator Biden and Professor Adler to argue that no one ought to be appointed to the highest appellate court if they evince no historical or moral understanding of natural rights. For this is only to say that the judge ought to "cognize" the rights traditionally recognized in the law, and that the judge ought not to remove from his consideration certain rights because he finds the philosophy of inalienable rights intellectually repugnant. However, it is quite another thing to suggest that the existence of a natural right necessarily binds a judge apart from any consideration of the positive law.[53]

Second, preoccupation with judicial appeals to natural law can easily fall into the trap that Aquinas himself discussed. Recall that in the passage cited earlier Aquinas pointed out that insofar as a judge proceeds case by case the laws are apt to be disconnected. The business of a judge is litigation, and, on the whole, litigation is not the best context for taking stock of what the natural law requires: (1) litigation gives the judge little time for reflection; (2) it moves along according to adversarial procedures, which are not the best way to develop a systematic position on the moral quality of laws;[54] and (3) the interests of the various parties are usually narrowed so drastically that it is difficult to find generalizable principles for the common good.

Third, because Americans gravitate toward the branch of government that has the power to invalidate laws, and because we bring to the judiciary rights-claims which brook no compromise, natural law theories tend to look extravagant, quarrelsome, and inimical to the common good. Our reliance upon the judiciary to speak the natural law in the course of its ordinary obligation to *ius dicere*—and correlatively, our tailoring of natural law theory to influence what judges do—puts a bad face on natural law theory. For, upon historical examination, what we find is a miscellany and patchwork of case law that is not coherently organized. Historically speaking, appellate judges have lurched from natural law views of property rights to privacy rights and everything in between. Rather than making natural law effective in the political community, this case law looks like nothing other than the *ad hoc* decisions of judges in the service of one or another ideological agenda—or, at the very least, under the political pressures of the moment.

Thus far, I have made two points. *First,* a natural law theory of law and politics can be distinguished from the issue of whether legislatures or courts should have the principal authority to render the natural law effective. Unless we sort out these two problems, and take the measure of each at its own proper level of detail and complexity, the public debate over natural law will become fruitless and tiresome. *Second,* not only does the preoccupation with judicial uses of natural law provide a very narrow, and probably misleading, *theoretical* picture of natural justice, but it also furnishes an unsteady *practical* approach to how a body of positive law is to be made congruent with the natural law.

From an abstract philosophical point of view, there is no reason why legislatures and courts cannot have different, yet complementary, roles to play with regard to the natural law. In order to suggest how this is the case, I now turn from Bork's critics to Judge Bork himself. Thus far, I have at least indirectly defended Judge Bork against his naïve critics. But Judge Bork has also failed to attend to the different levels of the problem.

In a 1992 article Robert Bork writes: "Having endured for half a century a Court that seized authority not confided to it to lay down as unalterable law a liberal social agenda nowhere to be found in the actual Constitution of the United States, conservatives must decide whether they want a Court that behaves in the same way but in the service of *their* agenda."[55] Bork reproves some conservatives for arguing that there are proper judicial uses of natural law.[56] He contends that, regardless of differences in the content proposed by conservative proponents of natural law jurisprudence, the method is essentially no different than that of the liberal, activist Court. The "prospect," he says, "of 'correct' natural law judging is a chimera."

One of the problems in dealing with Bork's criticism of natural law jurisprudence is that he has said quite different things at different times about what, precisely, is wrong with judicially cognizable natural law. For example, he has written that: "If a judge should claim . . . to possess a volume of the annotated natural law, we would, quite justifiably, suspect that the source of the revelation was really no more exalted than the judge's viscera."[57] In a similar vein, in *The Tempting of America,* he writes: "in today's situation . . . there is no objectively 'correct' hierarchy to which the judge can appeal. But unless there is, unless we can rank forms of gratification, the judge must let the majority have its way."[58]

These remarks reduce the issue of judicial uses of natural law to the philosophical problem of moral relativism and emotivism. We can agree that if emotivism is a correct picture of moral judgment, it would not make much sense to invoke natural law as a principle in law, whether by a legislature or by a judge. The problem, however, is that Judge Bork tries to prove too much. If the argument from emotivism is taken seriously, the arguments that avail to that end undermine the moral basis for imposing the judicial discipline championed by Judge Bork himself. Surely, the basis for judicial discipline consists in something more than the rules of art imposed by a written text. If there is a good reason for imposing limits on the kind of moral argument available to the judge, the reason will be drawn from specifically moral considerations; that is, considerations that represent something more than the idiosyncratic "viscera" of either those who allocated the powers of government or those who operate under the constraints of those delegated powers.

Just as Adler makes the issue of the moral teleology of law depend upon what judges do, so too Bork makes the issue of the moral responsibility of judges dependent upon propositions that, if true, guarantee that there can be no moral telos to human law, much less to that part of morality which ought to apply to the judiciary. Here, I do not pretend to present a systematic appraisal of Judge Bork's judicial philosophy. Rather, I only wish to make the point that Judge Bork, like many other friends and foes of natural law, cannot resist the temptation to make the answer to the question at the second level (who decides?) depend upon generally stated propositions that ought to be debated at the first level (is there a natural law?). The difference, however, consists in the fact that Judge Bork pulls the moral rug out from under himself precisely where his argument is the strongest, which is on the issue of authority.

His argument is the strongest when he sets aside the debate about moral theory, and attends to the moral requirements of authority. Bork writes: "If there was evidence that the framers and ratifiers intended judges to apply natural law, I would accept that judges had to proceed in that fashion. When an institution is intended and designed to operate in a particular way, when its members take an oath to operate in that way, it seems appropriate that the institution and its members should do so. I suppose it could be said that this duty of fulfilling an obligation is itself natural law. If so, it is a piece of natural law that requires the judge to confine himself to positive law in all else."[59] Perhaps Bork could be persuaded to see that his case does not need to rest upon the epistemological debunking of natural law. Rather, he need only cogently and firmly state his arguments for why no judge under the Constitution has authority to invalidate positive laws, except where the positive law has given him authoritative warrant to do so.[60] As Aquinas himself argued, this discipline is a moral matter; and I might add that it is only cluttered by ruminations about emotivism.

Furthermore, we have seen that Judge Bork is prepared to admit that a judge can be expected to address natural law in the course of discerning "what the framers and ratifiers meant"—a discernment, he says, which must be distinguished from making up "new rights the judge regards as 'natural.'"[61] Granting the cogency of the argument that the judge must never read his private theory of "nature" or "justice" into the law (a point on which both Bork and Aquinas agree), the question is whether one is already there, and whether it sets a norm for interpretation of the law. When we suggest that one is already "there," we can mean a number of different things: (1) we can mean, for instance, that the entire system of positive laws represents a general effort to make natural justice effective; (2) we can also mean that the moral requirement that a judge adhere to the disciplines and limits of his office bespeaks not merely a rule of art, but a precept of morality; (3) we can mean that there is a morality inherent in the fair procedures of judgment. But we can also mean that there is a discernible (as the lawyers say, cognizable) moral conception of justice that shaped the written law, and that expresses what the legislator intended to make effective.

Even Aquinas, who, as we said, clearly favored legislative rather than judicial authority in rendering the natural law effective, also held that equity is the highest justice. Equity—what the Greeks called *epieikeia*—is the act whereby a judge reaches beyond the letter of the law in order to achieve its purposes. Interestingly, Aquinas argued that a judge who refuses equity—who cleaves to the letter of the law where the letter is defective—does not obey, but rather disobeys the will of the legislature.[62] Giving equity is not opposed to judicial discipline. Aquinas points out that although "it would be passing judgment on a law to say that it was not well made [*non esse bene positam*]," to say that "the letter of the law is not to be observed in some particular case is passing judgment not on the law, but on some particular contingency."[63] Given the fact that a legislature must frame laws very generally, there will always be work for judicial interpretation in order to assist the legislative intent in the resolution of singular cases. Section one of the Fourteenth Amendment, for example, was debated and framed in the light of natural law principles. That is a matter of historical record.[64] To rule out in advance any judicial consideration of natural justice would seem to be the imposition of the judge's private opinion, which, according to both Aquinas and Judge Bork, represents a violation of, rather than obedience to, judicial discipline.

We can agree with Judge Bork that if the administration of justice in a polity were to evolve such that *only* courts exercised the authority to adjust the law to achieve its purposes—a situation, perhaps, in which legislatures remain naïvely or maliciously indifferent to the defects in laws they make, or defects in the scope of their application—then we would have a polity in a real mess. The draftsmen of the Constitution and of its subsequent amendments enacted broad and sweeping clauses into the fundamental law. To be sure, much of the fundamental law evinces the lawyerly arts of making words mean what they say. This is particularly true of the unamended Constitution, which is mainly concerned with the allocation and enumeration of powers. But the parts of the fundamental law that ignite debates are those which are broadly drawn. Moreover, these also tend to be the parts that are morally fraught, touching upon the rights and liberties of citizens.

Perhaps part of the problem, for Judge Bork and other conservative proponents of judicial discipline, is not judicially cognizable natural law, but rather the fact that the amendments are deficient at the level of art. Unlike the European civil codes, which more carefully specify the order of moral axioms and postulates governing the written laws, our tradition has left these things very general. The First Amendment, for example, does not define the meaning of the word "religion." Section one of the Fourteenth Amendment does not provide us with an annotated list of what count as "privileges and immunities," much less what the term "liberty" means in the due process clause. A Supreme Court majority, in its 1992 *Planned Parenthood v. Casey* opinion, defined "liberty" so capaciously as to include "the right to define one's own concept of existence, or meaning, of the universe, and of the mystery of human life."[65]

My interest here, however, is not in constitutional case law. I only wish to point out that deficiency at the level of legislative art can unintentionally force judges to engage in a kind of speculation that makes it difficult to retain judicial discipline. Given the almost continual perturbations caused in the body politic by debate over constitutional rights, one might wonder not only whether Jefferson's standard of "written reason" has been fulfilled in our written law, but also whether the Federalists were correct when they originally insisted that it was both imprudent and unartful to attach a Bill of Rights to the Constitution.[66] In any case, we should not rule out the possibility that part of the problem of natural law in constitutional interpretation is due to a deficiency at the level of legislative art. And, to the extent that this is true, we can begin to understand why much of the debate about natural law is misplaced. Failure at the level of art is not, in the first instance, a problem of the moral content of the natural laws, nor a problem concerning who has authority. Rather, it expresses the problem of making justice effective through the medium of written words.

Contrary to simplistic views of either conservatives or progressives
in our legal culture, our exposition of Aquinas's position showed that
one can at once hold a robust theory of natural law, constrain the
adjudicative office to the written law, and recognize that judges will
from time to time need to search out the moral intent of laws in order
to assist their completion in individual cases. The non-negotiable core
of Aquinas's position rests upon two principles. First, that human
lawmaking is an expression of the telos of natural law, made effective
through human prudence and art. Second, that, by moral necessity,
human law can make the natural law effective only insofar as it is done
by proper authority.

The remaining issues concern the application of these principles—
applications that must rely upon prudence and art rather than philosophy. How a particular polity ought to delegate lawmaking and adjudicating powers depends upon any number of contingencies and exi-
gencies regarding the condition of the people. Aquinas thought it wise
to rely upon the virtue of a select group of legislators, rather than
judges. However, there is nothing in Aquinas's theory that would prohibit a large democratic state from looking to a select number of judges
to act as a check against willful legislative majorities. So long as this
power is not usurped, there is no absolute reason in the order of moral
necessity why law cannot be made by judges.

My aim in this chapter has been to untangle and clarify these
questions, and only incidentally and imperfectly to suggest solutions
to them. By sorting out their different levels, we might take a less simplistic and naïve measure of the issue of the general problem of natural
law in the positive laws. Any theory that aspires to interrelate the different levels of the problem of natural law in the positive law will succeed
only if it attends to the role of authority. It often seems to be the missing
piece of the puzzle in this debate. But even with a theory of authority
supple enough to interrelate the first and second levels of the problem,

there will remain issues of prudence and art in what judges do when they interpret law and apply it to concrete cases. Because the issues stand at different levels, bestriding questions of principle, prudence, and art, we should be cautious about appealing to what the natural law requires.

CHAPTER FOUR

Authority to Render Judgment

S t. Thomas Aquinas observes that in the broadest sense of the term, the word *iudicium* (judgment) signifies an act whereby "a cognitive power judges of its proper object."[1] Given the natural capacity of the intellect to apprehend and to particularize universal forms,[2] everyone has some competence to render judgment: "to say that such and such is the case."[3] Thus Aristotle's dictum that "everyone judges well of what he knows."[4] Thomas also teaches that by an influx and impression of created light, every rational creature has competence to make judgments according to law. Not just to say that such and such is this case, but to say that such and such *ought* to be the case.

Finite intelligences also have competence to judge others. Hence, Thomas notes that the word *iudicium* can also signify "a superior judging of a subordinate by a kind of practical judgment, as to whether he should be such and such or not."[5] In this sense *iudicium* is an inherent feature of authority, wherever it might be found, with or without a further capacity to make or impose laws. When a parent judges that a child should go to bed, or an abbot judges that a brother should be a bell-ringer, the legal competence to render such judgments according

to natural, civil, or ecclesiastical law does not necessarily mean that
these judgments are legal sentences that bind subordinates under penalty of law.

Thomas teaches that *iudicium* "properly denotes the act of a judge
as such [*iudicis inquantum est iudex*]." For the judge binds others to render
to each what is his due (*ius*), and in this way the judge is said to be the
"personification of justice."[6] He has authority to take cognizance of a
fault or obligation, and to issue a sentence that binds or looses, con-
demns or absolves. The *iudex* then does something more than judge
what he knows, or judge the conduct of a subordinate; he issues decrees of guilt or innocence according to law. This, then, is judgment
properly speaking, without qualification. It is competence to judge
according to law and to make the judgment legally binding.

Interestingly, Thomas holds that only one human being has a natural
right and title to judge in this latter and proper sense of the term *iudicium*.
"To judge belongs to God in virtue of His own power," he writes,
"wherefore His judgment is based on the truth which He Himself
knows, and not on knowledge imparted by others." Therefore, only
Christ, "Who is true God and true man," may *as human* judge "in
virtue of [his] own power."[7] Other judges must receive authority (*potestas
iudiciaria*), perhaps like Daniel, who exercised judgment by divine instinct; or exercise judgment by delegation from the sovereign.

With this brief summary of definitions and terms, we can move to
the disputed question of this chapter. What is the obligation of the
iudex with respect to the natural law, and how does it differ from that
of the *legislator*? Does a judge *qua* judge have authority to ignore or
change laws, or to remit sentences required by laws, on the basis of his
judgment of what is required by natural law? What is he entitled to do
or not do when a law conflicts with the natural law?

To answer this question, I will need to do three things. First, I need
to make some general remarks about the natural law. Since this is itself

an enormous subject I shall focus upon a few aspects of Thomas's natural law doctrine that are useful for answering the question about the authority and scope of the judicial authority. Second, I will try to answer the question at hand: namely, how the *legislator* and *iudex* stand respectively within the orbit of natural law and human jurisprudence. Finally, I will turn to three cases discussed by Thomas in which the judge seems to be in an awkward position vis-à-vis the legislator with respect to laws that either on their face or as applied seem contrary to natural law.

What Is Law "In"?

Thomas's definition of law is well known. Law is a binding ordinance of reason for the political common good, actually promulgated by a competent authority.[8] Thus, there are four principles: ordinance of reason rather than force, for the common good, made by a competent authority, and promulgated; each is a necessary but not a sufficient condition for something to be a law. We could easily spend the remainder of this chapter discussing this definition. For now, let us suppose that in a given case all four conditions are met and that an ordinance is entitled to be called a law.

The question that I want to bring into view will seem at first rather odd: "What is law *in*"? This is a question that Thomas took some pains to answer correctly, and I hope to show why it is crucial if we are to understand the relationship between the legislator and the judge.

In the *Summa Theologiae*, Thomas takes his first stab at the question in answer to the objection that St. Paul speaks in Romans 7 of "another law in my members"—the so-called *lex membrorum*.[9] Thus, when St. Paul confesses that he would do the right thing, were it not for another law in his members, he conjures the idea of his will being moved by appetites contrary to his will. The apostle seems to suggest that law is "in" a man in a physical sense. And if this is so, how can we say that law is a command of reason? Thomas replies:

> [I]t should be said that since law is a kind of rule and measure, it may
> be in something in two ways. First, as in that which measures and
> rules. Since this is proper to reason, it follows that, in this way, law is
> in the reason alone. Second, as in that which is measured and ruled.
> In this way, law is in all those things that are inclined to something
> by reason of some law, so that any inclination arising from a law may
> be called a law, not essentially but by participation as it were.[10]

In answer, then, Thomas teaches that Law is "in" the intellect that
actually performs the act of measuring and ruling; in a derivative
sense, law can be said to be "in" whatever is measured and ruled.
Properly speaking, law is always "in" the active principle,"[11] which is
to say, in a mind; and when two coordinate powers (or minds)
combine to produce the effect in the passive principle, the formal
notion is taken from the superior active principle (mind).[12]

Let's take a concrete example. We observe an ordered or a law-
abiding pattern of traffic. If we ask where the law abides properly and
essentially, we would have to say in the mind of the legislator who
imposed the rules and measures—"all traffic to the right," "stop on
red," etc. Derivatively, of course, it is in the minds of motorists who
partake of the rules and measures. What causes the traffic to stop at the
red light? Answer: The law that resides in the mind of the legislator *and,*
coordinately but secondarily, the minds of the motorists who stop their
cars. In a very extended sense of the term (*per similitudine*) law is "in"
things devoid of reason: the law books, the red light, the physical flow
of traffic itself.[13] In the case of the *lex membrorum*, Thomas explains that
the law is not *in* the bodily members except in this extended sense of
the term, and it is *there* only as the effect of a punishment for sin; in
other words, it is the effect of a judicial sentence.

As we will see, the proposition that law is predicated properly of the active principle, which is always an intellect having authority to impose a rule and measure of action, is the ground for Thomas's doctrine of original intent, as well as his insistence that the judge must sometimes favor the intent rather than the written words of the legislator.

This distinction between a regulating principle and the thing regulated applies no less to natural law. In answer to the question whether there is a natural law *in nobis*, Thomas answers that it depends upon what is meant by "in."[14] Since law is properly and essentially in the intellect of the legislator, natural law is "in" the divine mind. Hence, in answer to the further issue of the immutability of natural law, Thomas points out the obvious. The human mind is changeable and imperfect. Natural law, therefore, "endures without change owing to the unchangeableness of the divine reason, the author of nature."[15]

Does this mean that natural law is "in" man merely in the extended sense that a traffic law is in the law books or in the red light? No. Thomas contends that the human mind participates or has a share in the active principle of the eternal law. The human mind is a measured measure (*mensura mensurata*) not a measuring measure (*mensura mensurans*).[16] Having received a law, the human mind can go on to judge and command according to that law.

Thomas is very careful never to say that nature is a law, or to say that law is "in" nature in a proper sense of the term. Rather, the word "natural" is predicated of our share in the eternal law for two reasons. First, it is by the natural power of reason that we partake of the law; second, by mode of promulgation the law is instilled or indicted in us so as to be known naturally [*naturaliter*].[17] Even so, natural law is not law because it is "in" us.[18] The law is called natural according to the mode of promulgation and reception, not the pedigree of legislation.[19]

Modern philosophers will stand all of this on its head, and will speak of the "laws of nature" that reflect a deistic god who no longer governs. This should not be confused with Thomas's doctrine.

For Thomas, all human judgment is set within an already existing legal order, although to be sure not every human judgment is a legal judgment. Thus we find in *Summa* I-II, 94.2 the proposition that the habit of *synderesis* holds the "first precept of law" (*primum praeceptum legis*): "the good is to be done and pursued and evil resisted." Notice that Thomas does not say the *first principle of practical reason*, as some contemporary Thomists have paraphrased the passage; rather he says *first precept of law*. Thomas means exactly what he says. By the impression of created light God induces the creature to share in the rules and measures of the eternal law.[20] The radical implications of Thomas's teaching should be evident. Every created intelligence not only has a competence to make judgments, but to make judgments according to a real law—indeed, a law that is the form and pattern of all other laws. Thus, the legal order of things does not begin with an acquired virtue, possessed by a few; nor does it begin with the offices and statutes of human positive law; nor does it begin with the law revealed at Sinai. God speaks the law, at least in its rudiments, to every intelligent creature. "The right ends of human life are fixed," Thomas explains, and therefore there is a "naturally right judgment about such ends."[21] Thomas groups these under the triad of *to be, to live,* and *to know*—effects of God that are desirable and lovable to all and represent traces of the fully transcendent trinitarian God.[22]

This teaching has always proved distressing to kings and authorities of this world who perhaps admit that all men have a moral sensibility but not authority to make judgment according to a law. If, then, every created intelligence has competence to make judgments according to the natural law, we must inquire into what delimits the natural competence to judge, and whether the limits are merely arbitrary.

Judgment and *Prudentia Regnativa*

For our present purposes let's imagine an agent whose natural capacity to judge is reasonably well perfected. What is he entitled to judge and command? Since *imperium* is the chief act of practical reason, and hence of prudence, we can outline the diversity and scope of things to be judged according to the species of prudence (individual, domestic, regnative).

Individual prudence takes the antecedent (natural) law and renders it efficacious for one's own actions. The perfection of individual prudence consists in rendering action adequate to the singular case—to this choice, in this context and web of facts. Thus, individual prudence begins with law but terminates in an ordering-judgment adequate to singular, contingent facts. Indeed, as Yves Simon insisted, this species of prudence would appear to complete itself in an act that looks like the very opposite of a law. For laws must have adequate generality if they are to peremptorily bind the actions of many agents. The authenticity or accuracy of the judgment of individual prudence, on the other hand, does not consist in its ability to be repeated by others, nor even to be fully communicated to others. Thus, we say that individual prudence proceeds from the rules and measures of law, but its perfection does not entail any additional commands or laws to others.

Domestic prudence delivers ordering-judgments for a family (but by extension to other societies as well, e.g., the corporation, the monastery, etc.). Like individual prudence, this too proceeds from law, but unlike the former its end term is a command that moves others. Thomas is prepared to call these commands "ordinances or statutes" (*facere aliqua praecepta vel statuta*), but they lack the *ratio* of law.[23] When one commands one's children to go to bed, one has not issued a curfew.[24]

The kind of prudence that proceeds from law to law is *regnative prudence (prudentia regnativa)*. The word is taken from *regnum* or kingdom because it is the "best of all governments." But it comprehends

"all other rightful forms of government."[25] This is essentially legislative prudence, the capacity to make and impose laws (*leges ponere*).[26]
The chief act of a political authority (*principatus regalis*) is directing by
law a multitude to a political end. What makes his ordering-judgment
unique is that it remains totally within the genus of law. Having received law he makes more law. Legislation is the epitome of participation in the eternal law, for it is in issuing the ordering-judgment that
we are most imitative of God, who spoke such a word to his creation.
(Incidentally, this is one reason, among others, why Thomas insists that
Christ was a lawgiver, why the New Law cannot be reduced to individual or domestic prudence, and why, finally, the Church has authentic and unique legal powers.)

Before I try to answer the question posed at the beginning of this
chapter, I need to introduce one more virtue. In those subject to the
law, the corresponding prudence is called *political prudence* (*prudentia
politica*). Thomas explains: "men who are *servi* or *subditi* in any sense, are
moved by the commands of others in such a way that they move themselves by their free will; wherefore some kind of rectitude of government is required in them, so that they may direct themselves in obeying their superiors; and to this belongs that species of prudence which
is called political."[27] Both the human legislator and judge need this
virtue with respect to God, the *principatus regalis* of the natural commonwealth. Because every human legal official first receives a natural
law before he makes or adjudicates a human law, the human authority—legislator and judge—is always a *servus* or *subditus* (not, in the first
place, a servant of the people but of God.)

But here is the crucial difference between legislator and judge.
The human legislator, having obediently received a (natural) law, goes
on to make more law. The *iudex* (the judge), however, must exercise a
twofold obedience before he can render judgment: first, he must dispose himself to obey the natural law (such is the case for every human

being); second, he must obey the law made by the human legislator. He is, as it were, twice moved before he can move others. And for this reason, among others, the judge has a quite imperfect share in regnative prudence. As a subordinate in the chain of legal causality, his virtue consists chiefly in *prudentia politica*. (Today, when we hear it said that judges should not be "political," we mean by this word something quite different than what Thomas means by political prudence; Thomas means the free and intelligent disposition to obey a law made by another.)

Subordination of the Judge to Inanimate Law

Medieval theorists routinely spoke of animated justice: *iustum animatum, lex animata, lex viva*. "[I]t is better to be ruled by a good king than by good law."[28] Such proverbs were intended to express the following idea. Justice is best served among men by not requiring judges to consult written law (*lex inanimatum*), but rather by finding judges who, like Solomon, can judge in the light of their own virtue.

Thomas does not disagree, so far as it goes. What's important for our purposes is why he disagreed with the rubric of animated justice, especially as it applies to the *iudex*. We saw in chapter 3 that in response to the objection that recourse to a judge is more useful than statutes, Thomas replies:

> As the Philosopher says (*Rhet.* i, 1), "it is better that all things be regulated by law, than left to be decided by judges": and this for three reasons. First, because it is easier to find a few wise men competent to frame right laws, than to find the many who would be necessary to judge aright in each single case. Secondly, because those who make laws consider long beforehand what laws to make; whereas judgment on each single case has to be pronounced as soon as it arises: and it is easier for man to see what is right, by taking many instances

into consideration, than by considering one solitary fact. Thirdly,
because lawgivers judge in the abstract and of future events; whereas
those who sit in judgment judge of things present, towards which
they are affected by love, hatred, or some kind of cupidity; wherefore
their judgment is perverted.

And again, he concludes: "Since then the animated justice of the
judge is not found in every man, and since it can be deflected,
therefore it was necessary, whenever possible, for the law to determine how to judge, and for very few matters to be left to the decision
of men."[29]

Thomas's argument against a system of animated justice is prudential; he is trying to establish in the order of utility (*utile*) that inanimate justice is better (*melius*) wherever possible (*in quibuscumque possibile*).
Every polity needs a fresh supply of binding directives drawn from the
natural law by way of *determinationes*.[30] Human laws determine the *iura*
left indeterminate by natural law: in political justice, the *iura* to be
given by the individual to the polity; in distributive justice, the *iura* to
be given by the community to the individual; and in commutative
justice, the *iura* to be given by private parties to other private parties.
Until or unless someone can rightfully claim "this is owed to me [him,
or them]," there is no issue of justice, or what's worse, the issue of
justice is in doubt.[31] Human law is necessary not merely because we
need a proximate or human authority to give notice and sanction to
precepts of natural law; it is also needed for the purpose of making,
changing, and applying rules left indeterminate by natural law.

Thomas is saying that the animated justice of a judge is not suitable for achieving this end—at least not in a systematic fashion with
respect to legal and distributive justice. Judgment in the individual case
does not yield general standing laws—rules that have adequate generality and prospectivity.[32] Judicial judgment stands more closely to the

kind of prudence that gravitates to the particular facts of a singular case rather than the prudence that considers the prospective well-being of a multitude; were we to find a judge considering the merit or demerit of policy decisions that affect the body politic, we might wonder whether he is attending to the litigation at hand.[33]

If the judge does not apply a known law to particular facts, he fails as a judge. But Thomas suggests that if he were to shape his ruling to affect the entire body politic he would also fail as a legislator, because his sentence resolving the disputes of litigants is not apt to have sufficient generality to move a multitude toward a common good. In sum, the judge will not govern men in the fashion of law, for to govern men by laws one must supply ordering-judgments of adequate generality.

Thomas always supposes that the *iudex*—in our usual sense of the term—is a *iudex inferior:* a judge who enjoys delegated authority, and whose proximate rule for judging is the law that abides in the mind of the legislator.[34] So, the judge has no authority to render judgment except according to that rule. If, on the basis of his estimation of the natural law, he should choose to ignore the law in the legislator's mind, the judge inflicts injury upon the commonwealth.

The injury is threefold. First, by taking more than one's fair share of authority (even when that share was determined by positive law), usurpation is an offense against natural justice. Because usurpation is an offense against the common good, it will never do to cite the common good as the reason for usurping the authority. Second, the judge deflects that part of the natural law which the legislator was trying to make effective in the positive law. Third, he almost inevitably fails to produce a command that can function in the manner of a law.[35] "Hence it is necessary to judge according to the written law," Thomas concludes, "else judgment would fall short either of the natural or of the positive right."[36]

But what is the judge to do if he has reason to believe that the human law somehow falls short of the natural law? No human legislator has authority to make and impose laws contrary to natural law; nor would it seem that such laws have a presumption in favor of the common good. Is the judge now at liberty to plough ahead, changing or remitting deformed laws according to his understanding of the natural law?

Let us turn to three cases mentioned by Thomas. I shall take them in the order of difficulty, beginning with the easiest.

Three Cases

In the question devoted to homicide in the *Summa,* Thomas asks whether it is ever lawful to kill the innocent.[37] As we would expect, he answers that it is in no way lawful to slay the innocent. But what about the case of a judge who knows that a defendant in a capital case is the victim of false testimony? Thomas writes:

> If the judge knows that a man who has been convicted by false witnesses is innocent he must, like Daniel, examine the witnesses with great care, so as to find a motive for acquitting the innocent: but if he cannot do this he should remit him for judgment by a higher tribunal. If even this is impossible, he does not sin if he pronounce sentence in accordance with the evidence, for it is not he that puts the innocent man to death, but they who stated him to be guilty. He that carries out the sentence of the judge who has condemned an innocent man, if the sentence contains an inexcusable error, he should not obey, else there would be an excuse for the executions of the martyrs: if however it contain no manifest injustice, he has no right to discuss the judgment of his superior; nor is it he who slays the innocent man, but the judge whose minister he is.

We might be reminded of Pontius Pilate, who, as Thomas notes elsewhere, properly fulfilled his office as a *iudex inferior* under Caesar.[38] According to the Roman procedure of *cognitio extra ordinem*, the imperial authority is at liberty to receive a free formulation of charges and penalties (in this case from the Sanhedrin). After a formal accusation, the *imperium* may proceed according to the principle *arbitrium iudicantis*; that is to say, he is at liberty to take the *consilium* of his cabinet or friends, and go on to issue the verdict and assign a punishment. From this point of view, the trial of Jesus is a spectacular instance of the problem of animated justice. For the Roman practice of *cognitio extra ordinem* is nothing more nor less than the animated justice of the Roman *imperium*, free to proceed with almost no artificial constraints of law, and entirely vulnerable to the passions of the moment.

Thomas's case is much simpler. Here we have an inferior judge with no authority to proceed *extra ordinem*. He has no power to introduce evidence or to fashion sentences on his own recognizance. But what makes this hypothetical case especially easy to resolve is that there is no flaw in the law. The law is not contrary to the *ius naturale*. Nor is there reason to believe that the instruments and procedures of the law are inherently flawed, nor that the judge neglected to use the procedures available to his office. Provided that appeals to a higher tribunal have been exhausted, the conclusion is clear: the judge must pronounce sentence according to the law. In so doing, Thomas says, the judge commits no injustice. He would, however, act unjustly were he to introduce private evidence or fashion a sentence contrary to what the law demands.[39] "In matters touching his own person," Thomas writes, "a man must form his conscience from his own knowledge, but in matters concerning the public authority, he must form his conscience in accordance with the knowledge attainable in the public judicial procedure."[40]

The second case concerns judgment rendered *praeter verba legis*, outside the letter of the law. Thomas gives different examples. (1) in order to protect the city during a siege, an ordinance prescribes that the gates be shut: May they be opened to save the lives of citizens pursued by the enemy?[41] (2) The law requires that deposits be restored: Is one obligated to command that the *ius* be given in the case of a madman who wants his weapon returned?[42]

While the success of individual prudence is measured by adequacy of judgment to the particular, jurisprudence succeeds only if the lawmaker can frame general, standing statutes. But he can never legislate so successfully as to eliminate a certain material (not a moral) deficiency, namely, consideration of unusual events or facts that render the scope of the statute problematic or its application doubtful. Thus, the perfection of judgment called *gnome* renders a verdict on the basis of the "natural law in those cases where the common law fails to apply."[43] In such cases, the judge follows the principle of *epikeia*, and gives equity (*aequitas*). Indeed, Thomas contends that it would be sinful for the judge not to give equity.[44] The question is whether this obligation authorizes the judge to put aside the positive law and revert to his estimation of what natural law requires in the case at hand.

The answer to that question is: No. Thomas's treatment of *gnome* and *epikeia* do not open the door to a judicial consideration of facts only in the light of natural law. To explain why this is so, we should begin with the obvious. Notice, in the first place, that Thomas does not ask whether it is permissible to judge *contra legem*, but rather to judge *praeter verba legis*—not judging contrary to the positive law, but outside of its letter(s). In the second place, in none of the examples discussed by Thomas do we have reason to worry that the law is unjust. *Gnome* and *epikeia* presuppose (a) that there is a valid law inherited from the legislator, and (b) that the law is not contrary to natural justice. Should the law fail in either of *these* two respects it is no law at all, and thus all questions of giving equity or judging *praeter verba legis* are moot. In the third place, we need to take note of why Thomas says it is sinful not to give equity: "Without doubt he transgresses the law who by adhering to the letter of the law strives to defeat the intention of the lawgiver."[45] In other words, the moral fault does not consist merely in the fact that the litigant or defendant doesn't receive his *ius,* but in the fact that the judge disobeys the law that is in the mind of the legislator.

Legitimate judgments of equity always require the judge, as Thomas says, to "follow the intention of the lawgiver."[46] When the judge gives equity he gives the equity that the lawgiver has in view.[47] Thomas is quite insistent that the judge may not pass judgment on the law itself, or even declare that "it was not well made."[48] And when the interpretation of the legislator's intent is doubtful, the judge's first responsibility is to remit the question to the sovereign.[49]

Therefore, Thomas's understanding of equity does not permit the judge to prefer natural law to the law of the human legislator. The judge can bring natural law into the picture only on the assumption that this or that precept of natural law is what the legislator had in mind and is contained in a materially defective (but not morally defective) way in the written statute.

The third case is the more difficult. Consider a human ordinance that requires acts contrary to the natural law—Thomas mentions idolatry, but it could be any act that is *malum in se*—murder, theft, adultery, etc. Unlike the first two cases, the judge cannot take refuge in procedures or repair to the legislator's original intent. Concerning such ordinances, Thomas answers straightaway: "judgment should not be delivered according to them [*eas non est iudicandum*]."[50]

Two things make this interesting and a bit complicated. First, Thomas says that no judgment should be rendered according to the flawed measure; he does not say that one is entitled to make a new rule and measure, for that would imply legislative authority. A corrupt law does not give the judge a license to legislate. Second, Thomas delineates several ways that a law is corrupt, and depending upon the mode of corruption the prohibition against delivering a judgment might be more or less strict.

Laws, he explains, may be unjust in two ways.[51]

> First, by being contrary to human good, through being opposed to the things mentioned above—either in respect of the end, as when an authority imposes on his subjects burdensome laws, conducive, not to the common good, but rather to his own cupidity or vainglory—or in respect of the author, as when a man makes a law that goes beyond the power committed to him—or in respect of the form, as when burdens are imposed unequally on the community, although with a view to the common good. The like are acts of violence rather than laws; because, as Augustine says (*De Lib. Arb.* i, 5), "a law that is not just, seems to be no law at all." Wherefore such laws do not bind in conscience, except perhaps in order to avoid scandal or disturbance, for which cause a man should even yield his right, according to Mt. 5:40–41: "If a man ... take away thy coat, let go thy cloak also unto him; and whosoever will force thee one mile, go with him another two."
>
> Secondly, laws may be unjust through being opposed to the divine good: such are the laws of tyrants inducing to idolatry, or to anything else contrary to the divine law: and laws of this kind must nowise be observed, because, as stated in Acts 5:29, "we ought to obey God rather than man."

Under the first heading, a human ordinance can be unjust in three ways: *ex fine,* "laws" ordained to a private good; *ex auctore,* "laws" enacted by one who has usurped authority; *ex forma,* "laws" that unjustly distribute benefits and burdens. Thomas contends that on any of these three counts the ordinance does not bind. One might be obligated to comply with the command, but on grounds other than the *ratio* of the ordinance itself—for instance, to avoid greater harm to the community. Thus put, when one complies one does not judge according to the ordinance, but according to the natural law, which teaches one how to deal with the corrupt law.

But what about the act of the *iudex*? It is relatively easy to understand how a private person could comply with, rather than obey, an unjust law. The *iudex,* however, performs an essentially public act of speaking the law and authoritatively applying it to the case. He cannot sincerely say, "This is no law at all but I will issue a binding judgment having it enforced." If the legislator cannot make unjust laws bind in conscience neither can the *iudex.* And if the sentence of a judge is not binding, it is no sentence at all. That is to say, he has not judged as a judge.

Moreover, the three ways an ordinance can go wrong are rather different. Take an ordinance that fails *ex fine.* Let's say the sovereign makes himself the chief beneficiary of the profits drawn from the nation's industries; but at the same time, he pays everyone a decent wage. If a dispute over the ordinance should come into his court, must a judge refuse to render judgment according to the "law"? Suppose on the next count that a junta illegally, even immorally, seizes power and then promptly enacts a "law" changing the date on which income taxes are to be paid. Again, it is easy to see how a citizen would feel morally obligated to comply with the unjust ordinance. But can the judge render judgment according to that ordinance? Finally, with respect to ordinances flawed *ex forma,* how serious must the deformation be to put the judge into a situation where he must not render judgment? Thomas allows that this kind of deformation can satisfy the other two criteria: it can be made for the common good by a proper authority. So let us imagine that a Washington think-tank persuades Congress to tax only the poor and lower-middle class. It is a farfetched example for our own polity, but it is exactly what Thomas means by unjust *ex forma*. When we pause to consider the fact that human polities are frequently afflicted with ordinances that are unjust *ex forma,* we might suspect that the answer, no judgment should be rendered, is too rigorist. Even so, I think that this is the conclusion to be drawn from Thomas's understanding of the principles.

A constitutional court might enjoy authority to invalidate laws that are unjust in any of these three modes; especially, one would think, laws that are unjust *ex auctore*—provided, of course, that this court has access to some other law that is not corrupt, e.g., a constitution. Thomas however would not allow a freewheeling appeal to natural law, even for a constitutional court; in any event, I find no evidence in his writings of a principle or practice on which judges can invalidate unjust positive law for no other reason than the natural law. They can refuse to render judgment on no other ground than natural law, but that's a different issue than acts that officially invalidate a law or that make a new one.

The second way that a human ordinance is unjust is the case of a law that commands something directly contrary to divine law. The term *lex divina* can mean different things in Thomas, usually one or another mode of divine positive law. We can think, for example, of an emperor who, usurping the authority given to the apostles, makes laws on the number and administration of the sacraments. Clearly, in this case judgment should not be rendered. No one should comply with it.

But by the divine law Thomas also means the Decalogue, which is nothing less than the *conclusiones* of the natural law promulgated by divine positive law.[52] Here, we have the human legislator commanding his subjects to worship idols, to slaughter the innocent, to commit adultery, and so forth. He commands the people in the moral order of things to do what they must not do, or perhaps not to do what they must do. Whereas in the three earlier modes the principle of the common good permits some room, even obligation, for compliance by citizens, there is none here. For no appeal to the common good can defeat the truth that these actions can never be ordered to the common good. In the face of such ordinances the *iudex* must do the same thing as any private person: render no judgment according to the "law." Everyone must imitate the Egyptian midwives, obeying God rather than men.

The tricky part of this scheme is how we formulate the various aspects of injustice. Martin Luther King Jr., for example, seemed to think that the segregation laws were not merely corrupt *ex forma,* but contrary to divine law. And we ourselves might wonder where to place abortion law. That law is certainly corrupt *ex forma,* and probably corrupt *ex auctore.* Although the law does not directly command a violation of the fifth commandment, it certainly forbids legal officials and by extension ordinary citizens from doing what they must otherwise do: namely, to protect the lives of the innocent. Indeed, it makes not merely difficult, but impossible, the legal protection of those innocents who are most vulnerable to attack. This is not the place to untangle the knots of legal abortion in our polity; it does seem however that Thomistic principles would not permit subordinate legal officials—trial judges, executives, legislators, police—to issue an ordering-judgment according to that law.

Conclusion

Human judgment in any of its modes always proceeds from law. The nucleus of Thomas's doctrine of natural law is that in human action we find law (by analogy) all the way down, as it were; but it is not a matter of law all the way out. Every person may judge according to the natural law. Capacity to judge according to the natural law, moreover, is found wherever there is authority to judge other persons. In either case, the natural law must be preferred to any human ordinance that directly contradicts the divine law.

Only properly constituted political authorities may use the natural law to make more laws. The judge uses natural law only in conjunction with the legislator, and here specifically in cases where the written law, which is said to contain the natural right, needs assistance in reaching a certain set of facts. The judge's loyalty and obedience to the natural law require him to consider the law in the mind of the legislator. Therefore, the *iudex* is not torn between two jurisdictions. The human law is derived from the natural law. Moreover, the precepts of justice that forbid usurpation are themselves precepts of natural justice. Judicial preference for natural law over positive law is a contradiction in terms.

Loyalty to the higher law might obligate the judge not to render judgment; he may lawfully (by the natural law) refuse to be moved by a corrupt ordinance. In this case, however, the judge does not prefer the natural law to human law. Rather, he obeys the natural law in the face of commands that are no law at all. Yet even in the extreme case of refusing to render judgment, the judge, insofar as he is a judge, is not entitled to plough ahead and substitute his own law for that of the legislator, whether the legislator is divine or human.

Section Two

Natural Law in the Post-Christian World

CHAPTER FIVE

Natural Rights, Under-Specified Rights, and Bills of Rights

According to the dictum of the classic lawyers, justice is defined as "giving to each what is his *ius* [due, right]": *ius suum cuique tribuere.* Until or unless someone can rightfully claim "this is owned to me [him, or them]," there is no issue of justice. Whether we are speaking of natural or positive law, justice ensues only when two conditions are satisfied. First, there is a thing (*ius*) that belongs to someone else (*suum cuique*); second, there is an act that gives (*tribuere*) the *ius*.[1] For the lawyers of antiquity, justice can be exercised "only after something has been attributed to someone, that is when someone can say—at least in a certain manner and under a certain aspect—that that something is his."[2]

An enduring philosophical problem is the ground of things-that-are-owed. How is it that someone can claim "this is owed to me [or him, or them]"? At least some positivists (e.g., Hobbes) have held that the command of the sovereign creates both the thing to be given (the *ius*) and the obligation to give it (the *debitum*).[3] On this view, the human legislator has the unenviable task of attributing to persons things (*iura*) that hitherto were not assigned to them. By and large, natural lawyers have held the opposite: that there exist certain *iura* to be given—

by the individual to the community (legal justice), by the community
to the individual (distributive justice), and by individuals to one another (commutative justice)—prior to obligations that arise from
contract and statute.[4]

Bills and charters of rights, of course, tend to emphasize natural
rights in the mode of distributive justice, because they typically aim at
limiting and directing the actions of government by listing what the
government owes to citizens or persons.[5] In *The Natural Law*, the anti-
Nazi lawyer and activist Heinrich Rommen observed that wherever
there is a Bill of Rights, there is a "strong presupposition" that the
human law must be in harmony with natural law.[6] Rommen uses
appropriate terminology when he says there is a "strong presupposition." To say more than that would be to say too much, because a positivist
can hold that bills and charters of rights are simply a template of positive law laid over the rest of the system of positive laws, and that what
is assigned to each as "his own" is entirely a creature of legal convention. Yet Rommen is certainly correct from a historical point of view.
The post–World War II human rights paradigm, symbolized by the
United Nations Universal Declaration of Human Rights (1948), was
imbued with the conviction that certain things belong to individuals
by the fact of their membership in the human species. The historical
record will also show that the American Bill of Rights was a prominent model for the framers of the postwar declarations and covenants
concerning human rights. Rightly or wrongly, it was assumed that a
profitable lesson could be learned from the American polity: namely,
that government should be limited not only by institutional alloca-
tions of power (the constitutional principle) but also by lists of rights
that hold governments to superordinate moral duties to give to each
what is his own.

Let's assume, for the sake of argument, that there exist natural rights
that can be discovered and then enumerated in bills or charters of

rights. Let's also assume that there is in place a government to recognize, enumerate, and enforce these rights—to command that the *iura* be given. Even so, a list of natural or human rights along with a government disposed to enforce them is not enough. The *iura* must be formulated at a proper level of specificity before anyone (notably the government, in cases of charters and bills of rights) can be bound by claims that *this belongs to me, him, them.* Take for example Justice Brandeis's famous dictum in *Olmstead v. United States* (1928) that the Bill of Rights includes "the right to be let alone." Brandeis articulated a general ground of a potential right—an important area of concern, as it were.[7] So far forth, however, "the right to be left alone" is not a *ius* or a thing sufficiently specifiable for the purpose of anyone knowing precisely what is to be given. Are we speaking of privacy in the matter of government wiretaps (which was the issue before the Supreme Court in *Olmstead*), or are we speaking of a broad array of religious, familial, reproductive, and other lifestyle matters? The United Nations International Covenant on Economic, Social, and Cultural Rights (1966) declares that states have an obligation to bring about "continuous improvement of living conditions."[8] This declaration is so under-specified that it is exceedingly difficult to grasp the nature and content of the putative obligation on the part of the government.

One needn't be a skeptic about natural or human rights to understand the problem posed by under-specified rights, which so often find expression in bills and charters of rights. The *ius* will have to be specified by some legal procedure subsequent to the declaration of the right. Thus, people believe they have a right prior to anyone knowing precisely what it is. Notice that this problem is quite different than the problem of having to consider myriad contingent facts in order to assess a particular claim. Such complications often attend efforts to apply laws or to enforce contracts. We are speaking rather of a situation in which claims are made in advance of a *ius* or right. A generic area of concern entitles one to make a claim before anyone else (even the claimant) knows what is the *ius*. Where this situation prevails, courts must do something more than apply law to facts; they must specify what in fact someone is entitled to in the first place. This not only leads to the problem of "having" a right prior to anyone knowing precisely what it is or who is duty-bound to satisfy it, but also leads to rather arbitrary modes of specification in the work of constitutional or appellate courts.

In varying degrees, the problem of under-specified natural rights afflicts the United States, Canada, and, increasingly, the European Union. Despite the good will to submit themselves to bills, charters, and other instruments that hold government to the dictates of natural justice, these polities chronically find themselves in the situation where citizens believe they "have" rights not merely prior to the state, but prior to the specifications that would allow anyone to know precisely what rights they enjoy. Not surprisingly, there is considerable controversy when courts are called upon to specify the enumerated rights.

In this chapter, I shall make two sets of points. First, I will consider why the framers of the U.S. Constitution resisted any constitutionalization of the rhetoric of natural rights and why, in fact, they resisted the adoption of a bill of rights. It is true that this Constitution and constitutional mentality no longer exist in the United States. The Bill of Rights was adopted in 1791, and since the 1890s it has been developed by federal courts to such an extent that most Americans sincerely believe that ordered liberty is chiefly a creature of the Bill of Rights rather than the articles of the original Constitution. Here, I shall not recount this history in any detail. Rather, I want to look at the problem of trying to enumerate natural or human rights, using U.S. constitutional law as our main example. This would seem especially important, if for no other reason because the American model has exerted such influence elsewhere. Second, I will make some more

properly philosophical observations about the problem of enumerated, but under-specified, rights.

Responsibility for Making Natural Justice
Effective in Human Law

If one surveys the great treatises on natural law, from Thomas Aquinas
to Hugo Grotius, one will be struck by the fact that philosophers and
jurisprudents took it for granted, first, that natural justice is of primary
interest to legislators, and, second, that lawmakers legislate for a
government of general jurisdiction, having moral police powers.

Given the conviction that there exist rules and measures of justice
antecedent to the positive law of the state, it would seem to follow that
whoever makes law is most immediately responsible for ensuring that
statutes and policies are in harmony with the natural law. This is not to
say that judicial and executive powers in a polity have no interest in the
natural law. Rather, it is only to make the obvious point that human
law first connects or disconnects with the natural law in the act of
legislation. Without a legislative act, there is nothing of a public nature
to execute and nothing to adjudge.

On the model of a government of general jurisdiction, having
moral police powers, it is not difficult to picture, in a general way, how
political institutions are related to natural law. The human legislator
has the task of making the natural law effective in the political community. In the first place, this will involve using principles of natural
justice for remedial purposes. Some natural principles of justice will be
re-presented, by way of codification. For example, natural law precepts
forbidding murder and theft will be acknowledged in criminal codes.
In the second place, the human law will recognize certain limits on its
own power. At least in the Western constitutional polities, the rights
and duties of persons at private law, the rights of the church, and the
rights of persons are typically recognized as setting some limits to the

jurisdiction of the state. In the third place, the human legislator will use creatively the rules and measures of the natural law for the purpose of making more determinate rules and measures such as are needed by the people.

This scheme, only briefly elaborated here, corresponds rather nicely to the work of state governments. The governments of the several states are (or were) governments of general jurisdiction having police powers. In the *Commentaries,* William Blackstone described police power as "the due regulation and domestic order of the kingdom, whereby the individuals of the state, like members of a well-governed family, are bound to conform their general behaviour to the rules of propriety, good neighbourhood, and good manners: and to be decent, industrious, and inoffensive in their respective stations."[9] Police power, then, covers (very generally) the power of a *civitas* to legislate on those things which concern the entire body politic. Notice that Blackstone said "like members of a well-governed family." Such a polity is more or less like that of the state governments, thirteen of which preexisted the U.S. government.

But the U.S. Constitution is a different kind of instrument because this government is not (or was not) a government of general jurisdiction, having an indefinite scope of police powers. As one of the framers, James Wilson, observed, the government created under the U.S. Constitution was "a system hitherto unknown."[10] For the U.S. government was not merely limited by rules of law, nor limited by a feudal-like system of customs and common laws; nor was it limited merely by the separation of powers. This government was limited by other governments, according to the principle of dual sovereignty.

In *Democracy in America,* Tocqueville contended that the entire genius of this new government is summarized in the following four sentences of *Federalist* 45:

The powers delegated by the proposed Constitution to the federal government, are few and defined. Those which are to remain in the state governments are numerous and indefinable. The former will be exercised principally on external objects, as war, peace, negotiation, and foreign commerce, with which ... the power of taxation will, for the most part, be connected. The powers reserved for the several states will extend to all the objects which, in the ordinary course of affairs, concern the lives, liberties, and properties of the people, and the internal order, improvement, and prosperity of the state.[11]

According to Madison, the political rule of this new regime consists of two quite distinct kinds of government—different kinds, not merely different orders of magnitude. In *Federalist* 51 he writes: "In the compound republic of America, the power surrendered by the people is first divided between *two distinct* governments. . . . Hence a double security arises to the rights of the people."[12] On the one hand, there are governments of general jurisdiction, having moral police powers. As Madison says, their powers are "numerous and indefinable" because their objects extend to all of the things "in the ordinary course of affairs" that bear upon the common good. On the other hand, there is a government of delegated and enumerated powers. Many, if not most, aspects of human well-being—marriage, religion, education, crime— do not (immediately) fall under its direction. Rather, they fall under the direction of governments of general jurisdiction, which were the states.

From this, we can adduce two institutional reasons why the U.S. Constitution is so abstemious in mentioning rights. First, given a government of "few and defined" powers, one is chiefly interested in whether that government has a power, and only secondarily (but not unimportantly) in how it is used. In this respect, an abundance of moral language would prove counterproductive. To worry whether the use of a power is morally adequate to various objects and ends (education, health, religion, etc.) is to put the cart before the horse. The first question is whether that government has been delegated power over a specific object or end. Second, because it is not a government of general jurisdiction, having moral police powers, many areas of human conduct that are most immediately and vividly related to moral considerations fall outside its jurisdiction. In the original Constitution, even slavery was left primarily to the states. The states, having "numerous and indefinable" powers, reach many more ends. Thus, it is entirely appropriate that the state constitutions should expressly include the moral axioms and theorems that guide these powers.

It should be emphasized, however, that this does not mean that the U.S. Constitution is not informed by moral principles; it is only to say that their exposition is indirect, in keeping with the nature of the instrument and its ends. This indirection represents a deliberate effort by the framers to discipline how we should think about the limits of governmental power. Rather than listing all the moral norms that ought to guide the use of legislative, executive, and judicial powers, the Constitution tries to state as precisely as possible who has authority over a certain scope of objects.

Enumerated powers do not necessarily tell us whether any particular law made in pursuance of a power satisfies or thwarts natural justice; nor does it immediately tell us whether a liberty exercised in the absence of a power is exercised rightly or wrongly, from a moral point of view. So, for example, Article I (§8) of the U.S. Constitution gives Congress authority to grant temporary rights to authors and inventors for their respective writings and inventions. Interestingly, it is the only place where the word "right" is mentioned in the original Constitution. This article does not, however, tell us how this Congressional power ought to regard a Kevorkian suicide machine, much less which, if any, writings have redeeming social value. Unlike ordinary moral reasoning, which is only satisfied when the choice is fully adequate to the concrete particular, the articles of the Constitution merely tell us who has what power, not how the power is to be used to secure the moral right.

It is indeed a moral question whether Congress ought to underwrite inventions likely to serve immoral purposes. We can assume that implicit in the grant of power is a norm requiring those who use the power to use it reasonably, in accord with the common good. This level of reasoning, however, is not *constitutionalized* by the Constitution. It is left to the judgment of Congress, and ultimately to the people who are represented therein. The Constitution leaves to Congress the responsibility of using its delegated power in ways that make natural justice effective in the political community—or at least in that part of the political community over which the national legislature has power to act. If it does not have delegated power over a certain object or end, there is no need to inquire further into the moral specifications of its legislation or policies. It is assumed that in the absence of delegated power, some other agent (private or public) has responsibility to address the matter at hand.

To summarize: it is one thing to ask whether a government has been delegated a power; it is quite another thing to ask whether a power is used rightly (from a moral point of view). If a government has plenary powers, then a bill of rights can do nothing more nor less than provide additional rules concerning how those powers are to be used. Hence, natural law or natural rights will make their appearance as moral limits on the government. If, however, a government does not have, as Madison said, "numerous and indefinable" powers, a bill of rights will have to have a completely different function. In this case, a bill of rights will have to make clearer precisely which powers the government lacks.

From the very outset, critics of the U.S. Constitution complained that its lack of explicit moral language was a defect. Anti-federalists urged that the Constitution be adopted only if it included a bill of rights. And in this century, Article III courts came to believe that the sparse and lawyerly language of the U.S. Constitution contains hidden moral substance that courts must make explicit.[13] This is not the place to review the complex historical reasons for this new perspective. Here it will suffice to say that the U.S. government became over time a regime that certainly appeared to be a government of general jurisdiction with "numerous and indefinable" powers. This was the fear voiced in the late eighteenth century by the anti-federalists, who believed that the new government would inevitably become a regime of plenary powers, and hence a bill of rights was needed to correct or at least mitigate its use of such power. In any event, from the judgment that the U.S. government is no longer a regime of "few and defined" powers, the interpretation of the Bill of Rights would have to change accordingly. It would become a device not for saying whether government has a power, but rather for judging how that power ought to be used. Thus, the Bill of Rights would become a sluice-gate not merely for a moral debate about the actions or inactions of the U.S. government; of necessity, it would also become a constitutional debate.

In a rare moment of candor, Justice Jackson took note of the change in perspective in *West Virginia v. Barnette* (1943).

> True, the task of translating the majestic generalities of the Bill of Rights, conceived as part of the pattern of liberal government in the eighteenth century, into concrete restraints on officials dealing with the problems of the twentieth century, is one to disturb self-confidence. These principles grew in soil which also produced a philosophy that the individual was the center of society, that his liberty was attainable through mere absence of governmental restraints, and that government should be entrusted with few controls and only the mildest supervision over men's affairs. We must transplant these rights

to a soil in which the laissez-faire concept or principle of non-interference has withered at least as to economic affairs, and social advancements are increasingly sought through closer integration of society and through expanded and strengthened governmental controls. These changed conditions often deprive precedents of reliability and cast us more than we would choose upon our own judgment. But we act in these matters not by authority of our competence but by force of our commissions. We cannot, because of modest estimates of our competence in such specialties as public education, withhold the judgment that history authenticates as the function of this Court when liberty is infringed.[14]

In *Barnette*, the Supreme Court had to decide whether state governments could require public school students to join in a flag-salute ceremony. Jehovah's Witnesses had refused to do so, on grounds of religious conscience. The Court ruled that individuals enjoy a right not to be compelled to utter what is not in their mind. Although the majority of the Court could find no particular text of the Constitution that recognized such a right, much less one that recognized such a right as a federal matter, they reasoned that this immunity from state-imposed symbols could be inferred from the meaning of the First Amendment. Justice Jackson, writing for the majority, contended that the laissez-faire philosophy had been dealt a blow by the New Deal, at least as regards matters of economic liberty. The Court, by Jackson's admission, was unable to check the U.S. government's surging powers, which attended the Great Depression, the New Deal, and national mobilization during World War II.[15] Having lost the battle of delimiting power according to a strictly constitutional criterion of whether a power was delegated in the first place, Justice Jackson and the Court decided to limit power by a moral argument keyed to individual rights. This betokened a great change in the habits of American constitutional law. Implicitly, government was now thought to have plenary powers that needed to be checked by appeals to unenumerated individual rights.

Justice Jackson also points to another problem. How can the Court move from the "majestic generalities" of the Bill of Rights to rights adequately specified? Without specification these rights are virtually useless for the purpose that Jackson has in mind. After slight hesitation, Jackson asserts that the Supreme Court will have to specify the rights, presumably on a case-by-case basis.

Enumeration of Powers and the Enumeration of Rights

The potential problem of vaguely formulated rights was not unknown to the founders. In his magisterial *Commentaries on the Constitution of the United States* (1833 edition) Chief Justice Story wrote:

> That a bill of rights may contain too many enumerations, and especially such, as more correctly belong to the ordinary legislation of a government, cannot be doubted. Some of our state bills of rights contain clauses of this description, being either in their character and phraseology quite too loose, and general, and ambiguous; or covering doctrines quite debatable, both in theory and practice; or even leading to mischievous consequences, by restricting the legislative power under circumstances, which were not foreseen, and if foreseen, the restraint would have been pronounced by all persons inexpedient, and perhaps unjust. Indeed, the rage of theorists to make constitutions a vehicle for the conveyance of their own crude, and visionary aphorisms of government, required to be guarded against with the most unceasing vigilance.[16]

Story's point was aimed at the anti-federalists, who (in Story's view) misunderstood the nature of the U.S. Constitution. But his deeper point touches upon an important question of practical philosophy. Do vaguely formulated principles of natural rights really limit government in the ways their proponents imagine?

Before turning to the philosophical issue, it would be useful to recall the historical context of the dispute over the Bill of Rights. Story's remark was made in reference to Alexander Hamilton's famous argument in *Federalist* 84 that a Bill of Rights is unnecessary. Hamilton contended that "the Constitution is itself, in every rational sense, a Bill of Rights."[17] Insofar as a constitution delegates and enumerates the powers of the state (here, the U.S. government), there is no need to limit the state by the addition of natural rights claims, nor indeed any kind of rights claims. Hamilton asked: "[W]hy declare that things shall not be done which there is no power to do?"[18] Accordingly, the internal structure of the government protects rights, by spelling out precisely what the government cannot do. If Article I (which enumerates Congressional powers) gives Congress no power to make laws respecting an establishment of religion, there is no reason to reiterate that want of power in an amendment. Hamilton concluded: "Here is a better recognition of popular rights than volumes of those aphorisms which make the principal figure in several of our State bills of rights and which would sound much better in a treatise of ethics than in a constitution of government."[19]

The options presented by Hamilton are simple. We could, in the fashion of moral philosophers, first identify a body of moral rights, and then erect institutions of government as so many implications of those rights. For example, from the proposition that individuals have an inalienable right of conscience, we could declare in the Constitution that government may not abridge the right of religious conscience. Or, we could, in the fashion of the framers, limit the institutions and activities of the government, from which there would flow certain liberties to be enjoyed by the people.[20]

On the first model, the duties of government are derived and exposited from antecedent rights claims; on the second model, rights are enjoyed as liberties exercised in the absence or specification of a governmental power. On the second model, public and justiciable rights do not appear prior to the actual institutions of law and government. The same result can be generated by either starting point, for citizens cannot be molested or impaired in their religious duties whether we start from the want of power on the part of Congress to make such laws or whether we start from the right of citizens to religious conscience. However, the framers, by eschewing the first model, avoided the problems characteristic of natural rights discourse: (1) there are no rights antithetical to the rule of law; (2) there are no vague propositions about justice; (3) there is no lack of clear and precise instructions to the government about the nature and scope of its powers, for the government is not being asked to interpret its powers as though they were the implications of a list of human rights.

James Madison wrote in *Federalist* 51: "In framing a government which is to be administered by men over men, the great difficulty lies in this; you must first enable the government to control the governed; and in the next place oblige it to control itself." The federalist argument was that while it is relatively easy to enumerate governmental powers, it is relatively difficult to formulate abstract principles of justice or of natural rights that have sufficient specificity or adequacy to the matters that come under dispute. A government that will not conform its activities to the powers delegated to its people is not apt to be a government that will limit its activities to the abstract aphorisms of natural rights. In fact, rather than limiting the government, abstract rights, Hamilton warned, "would furnish to men disposed to usurp, a plausible pretense for claiming that power." Once government is commissioned to secure the end of generally stated moral desiderata, government will not only claim the power to interpret the scope of these ends, but will also claim power over the means to achieve them. Since the former are general and indefinite, so too are the latter. Everyone believes that they have rights, but no one actually knows what they are until an organ of the government specifies them.

Here we can recall Justice Story's criticism of state bills of rights, which "contain clauses of this description, being either in their character and phraseology quite too loose, and general, and ambiguous; or covering doctrines quite debatable, both in theory and practice; or even leading to mischievous consequences, by restricting the legislative power under circumstances, which were not foreseen, and if foreseen, the restraint would have been pronounced by all persons inexpedient, and perhaps unjust." Examples of this problem are abundant, especially in the dicta of the courts. Take the case of *Planned Parenthood v. Casey* (1992), where the Supreme Court tried to expound the principle of justice limiting the moral police powers of the state governments on the issue of abortion. The Court maintained that "[a]t the heart of liberty is the right to define one's own concept of existence, of meaning, of the universe, and of the mystery of human life. Beliefs about these matters could not define the attributes of personhood were they formed under compulsion of the State."[21] This particular right, without further qualification, would give citizens an immunity from virtually all positive law. So stated, it could mean anything. A right that can mean virtually anything does not limit the government. Rather, such a right authorizes the government both to meddle in social relations for the purpose of securing open-ended claims of justice, and (paradoxically) to make constant exceptions to the alleged right whenever its open-ended character seems to conflict with some compelling governmental function. Vaguely formulated "rights" must prove extremely difficult to adjudicate in a fair, public way. *À propos* of the *Casey* dictum, in the context of litigation, how can the right to define the meaning of the universe be ascertained by a judge, since the right is essentially a right to enjoy private, if not idiosyncratic, meanings? As Simone Weil said, "To set up as a standard of public morality a notion which can neither be defined nor conceived is to open the door to every kind of tyranny."[22]

There may well be a kernel of moral truth in the *Casey* dictum, but as it stands the "right" is under-specified. Until it is further specified, no one can know who is bound to do (or not do) *what* to *whom*. And so long as that condition persists, there is no *limit* to the government.[23] On the one hand, we have a principle of unbounded individual liberty; on the other, a government responsible for enforcing that principle in a very arbitrary manner.[24]

Consequences for Constitutional Limits on Government

Inadequately specified moral or human or natural rights claims have some very deleterious consequences for constitutionalism.

First, generalized rights claims do not always limit the government, for government will inevitably have to make exceptions to the exercise of the alleged right. It is not merely coincidental that the U.S. Supreme Court invented the criterion of "compelling state interest" at the same time it (the Court) started down the path of interpreting the Constitution in the light of substantive rights rather than in the light of enumerated powers of government. Under-specified rights, then, not only permit the individual to make a claim in advance of a truly binding term of justice, but such rights also permit the government to brush aside the right when it can demonstrate some compelling utilitarian reason for doing so.[25]

Second, even under optimal conditions of a government that sensibly deliberates about how to fill the "gap" between rights and rights exercised rightly (which is the same thing as the gap between merely putative rights and actual rights), the government does not have a sufficiently precise idea of how to direct and limit its powers. For every under- or over-specified rights claim we will have to commission the government to discover precisely what it is that the government must promote, protect, and secure. Since no one knows precisely who is obligated and what they are obligated to do or not do, the constitutional system will become dystelic, and ultimately unjust. It is one thing to suffer morally confused individuals; it is far more dangerous to suffer a government that acts blindly and without direction—especially when the confusion stems from the fundamental law of the constitution rather than from a stupid or unjust policy or statute.

Third, whereas a crudely framed policy or statute can be corrected through the ordinary political process, a morally improper right at the constitutional level can generate a crisis of conscience for the entire polity. This problem surfaced in an especially critical way with the *Dred Scott* decision of 1857. With regard to the notion that owning slaves is a fundamental or natural right, Abraham Lincoln observed: "Its language is equivalent to saying that it is embodied and so woven into that instrument [viz. the Constitution] that it cannot be detached without breaking the constitution itself."[26] "If slavery is right," Lincoln said, "all words, acts, laws, and constitutions against it, are themselves wrong, and should be silenced, and swept away."[27] In the same vein, James Madison, a slaveholder, argued at the Constitutional Convention that it would be "wrong to admit in the Constitution the idea that there could be property in men."[28] With consummate clarity, Madison understood that to recognize such a right in the fundamental law would forever take the matter of slavery out of the sphere of governmental prudence and would bind the entire polity to the protection of a wrong. Such "wrongs" can enjoy a kind of legal immunity in the case of legislative toleration, or in the case where a constitution does not delegate to government (or a certain sector of it) the power to address the wrong.

But as both Madison and Lincoln understood, toleration and the want of power are entirely different than grounding the wrong in a claim of natural right.

Fourth, the constitutionalization of natural rights tends to erode civil amity because citizens are encouraged to play a legal version of atomic warfare. Partisan groups look to the courts to rewrite the fundamental law on their behalf. Rather than winning a right in an ordinary civil action, victory in a constitutional court wins the power to shape basic constitutional values. This, then, produces an atmosphere that is very nearly the opposite of what is supposed to be achieved by a bill of rights. A bill of rights is supposed to limit the arbitrary power of the government by placing exacting restrictions on how the people can express their will through the organs of government. Some rights are not supposed to be up for grabs. Yet, to the extent that ordinary politics is displaced in favor of constitutional or bill-of-rights politics, people inevitably come to believe that their rights are only as good as their success in bringing their own partisan agenda before the bar. The stakes of winning and losing are so severe that there can be no compromise. This problem of overheated constitutional politics is especially to be avoided in polities like Canada and the United States, which are deeply pluralistic societies. In such societies, it is essential to ensure that the organs of power are not commandeered by one group. Civil amity requires that every group learn how to engage in civil conversation. How can I live with my neighbor, if he or she need only convince a court (rather than the rest us) to recognize a right to "define the meaning of the universe"? Imagine a society that suffers a perpetual constitutional convention that, case by case, rewrites the social contract. Then imagine the resentment of citizens who discover that they have no effective voice in that process. This is precisely what happens when partisan groups bring their agenda to constitutional courts. Only the litigants win the power to reshape the social contract.

The framers and ratifiers of the U.S. Constitution certainly believed in natural rights. But to their credit, they were exceedingly cautious about writing these principles directly into the fundamental law. Instead, they opted for a Constitution of enumerated powers, which spelled out precisely what the government cannot do. How, from a moral standpoint, the government should do the things it is constitutionally enabled to do is left mostly to the judgment of the people and their government. In framing this kind of fundamental law, they believed that the institutions of government would be broadly congruent with natural principles of justice. How the actions of government are to be made more adequate to the requirements of natural justice is deferred to the deliberative skills of ordinary legislation.

They understood that from unbounded individual liberty comes despotism. An under-specified right is nothing other than an unbounded liberty. But since only a court can discover the limits to such a right, judicial power (willingly or unwillingly) comes to share in that unboundedness. And thus, one of the best ways to limit the despotic tendencies of government is to eschew broad and under-specified rights claims. Far from disparaging principles of natural justice, the American framers took care to protect those principles from the exuberance of ideologues. The specific institutional character of the U.S. Constitution is one among many different kinds of constitutional orders. It differs sharply from those constitutions which display the powers and ends of a government of general jurisdiction.[29] To this extent, it is not necessarily a model for any other polity. But its institutional wisdom about the problem of rights drawn too broadly has value for political and legal philosophers.

CHAPTER SIX

Private Uses of Lethal Force:
The Case of Assisted Suicide

J ustice Brandeis's dictum in *Olmstead v. United States* is
familiar to every student of constitutional law:

The makers of our Constitution undertook to secure conditions
favorable to the pursuit of happiness. They recognized the significance of man's spiritual nature, of his feelings and of his intellect.
They knew that only a part of the pain, pleasure and satisfactions of
life are to be found in material things. They sought to protect Americans in their beliefs, their thoughts, their emotions and their sensa-
tions. They conferred, as against the Government, the right to be left
alone—the most comprehensive of rights and the right most valued
by civilized men.[1]

Brandeis's dictum has become a permanent feature of our judge-
made law, cited not merely as dictum but as a kind of self-evident norm
regulating the relationship between government and the citizens. The
proposition that a comprehensive "right to be left alone" is the right
"most valued by civilized men" is an odd one, since the word "civilized" derives from *civis*, or citizen. If we were to make a short list of
those rights most prized by citizens, we might start with the political

franchise itself; from there, one might go on to mention the right to hold office, to engage in mutual deliberation with one's fellow citizens in legislative assemblies; one might at least call attention to the First Amendment right of being able to petition the government for redress of grievances. These rights are specifically "political" because each one guarantees access to and participation in the political process. We might also mention those goods and privileges which accrue to anyone who enjoys political order: for example, protection against arbitrary violence; the ability to settle disputes in public courts according to known and standing laws; and the orderly and just distribution of common resources, such as education and healthcare.

The privatizing of public things is perhaps characteristic, in varying degrees, of all the Western polities as they enter postmodernity. The modern states that emerged after the Napoleonic wars served as the exemplars of national culture, as the patrons of industry and military science, and above all as the great teachers of society (*l'État enseignant*). Massive systems of mandatory education were put in place. It was not uncommon for the state to claim a *de facto* if not a *de iure* monopoly on education. Governmental bureaucracies increasingly brought society under the guidance and control of administrative law. In creating a new kind of society-state, the modern regimes did not hesitate to render judgments of truth and falsity about what they deemed good or enlightened for their own societies, and beyond that, for societies across their national borders. Censorship of subversive or indecent literature was practiced in virtually all the modern, Western states. In 1890, the German *index expurgatorius* contained names of 13 periodicals, 83 newspapers, and 60 foreign publications. In 1910, England enacted a press act that banned 121 publications in India. In the 1870s, the "Comstock" laws in the United States empowered the federal government to suppress the interstate shipment or importation of articles and literature concerning sexuality or reproduction.

The postmodern state, however, is far less sure of its powers. It claims to be axiologically blind and deferent to individual conceptions of the good. It may not approve of the consequences of abortion, euthanasia, reprogenics, and homosexual marriage, but it feels helpless to use political authority to prohibit—and often, even to publicly discuss—the justice or injustice of these acts. Unsure of the scope of their own sovereignty, postmodern states are prepared to relocate sovereignty in the individual; in other words, postmodern states are prepared to be the guarantor of the rights of individual autonomy. We should not be surprised that individuals now claim private authority to say who shall die and who shall live, who should receive justice and who shall not. Hence we see not merely the privatization of industry and what were once deemed public services (a process that may in some cases be quite defensible and desirable from an economic standpoint), but a privatization of judgments that indisputably belong to public authority: judgments about uses of lethal force and who deserves to live or die, judgments about how the strong treat the weak, and judgments about whether private parties can claim power over something as common as the genetic infrastructure of the *humanum*.

In this chapter, I shall address one particular move toward privatization that provides a test case for how far we can go in enjoying a right "to be left alone" and still remain "civilized." The test case is the alleged right or "liberty interest" to physician-assisted suicide—a right recently discovered by the Ninth Circuit Court of Appeals.[2] In brief, my argument is that the use of lethal force is fundamentally unlike tax vouchers, airline and cable deregulation, consensual sex, or religious worship. Men and women, I argue, cannot exercise a private franchise to use lethal force and still enjoy political order. Before I turn to the argument of the Ninth Circuit, and then to my own argument, two comments are in order:

First, the critical and polemical aim of this essay is not directed exclusively at the federal judiciary. We shall focus upon the Ninth Circuit's discovery of a constitutional right to physician-assisted suicide for the good reason that Judge Reinhardt's opinion is the first serious effort to constitutionalize such a "right."[3] Regardless of how the Supreme Court might dispose of this particular case, Reinhardt's opinion is a compendium of the sorts of arguments (moral, historical, legal) that can be made for the right of individuals to physician-assisted suicide. That this liberty (by way of exception or by way of right) is moved from the federal to the state level is irrelevant to the argument advanced in this chapter. My argument is that a private franchise to use lethal force is inconsistent with political order.

Second, everyone knows that direct and deliberate killing of another human being is the sort of act that requires justification. In virtually all developed legal systems, justification must satisfy two criteria, each of which is a necessary, but neither of which is a sufficient, condition. First, the person killed must deserve the harm inflicted. Let's call this the horizontal issue of justice. It forbids the giving of undeserved harm to one's neighbor. Second, killing is judged not only by the standard of whether the victim is owed such harm, but also (even primarily) by the standard of whether the killing is done on proper authority. The private person who takes upon himself the task of punishing the wicked is accused of a crime. Unlike a civil action, where one private party accuses another of harm or dereliction, crime is regarded as a harm against the community (or state). All relatively well-developed legal and political systems believe that the state has a monopoly on lethal force, and that the state's exercise of that right is to be limited by rules of law. When private individuals, acting alone or in concert, try to vindicate justice by recourse to lethal force, we understand that a new and distinct harm comes into being. For this reason, the issues of abortion, euthanasia, and physician-assisted suicide are

Janus-faced. They look in one direction toward the moral reasons that might justify the taking of human life, especially when we are speaking of killing the young, the old, the infirm, or for that matter anyone who is in no dereliction of duty. But they also look in the other direction toward society itself, raising the question of whether political order can tolerate or recognize a private license to use lethal force.

The state of Washington repealed its criminal prohibition of suicide in 1975. Its criminal code, however, prohibits persons in its jurisdiction from "knowingly caus[ing] or aid[ing] another person to attempt suicide."[4] This statute was enacted in 1854, within the first year that Washington became a territory. An effort to repeal this provision by referendum narrowly failed in 1991. Soon afterward, Compassion in Dying, a group devoted to assisting terminally ill patients contemplating suicide, filed suit, seeking a declaration that the Washington statute violates the due process and equal protection clauses of the Fourteenth Amendment. Chief Judge Barbara Rothstein, of the District Court for the Western District of Washington, found for the plaintiffs.[5] Relying heavily on *Planned Parenthood v. Casey*,[6] Judge Rothstein wrote: "Like the abortion decision, the decision of a terminally ill person to end his or her life 'involv[es] . . . [a] choic[e] central to personal dignity and autonomy.'"[7] The joint opinion in *Casey* defined liberty as "the right to define one's own concept of existence, of meaning, of the universe, and of the mystery of human life. Beliefs about these matters could not define the attributes of personhood were they formed under compulsion of the State."[8] According to Judge Rothstein's understanding of the issue, the Washington statute is unconstitutional "facially" and not merely "as applied."[9] Thus, from this point forward in the litigation, the individual's liberty right was to be judged in the strongest light available to constitutional law.

On appeal, a three-judge panel of the Ninth Circuit Court of Appeals reversed the district court.[10] Judge Noonan ruled that the analogy to the Supreme Court's decision in *Casey* was ill considered.[11] He argued that the Supreme Court's precedents in the area of sexual or reproductive privacy represent a *sui generis* line of jurisprudence that cannot reasonably be expanded beyond individual decision-making in matters of reproduction.[12] On March 6, 1996, in vacating the decision of the panel and in affirming the district court, the Ninth Circuit Court of Appeals, sitting *en banc,* ruled that the state of Washington is constitutionally incompetent to legally prohibit physician-assisted suicide.[13]

Writing for the majority, Judge Reinhardt understood perfectly well that, with the exception of the common law principle of self-defense—the right of private persons to kill is not to be found in the organic, statutory, or written constitutional laws of our polity.[14] The common law principle has never been construed to condone either (a) the deliberate use of lethal force by private agents, or (b) suicide. In cases of self-defense, the individual is not publicly authorized to use lethal force; he does not act as a policeman, jury, or executioner; rather, he acts to protect his life against extreme and imminent danger. The agent does not intend to kill, much less to kill himself; he only uses that amount of force sufficient to ward off coercion. The law has always pictured the defender as turning the force back against the aggressor. If such force does have a lethal effect, it is incidental to law's denomination of the act. Should the individual use force with the express purpose of killing, however, the common law of self-defense is of no avail; he is charged with wrongful homicide. In short, the common law principle of self-defense does not conflict with, nor may it trump, the state's monopoly on the use of lethal force. No private party has a right to judge that another person deserves to die nor to execute that judgment by way of lethal force.

It is also worth recalling that the common law principle of self-defense has not formed any part of the Supreme Court's case law on abortion. In *Roe v. Wade*,[15] Justice Blackmun listed five potential harms imposed upon a pregnant woman by state laws prohibiting abortion.[16] Only one of these—"[s]pecific and direct harm medically diagnosable"—provides anything analogous to the traditional principle and situation of self-defense.[17] This, however, was not at issue in *Roe*, for the state of Texas already had such an exception. The other harms enumerated by Blackmun are psychological, sociological, and economic in nature.[18] All of these represent forms of duress that have never been included under the common law right of self-defense. *Roe* and subsequent abortion decisions ground the right to abortion in the principle of personal or decisional autonomy, not in self-defense.

To his credit, Judge Reinhardt makes no bid either to reinterpret the common law principle or to smuggle it into the abortion precedents. Rather, he repairs to the Court's own common law regarding decisional liberties protected by the right of privacy.[19] After citing the Brandeis dictum concerning the right to be left alone, Reinhardt asserts: "The essence of the substantive component of the due process clause is to limit the ability of the state to intrude into the most important matters of our lives, at least without substantial justification. In a long line of cases, the Court has carved out certain key moments and decisions in individuals' lives and placed them beyond the general prohibitory authority of the state."[20] In the course of his one-hundred-page opinion, Reinhardt cites more than sixty Supreme Court cases on the privatization of sexual conduct, as well as a few cases that deal with the privatization of religion. There is not the space here to survey all of these cases. However, a brief report of the "long line of cases" might prove helpful.

Since the Second World War, the Supreme Court has developed two prominent lines of cases in which it has privatized individual decisions and actions that were once deemed amenable to the moral police powers of state governments. The first concerns religion, the second concerns sex and reproduction. In both lines of jurisprudence, the Supreme Court has made itself a central player in what we today call the "cultural wars."

In *Everson v. Board of Education*,[21] the Court, for the first time, incorporated the establishment clause of the First Amendment against the states.[22] The doctrine of incorporation, however, was not the main story; since 1833, all of the states had relinquished their established churches. The most important feature of *Everson* was the new meaning of "establishment" elucidated by Justice Black.[23] State governments were not merely forbidden to erect an official church, or from giving monetary preferments to a particular denomination; states were now also forbidden to "aid" or "promote" religion.[24] Religion was to be entirely a private matter.[25] Over the next three decades, the Court removed religion, bit by bit, from the public order. The best known case, of course, is *Engel v. Vitale*,[26] in which the Court prohibited prayer in public schools.[27] However, in its most important case in this area, *Lemon v. Kurtzman*,[28] the Court declared that even those laws and policies which are ostensibly "secular" can be ruled unconstitutional if there is evidence of religious motivation on the part of public officials.[29] Indeed, Justice Kennedy has gone so far as to maintain that the belief that "there is an ethic and a morality which transcend human invention"[30] is itself religious; thus, even the belief in a transcendent source of moral principles violates the First Amendment if it motivates or, in some detectable way, informs governmental action.[31]

In *Compassion in Dying*, Judge Reinhardt makes passing references to the Supreme Court's First Amendment jurisprudence. With respect to the Washington statute and referendum, for example, Reinhardt warns: "They are not free, however, to force their views, their religious convictions, or their philosophies on all the other members of a democratic society, and to compel those whose values differ with theirs to die painful, protracted, and agonizing deaths."[32] Laws prohibiting physician-assisted suicide, he concludes, do "injury" to some citizens for no other reason than "to satisfy the moral or religious precepts of a portion of the population."[33] Yet, for all of that, Reinhardt makes no systematic effort to mount a First Amendment argument for physician-assisted suicide.

Instead, he avails himself of the line of privacy cases that deal with matters of sexual conduct. Indeed, the Court's decisions in these cases do provide an impressive body of precedent for Reinhardt's argument that a constitutionally protected "right to die" exists. In *Griswold v. Connecticut*,[34] the Court concluded that married people enjoy a right of privacy to make uniquely marital decisions.[35] Seven years later, in *Eisenstadt v. Baird*,[36] the Court expanded the right of privacy: "It is true that in *Griswold* the right of privacy in question inhered in the marital relationship. Yet the marital couple is not an independent entity with a mind and heart of its own, but an association of two individuals each with a separate intellectual and emotional makeup. If the right of privacy means anything, it is the right of the *individual,* married or single, to be free from unwarranted governmental intrusion into matters so fundamentally affecting a person as the decision whether to bear or beget a child."[37] In the first part of this quote, Brennan extracts the privacy right from its marital context; in the second part, he suggests that the decision about reproduction and abortion is but one instance of a broader decisional liberty. In *Carey v. Population Services International*,[38] which invalidated state restrictions on the sale of contraceptives to minors, Justice Brennan wrote that the "right of personal privacy includes 'the interest in independence in making certain kinds of important decisions.'"[39] Here, Brennan makes it clear that the genus is decisional autonomy and that the sexual component represents a specific difference.

When we survey the Court's expansion of the right of privacy in the decade after *Griswold,* we see the right of privacy incrementally emancipated, first, from traditional protections afforded to married people, and second, from sexual conduct itself. At the time *Carey* was decided, the right of sexual liberty appeared to be a particular species under the broader genus of decisional autonomy. I will return to this point later because it is crucial to Reinhardt's argument that privacy is, as Brandeis asserted, a comprehensive right that is not limited to an individual's control over personal information, marital decisions, or various and sundry erotic or reproductive actions. For now, we must examine *Roe,* which is the proximate source of Reinhardt's analogy in favor of physician-assisted suicide.

In *Roe,* what was once homicide in all but three of the states be- came a private choice protected by the Bill of Rights.[40] We need to remember that neither in *Roe* nor in subsequent cases did the Court deny that abortion is homicide. In fact, one of the rarely mentioned oddities of *Roe* is that the Court refused to take a position, one way or the other, on the moral status of the entity being killed. The Court did not declare that the fetus is *not* a person in the moral sense of the term. Rather, the Court asserted that it could find no legal ground for such status, at least no ground sufficient to trump a woman's constitutional right of privacy (except in the third trimester when the interest of potential life may outweigh this right in some cases).[41] So, what made the framework established by *Roe* so unusual, and indeed such a pow- erful precedent for the issue of physician-assisted suicide, is that the Court declined to say whether the choice is homicidal in terms of the moral specification of the act. The moral specification of the act is, in effect, left to the private agent, which is precisely what will ensue from a constitutionally protected right to assisted suicide.[42]

In cases like *Webster v. Reproductive Health Services,*[43] where the state of Missouri had declared that unborn human beings are persons, the

Court refused to prohibit the states from expressing their concern that abortions are acts of homicide;[44] indeed, the Court has repeatedly said that the states may convey their opinion about this matter by asking a woman to think twice.[45] However, the Court *did* prohibit the states from effectuating that judgment in their criminal and civil laws. In the language of the joint opinion in *Planned Parenthood v. Casey*, the state may place no "undue burden" in the path of a woman's choice.[46] Again, the state may believe that a woman's choice to have an abortion is homicidal; but it may impose no criminal penalties or civil liabilities. For purposes of constitutional law, the woman may define the moral properties of her action; should the woman, in good conscience, believe that her act is wrongful homicide, that judgment must remain private.

The *Casey* decision did two things that provided a bridge from abortion to physician-assisted suicide. First, the *Casey* joint opinion jettisoned the trimester scheme.[47] For twenty years, the Court seemed to say that the state's effective valuing of human life is keyed to viability (even though, in effect, only a live birth on United States soil marked the right of the child). As everyone knows, even terminally ill persons are "viable." Hence, the viable/non-viable distinction weakened the analogy between abortion and physician-assisted suicide. Once this distinction was removed from the Court's abortion jurisprudence, the analogies between abortion and physician-assisted suicide became stronger, because we are no longer debating *whether* there is life and whether it is viable, but rather the meanings and values assigned to the life, as well as who has the power to assign those meanings.

Second, the joint opinion in *Casey* moved the abortion right from the category of an unenumerated right of privacy to the enumerated right of liberty in the due process clause of the Fourteenth Amendment.[48] The joint opinion defined the liberty at issue in the following way: "At the heart of liberty is the right to define one's own concept of existence, of meaning, of the universe, and of the mystery of human life. Beliefs about these matters could not define the attributes of personhood were they formed under compulsion of the State."[49]

By moving the source of the abortion right from privacy to liberty, the Court once again strengthened the bridge of analogies running from abortion to physician-assisted suicide. The issue of decisional liberty over matters of life and death was no longer limited by the context of marital, sexual, or reproductive privacy; it migrated to a much broader genus of a right to individual self-constitution. In the earlier line of privacy cases, Justices Blackmun and Brennan were constrained to treat individual liberty under the rubric of reproductive privacy. Almost everyone understood that this was an awkward and misleading category, for abortion is not especially private; nor does it exactly pertain to the decision whether or not to make one's sexual acts reproductive—presumably, reproduction has already taken place. What has not taken place are all of the sociological and economic consequences of reproduction. Again, recall Justice Blackmun's list of harms suffered by a woman who is forced to give birth: the stigma of unwed motherhood; psychological duress in the family; the limiting of vocational and economic choices.[50] In other words, the abortion right was essentially a right of the individual to control "intimate and personal" meanings, identity, vocation. Although it took twenty years, *Casey* simply liberated the abortion right from being ensconced in sexual and medical hocus pocus.

We can hardly criticize Judge Rothstein of the District Court,[51] and then, Judge Reinhardt, for making a bee-line to the *Casey* definition of liberty and noticing that the so-called right to "define one's own concept of existence" (not to mention "the universe") leaves plenty of room for the right to die—or, to put it more properly, the right of the individual, as against the state, to control the meaning of his life and death.

When *Compassion in Dying* went from the District Court to the three-judge panel of the Ninth Circuit, Judge Noonan tried to dismiss the apparent analogy between decisional, self-constitutive liberty in abortion and physician-assisted suicide:

> The inappropriateness of the language of *Casey* in the situation of assisted suicide is confirmed by considering what this language, as applied by the district court, implies. The decision to choose death, according to the district court's use of *Casey's* terms, involves "personal dignity and autonomy" and "the right to define one's own concept of existence, of meaning, of the universe, and of the mystery of human life." The district court attempted to tie these concepts to the decision of a person terminally ill. But there is no way of doing so. The category created is inherently unstable. The depressed twenty-one year old, the romantically devastated twenty-eight year old, the alcoholic forty-year old who choose suicide are also expressing their views of the existence, meaning, the universe, and life; they are also asserting their personal liberty. If at the heart of the liberty protected by the Fourteenth Amendment is this uncurtailable ability to believe and to act on one's deepest beliefs about life, the right to suicide and the right to assistance in suicide are the prerogative of at least every sane adult. The attempt to restrict such rights to the terminally ill is illusory. If such liberty exists in this context, as *Casey* asserted in the context of reproductive rights, every man and woman in the United States must enjoy it . . . . The conclusion is a *reductio ad absurdum*.[52]

Noonan is correct, of course, that the category is "inherently unstable." If every individual enjoys a fundamental right to define "one's own concept of existence, of meaning, of the universe, and of the mystery of human life,"[53] then virtually every positive law not justified by compelling state interest could be trumped by the right spelled out in *Casey*. It is such a broadly formulated right that one is easily tempted to regard it as mere dictum.[54] But so, too, are other conceptions of civil liberties proffered by the Court. Frankly, no one, including the Court, knows how to draw absolute boundaries around what might constitute "religion" for the purpose of interpreting either of the religion clauses of the First Amendment. In the Selective Service Board cases, for example, the Court virtually allowed individuals to define religion and religious conscience for themselves.[55] Beginning with broadly drawn conceptions of liberty, the Court typically will further specify or limit the right on a case-by-case basis. One can agree with Noonan's complaint that the *Casey* right is unwieldy[56] and still see that this complaint can just as well be lodged against the way the federal appellate courts handle any number of rights.

Most importantly, Noonan begs the question whether the liberty right in *Casey* is essentially, or exclusively, a "reproductive" right.[57] As pointed out earlier, the transition from privacy to liberty—a transition already under way in *Eisenstadt* before it became "officially" clear in *Casey* twenty years later—suggests that reproductive choices are only one species of a broader genus of liberty to make self-defining decisions. Therefore, to defeat the analogy between the *Casey* right and the alleged right to physician-assisted suicide, it will be necessary to show that, as far back as *Eisenstadt,* the Court erred when it transformed reproductive privacy into decisional autonomy.

Finally, in response to Noonan, we do not have to suppose that the exercise of the alleged right is "uncurtailable." Even the most expansive rights discovered by the modern Court have been regarded as amenable to time, place, and manner restrictions, as well as to various balancing tests when the state asserts a compelling interest. And this balancing test is precisely the move made by Judge Reinhardt: "If the balance favors the individual, then the statute—whatever its justifications—violates the individual's due process liberty rights and must be declared unconstitutional, either on its face or as applied. Here, we conclude unhesitatingly that the balance favors the individual's liberty interest."[58]

After considering the pattern of case law culminating in *Casey,* and after drawing out a right to die from that case law, Reinhardt turns to the interests of the state.[59] The chief and most traditional interest of the state, he avers, is the "preservation of life."[60] Given the right of decisional liberty defined by *Casey,* how should it be balanced against the state's general interest in preserving life? While tracking Reinhardt's opinion on the question, three things must be kept in mind: (a) the state (Washington) already permits physicians to accede to the patient's request to not be subjected to any further medical treatment; (b) the state of Washington has abandoned its law against suicide; and, (c) the train of abortion cases had already weakened the state's claim of having a monopoly on defining life (in fact, *Roe* had limited the states' power to unilaterally define the meaning and quality of life).[61]

As for the first point—"the similarity between what doctors are now permitted to do and what the plaintiffs assert they should be permitted to do"—Reinhardt begs the question.[62] Similarities do not imply that there are no important differences. Striking someone in the head in a sporting contest and striking someone in the head for the purpose of relieving them of their cash would not cancel out the very important difference between the two acts. Reinhardt much too quickly dismisses the moral and legal differences between complying with a patient's desire to forgo further treatment and performing an act that has as its express purpose the death of the patient.

So, too, does the Second Circuit Court of Appeals in *Quill v. Vacco,*[63] the companion case to *Compassion in Dying.* Noting that there is no "historic" right to die, the Second Circuit ruled that two New York statutes that penalized assistance in suicide violated the equal protection clause of the Fourteenth Amendment.[64] By permitting patients to refuse treatment at the end of life, but not allowing physician-assisted suicide, the state unfairly treats similarly situated persons.[65] The Second Circuit simply brushed aside the distinction between letting someone die (like *Cruzan*) and killing (assisted suicide). Judge Miner, writing for the majority in the Second Circuit, opined: "What concern prompts the state to interfere with a mentally competent patient's 'right to define [his] own concept of existence, of meaning, of the universe, and of the mystery of human life,' . . . when the patient seeks to have drugs prescribed to end life during the final stages of a terminal illness?"[66] He answers, "None."[67] In other words, given two patients, each of whom can define the meaning of the universe, the state of New York violates equal protection when it allows one patient to "define" himself by having treatment withdrawn, while it forbids the other patient from "defining" himself by requesting that a physician assist his suicide.

Reinhardt makes no equal protection argument. But once the patient's request to forgo further treatment is regarded as *properly* similar to the patient's request to have the physician hasten his death, the way is open to the conclusion that the individual may command the doctor to kill him. Remember that: (a) by repealing its criminal prohibition, the state has already weakened (though not completely abandoned) its interest in whether the individual commits suicide; (b) the privacy cases not only have established an individual right of autonomy over decisions that seem roughly analogous to the issue at hand, but also (along with the religion cases) have questioned the ability of the state to enforce its own definitions of what makes human life valuable. Reinhardt concluded that "[w]hen patients are no longer able to pursue liberty or happiness and do not wish to pursue life, the state's interest in forcing them to remain alive is clearly less compelling. Thus, while the state may still seek to prolong the lives of terminally ill or comatose patients or, more likely, to enact regulations that will safeguard the manner in which decisions to hasten death are made, the strength of the state's interest is substantially reduced in such circumstances."[68]

What is left of the interests of the state? Reinhardt answers that the state may regulate the conditions under which the free choice is made to preserve liberty against coercion.[69] What about the medical profession? Reinhardt acknowledges the potential problem of second parties exerting "undue influence."[70] Nonetheless, he opines that the medical profession will be a virtuous check because "the direct involvement of an impartial and professional third party in the decision-making process would more likely provide an important safeguard against such abuse."[71]

It is precisely at this point that one might suspect that something is missing from Reinhardt's representation of the state's interests, namely, the essentially public nature of lethal force. However, Reinhardt is not the only one to blame for an oversight in this regard. In fact, this view is missing from the Second Circuit's opinion in *Quill,* as well as from the various dissenting opinions in the Ninth Circuit's *Compassion in Dying* opinion. In his dissenting opinion, Judge Beezer enumerated four legitimate state purposes: "(1) the preservation of life, (2) the protection of the interests of innocent third parties, (3) the prevention of suicide, and (4) the maintenance of the ethical integrity of the medical profession."[72] The state's monopoly over lethal force is not mentioned; nor is it mentioned in the Solicitor General's brief where the state interests are summarized as follows:

> Overriding state interests justify the State's decision to ban physicians from prescribing lethal medication. The State has an interest of the highest order in prohibiting its physicians from assisting in the purposeful taking of another person's life. The view that there should be an exception to the State's general policy of protecting life for cases in which a competent, terminally ill adult voluntarily requests

life-ending medication strikes a responsive chord in many people. At this point in history, however, a State could responsibly conclude that creating such an exception would endanger persons who are not competent to seek lethal medication, persons whose decision to seek lethal medication is not truly voluntary, or those persons who are not in fact terminally ill. The difficulty that physicians have in determining whether requests for assisted suicide come from patients with treatable pain or depression, the vulnerability of terminally ill patients to subtle influences from physicians, family members, and others, and the continuing possibility that someone can be misdiagnosed as terminally ill all support a State's decision to ban all assisted suicides.[73]

The Solicitor General's position differs from Judge Beezer's in one important respect. Whereas Beezer emphasized the state's general interest in preserving life, the Solicitor General emphasized the specific interest in protecting the lives of those who do not, or cannot, give their consent to be killed. I do not wish to make light of this difference. Whether the state's legitimate interest is in preserving human life or in protecting individual choices *about* life is a question of great importance. The Solicitor General's position would permit the state to relinquish its laws against physician-assisted suicide if the state is convinced that the practice will not include unwilling victims. Carefully read, the state, in his view, does not claim a compelling interest with regard to the good of life, but with respect to individual liberty.

The critical question is still overlooked. What if the state's main interest is not (merely) the preservation of human life or choices about life, but also (indeed, chiefly) its own monopoly over uses of lethal force? This proposition is a matter of common sense. Many private persons have an interest in and responsibility for preserving human life: individuals, parents, family, physicians, and charitable organizations. After a moment's reflection, no one would say that the state has an exclusive interest in the good of life. In a myriad of ways, the state presupposes and defers to private decisions about how the good of life ought to be protected and nourished. The state, however, does have a unique and exclusive responsibility to adjudicate all contests over life and death.

In his opinion for the three-judge panel,[74] Judge Noonan came close to touching upon the point I shall now develop. Referring to the so-called right "to be left alone," Noonan remarked that "[t]ort law and criminal law have never recognized a right to let others enslave you, mutilate you, or kill you. When you assert a claim that another— and especially another licensed by the state—should help you bring about your death, you ask for more than being left alone; you ask that the state, in protecting its own interest, not prevent its licensee from killing. The difference is not of degree but of kind. You no longer seek the ending of unwanted medical attention. You seek the right to have a second person collaborate in your death."[75] Noonan is on the right track, especially in his reference to public law, because it is in public law rather than in tort law that the state traditionally makes something more than a moral judgment about what one private party owes to another. In public law, the state is always a party to the suit. Therefore, in public law (criminal or constitutional), the state must express its interest in maintaining the social contract. And this interest, of necessity, includes the issue of who has the right to use lethal force. Had Noonan focused more insistently upon this problem, the terms being "balanced" might have been completely different. As it now stands, we are required to balance, on the one hand, an all-purpose right to decisional liberty (Brandeis's comprehensive "right to be left alone"), and on the other hand, a general state interest in preserving human life.

Let us conceive of a different balance: the individual's decisional liberty against the state's interest in preserving its monopoly over lethal force. Only in this way can we locate an indisputable and unique interest of the state, for preserving the monopoly over lethal force is tantamount to preserving the conditions of the possibility of political order—an order in which private disputes about justice are forbidden the sword of lethal force. To be sure, political order means much more than the public monopoly over lethal force, but it must mean at least this much: A society that makes everything else public but leaves the execution of lethal force to private parties is not a political society.

Returning now to Reinhardt's remark about medical professionals, we can insist that although health-care professionals are often "impartial" third parties, they are not official legislators, judges, or executives. These third parties do not make laws regarding homicide; they have no public authority to resolve disputes between two parties; and, they have no executive powers to take away life, liberty, or property. If Reinhardt's argument prevails, however, we will have private parties exercising the right to use lethal force for the purpose of vindicating the order of justice as they see it. Moreover, in the case of physicians, these are no ordinary private parties, but rather are private agents whose professional competence is licensed by the state.

In other words, the patient who commands the physician to aid in his death not only is commanding the state to delegate to a physician the state's right to use lethal force, but also is asserting that the right be exercised without the ordinary constraints that the state must observe in using lethal force—constraints mandated in the due process clauses of the Fifth and Fourteenth Amendments. I propose that one cannot remain within a political order and exercise this type of right. Even if this right exists according to a natural or moral order of things, the exercise of this right is incompatible with political society.

Indeed, the relinquishment of such a right is the cornerstone of John Locke's theory of civil government. Let us recall Locke's understanding of the transition from a state of nature to a state of civil society. In his *Second Treatise of Government,* Locke has us imagine individuals in a condition of perfect liberty.[76] That liberty is comprised of two powers: (a) the power to make judgments about which acts are in accord with his own preservation or the preservation of others; and (b) the power to execute those judgments with whatever force is deemed necessary to secure the end of preservation. For Locke, and apparently for the federal judiciary, these are natural rights. Unlike the federal judiciary, however, Locke believed that natural law forbids suicide.[77] In the Lockean scheme, the natural right to preserve one's life is inalienable, for it binds the holder of right.[78] But, as I promised earlier, we will steer clear of the issue of suicide.[79] Can Locke still teach us anything else about private uses of lethal force?

At least in the state of nature, the preservation of life is the great commandment of the natural law. Every member of the species has an equal right to make and execute such judgments as are necessary to this end. But Locke insists that the exercise of such rights must be relinquished upon entering civil society. In civil society, the great law is not just the preservation of life but is also the preservation of life under public measures and constraints.

Why enter civil society in the first place? One reason is that brigands and miscreants will exercise their powers to the detriment of the rightful interests of others. Yet, we do not need civil society to afford us protection against the miscreants. This can also be accomplished Mafia-style—by individuals or families joining forces and constituting leagues to protect their interests. Locke emphasizes that the rationale for political order is the more general and persistent inconvenience of men being judges in their own case or cause, even while claiming a right to use executive force to enforce their judgment. Government is meant to address the problem of "the partiality and violence of men," including one's friends. The vigilante mob, the spurned son or angry wife, and the business partner are as much a problem as the gangster.[80] So long as any private individual retains the right to judge and execute issues of justice, the order of justice will prove uncertain and unstable.[81] If one individual has, or retains, the right to use force to vindicate his perception of justice, then everyone else must have the same right. So long as this situation prevails, there can be no political order. The counter-claim that such and such is (or ought to be) a merely private matter begs the question. For without the authority of the political community, every judgment and action is, from one point of view, a private matter.

According to Locke, the first act of civil society is a covenant whereby each agent relinquishes his natural and private rights to judge and execute the law of nature, transferring such powers to civil society, which enjoys a monopoly over judicial and executive powers. In the absence of such a covenant, no political order obtains. Some other kind of order might evolve, and other forms of contracts can be undertaken, but they are not political. Locke writes:

> And thus all private judgment of every particular Member being excluded, the Community comes to be Umpire, and by settled Standing Rules; indifferent to the fame of all Parties: and by men having Authority from the Community for the execution of those Rules, decides all the differences that may happen between any Members of that Society concerning any matter of right, and punishes those Offenses which any Member hath committed against the Society with such Penalties as the Law has established; whereby it is easy to discern who are, and are not, in Political Society together. Those who are united into one Body, and have a common established Law and Judicature to appeal to, with Authority to decide Controversies

between them and punish Offenders, are in Civil Society one with another; but those who have no such common Appeal, I mean on Earth, are still in the state of Nature, each being where there is no other, Judge for himself and Executioner; which is, as I have before showed it, the perfect state of Nature.[82]

Therefore, to assert that an individual has a private franchise to use lethal force is to assert that the individual is not a member of civil society; by the same token, for the state to transfer such powers back to individuals is tantamount to dissolving civil society.[83] Whether the delegation is done by a court, a legislature, or an executive is irrelevant.

Of course, an individual might wish to no longer be bound by this arrangement. He might calculate his interests differently and come to think that his properties, his decisional liberties, even his life, are best protected by reclaiming his natural right to be "left alone." But should he exercise an alleged natural right to judicial and executive powers, the rest of us are under no obligation to leave him alone. It seems unfair that an individual should enjoy a bubble of immunity to use lethal force while the rest of us have relinquished that right along with the right to be judge in our own cases.

The individual who asserts that government must recognize, and even assist, his private use of lethal force is not claiming a right to be left alone. Rather, he is asking for the state either (a) to cancel the civil contract altogether, (b) or to cancel it in his case, (c) or to admit that such a monopoly was never conferred upon the government in the first place. Any or all of these options imply the rejection of the principle of political order. A problem with physicians using lethal force is not only that they betray norms inherent to their profession; the deeper problem is that they no longer act like citizens who are bound by public measures of judicial and executive power.

In contrast, one could argue that in the case of assisted suicide the lethal force is being used with the consent of the recipient and that the state only recognizes a contractual exchange at the level of commutative justice. In short, there is no victim. However, that someone *is not* a "victim" by dint of having given consent, or, that someone *is* a "victim" by absence of consent, are considerations that cannot constitute an effective argument (pro or con) with respect to who has the authority to use lethal force in the first place. Whether one is a "victim" is an important consideration for morality in general, just as it is an important consideration for tort law, but it is not a sufficient criterion for determining who has authority, under the social contract, to use lethal force.[84]

By definition, a criminal offense is a wrong to society.[85] Thus, while the consent of one citizen marks the (subjective) fact that he does not regard the lethal act as an injury against his person, this act cannot trump the common good. The state's monopoly on lethal force, along with the limitations on use of that force at public law, is a common good. It cannot be understood on the model of commutative justice at private law where the consent of parties to a contract is a principal fact considered by the law.[86] Arguments for physician-assisted suicide bid us to confuse legal and commutative justice—namely, the obligations individuals have to the common good and the obligations citizens have to one another. The state, then, is given confusing, if not contradictory, directives. On the matter of life and death, the state must exact the obedience of every citizen to the common good (in matters of legal and criminal justice) and at the same time recognize the alleged right or liberty interest of one citizen to make a contract with another to use lethal force. Because the difference between public and private law is drawn only along the often indiscernible line of consent of an individual, no one could know with any assurance where crime begins or ends and, indeed, where the legitimate power of the state begins or ends. For this reason, private franchises to use lethal force are repugnant to government as such. Once again, it makes no difference whether the alleged franchise is the result of either a judicial discovery or a legislatively enacted "exception" at the state level.

If the state deputizes health-care professionals to use lethal force, these parties will have to be held to the requirement of due process. Due process is an inherently public procedure; traditionally, it has implied a fair finding of guilt or negligence or some cause for the state to take or impair the very goods it is pledged to protect. How this comports with giving death to a person who is not in dereliction of a moral or civil duty needs to be explained.

In *Washington v. Harper,*[87] the Supreme Court seemed to say that the judgment of a physician counts as procedural due process.[88] In this case, a ward of the Washington penal system was administered an antipsychotic drug against his will. The policy of the Special Offender Center (SOC) provided that any decision to medicate an inmate against his will be made by a committee consisting of a psychiatrist, a psychologist, and the center's associate superintendent.[89] Although none of the committee members may be involved, at the time of the hearing, in the treatment of the inmate, their diagnosis or treatment of the same inmate in the past does not disqualify them from sitting on the committee. Harper sued, claiming that the judgment of physicians under the employ of the state does not satisfy due process as required by the Fourteenth Amendment. Harper contended that due process protections required, at the very least, an official judicial hearing. The Washington Supreme Court agreed that a judicial hearing is a prerequisite for the involuntary treatment of prison inmates.[90] Relying in part on its holding in *Parham v. J. R.,*[91] the Supreme Court disagreed and held that "[n]otwithstanding the risks that are involved, we conclude that an inmate's interests are adequately protected, and perhaps better served, by allowing the decision to medicate to be made by medical professionals rather than a judge. The due process clause has never been thought to require that the neutral and detached trier of fact be law trained or a judicial or administrative officer."[92]

Writing in dissent in *Harper*, Justice Stevens complains about the notion that a "mock trial before an institutionally biased tribunal constitutes 'due process of law.'"[93] Citing the famous Brandeis dictum from *Olmstead*[94] concerning a "right to be left alone," Stevens argues that such a serious deprivation of liberty as the pharmacological alteration of a person's mind against his consent requires that the state not delegate its authority and responsibility to physicians, whose interests are easily compromised.[95] What Justice Stevens must now consider is whether physician-assisted suicide will raise the same problem: namely, state licensees (who, in many sectors of institutional health care, are the actual employees of government) making and executing decisions about who shall die without the formal constraints traditionally marking procedural "due process." All of the legal and philosophical nuances of "state agency" notwithstanding, the deliberate taking of life by a state licensee inevitably raises the question of the state's responsibility. The problem will remain whether the killing is allowed under a legislative "exception" at the state level, by a quasi-delegation, or by virtue of a judicially discovered right or liberty interest.

When, at the end of life, a citizen claims a right to be "left alone," not merely to die, but to contract with a second party to be killed, such a right does something more than expand the sphere of individual liberty of the contractors. It would also seem to expand the liberty of the state in a dangerous direction. For the individual is, in effect, claiming that the ordinary meaning of the due process and equal protection clauses does not apply in his situation. Due process requires that the state not take away life, liberty, or property without a fair finding and some procedure; equal protection requires that the state apply to everyone the protections afforded by general, standing laws. Hence, the individual is saying that his life can be taken without due process, and that the general, standing laws against homicide should not be applied when a person is terminal, infirm, or, in Judge Reinhardt's memorable phrase, "[W]hen patients are no longer able to pursue liberty or happiness."[96] The state, therefore, is allowed to regard some individuals as beyond the pale of common protections from the government itself. In a curious way, the individual stands in, or returns to, a state of nature in which he or she is no longer bound to other citizens in a specifically political common good. Why shouldn't the state, burdened as it already is by mounting health-care costs, regard the alleged right as a reason to lower its due process and equal protection standards with respect to the dying?

Earlier, I noted that the use of lethal force is Janus-faced. In one direction, it can be justified only in the light of moral rules and measures. The person being attacked or killed must deserve to be so harmed. In another direction, it can be justified only on the judgment of public authority. Perhaps we can remain "civilized" and enjoy a "right to be left alone" in matters of lifestyle. Perhaps we can regard the state as a kind of condominium that gives us options on various services such as health care, social security, fire departments, and schools. But the state's monopoly on lethal force, as well as the constitutional constraints upon the way the state uses such force, cannot be an option for individuals. This power is a necessary condition for the existence of political society. In principle, it cannot be delegated or transferred to private parties. The courts have no more business transferring that power than do legislatures. Courts and legislatures have authority only by virtue of the social contract. The fact that federal judges, as well as many citizens, perceive no danger in private franchises to use lethal force tells us much about our society. It tells us that people have forgotten what to fear. Apparently, many Americans believe that they have more to fear from the social contract and traditional criminal codes than they do from the private decisions made by physicians, insurance companies, and families. Yet, it is an illusion to believe that our suburban enclaves constitute an effective protection against the injustices and vagaries of private choices, especially when they concern the use of lethal force. *Compassion in Dying* raises the issue of why we need civil society in the first place. One hopes it will not have to be rediscovered from scratch.

CHAPTER SEVEN

The Supreme Court v. Religion

Yale scholar Harold Bloom has asserted that "[n]o Western nation is as religion-soaked as ours, where nine out of ten of us love God and are loved by him in return." Indeed, while polling data give only a fuzzy picture of the state of religion in America, the numbers indicate that, despite the secularization of culture, religious beliefs and practices stubbornly persist at relatively high levels, especially in comparison with Western European countries.

While the huge aggregate of religious believers defies any facile classification and analysis, it is possible to form a fairly clear picture of how the nine justices of the Supreme Court view matters religious. Since 1947, when the Court dramatically changed its jurisprudence of the establishment clause of the First Amendment, religion has been one of the most litigated issues in the judicial system. Before *Everson v. Board* (1947), the First Amendment's prohibition of "an establishment of religion" applied only to laws passed by the U.S. Congress; indeed, several of the states that ratified the Bill of Rights still had established churches of their own. In *Everson,* however, the Court incorporated the establishment clause, via the Fourteenth Amendment, against the states.

In his opinion in *Everson,* Justice Black argued that the establishment clause prohibits not just the establishment of a particular church by Congress, but also aid and promotion of religion "in general" by Congress or by any other sector of government. Thereafter, the Court found itself in the unenviable position of having to determine whether one or another government action aids, promotes, or endorses some amorphous reality called "religion in general." By its own novel interpretation of the First Amendment, the post-*Everson* Court was compelled to grapple with everything from tax policies to nativity scenes in public places. In short, it had to do the impossible, which was to draw clear and non-arbitrary lines not merely between church and state, but between religion and culture.

Scholars have argued that the post-*Everson* interpretation of "establishment" has led the Court into a maze of fruitless questions and conceptual dead-ends. The Court's church-state jurisprudence, says one scholar, is marked by "contradictory principles, vaguely defined tests, and eccentric distinctions." In terms of the craftsmanship of constitutional law, the Court seems to have lost any analytical control over the subject it aspires to adjudicate, and much of the problem is self-inflicted. A Court that finds itself having to determine, as it did in *Lynch v. Donnelly* (1984), whether plastic figurines and colored Christmas lights in a nativity scene constitute "religion" is one that has lost competence over the subject.

What Is Religion?

What follows is *not* a review of the legal doctrines and devices, but rather an examination of the Court's *substantive* (in contrast to legal) view of religion. For despite its contradictory and eccentric legal doctrines, a remarkably consistent view of religion emerges from the Court's church-state jurisprudence since *Everson.* This view is marked by extreme skepticism of, and often by outright hostility to, religion.

We might suppose ourselves to be cultural anthropologists, looking only at what religion means in the holdings and obiter dicta of the highest court. Looking only at that data, we would have good reason to conclude that religion is something that belongs in the category of dangerous poisons or mental illnesses.

There is no better place to start than with the Court's decision in *Lee v. Weisman* (1992). The case originated in Providence, Rhode Island. Robert E. Lee, principal of a middle school, invited Rabbi Leslie Gutterman, of the Temple Beth El in Providence, to deliver prayers at the 1989 graduation exercises. Such invocations and benedictions were a long-standing custom. The rabbi's prayers were in accord with the standing guidelines, requiring prayers to be composed with "inclusiveness and sensitivity." In the invocation, he addressed the "God of the Free, Hope of the Brave." In the benediction, he expressed gratitude to God as "Lord" for "keeping us alive, sustaining us and allowing us to reach this special, happy occasion." Daniel Weisman, father of one of the graduates, sought a permanent injunction barring Lee and other principals from inviting clergy to deliver invocations and benedictions at future graduations. The District Court enjoined the schools from continuing the practice on grounds that it violated the establishment clause. The Court of Appeals affirmed. On writ of certiorari, the Supreme Court heard the case.

In his opinion for the Court, Justice Kennedy agreed with the District Court that the establishment clause is violated not only when government "creates an identification of the state with a religion, or with religion in general," but also whenever "it tends to do so." Though the prayers were entirely nonsectarian, there could be little question that they did "create," and certainly "tended" to create, an identification between the school and religion ("in general"). While no one was coerced to pray, the prayers suggested that the invocation of divine blessing is a good and worthy thing to do on such occasions.

What is wrong with this practice? While we might expect a legal reason to be given, what is interesting is that the reasons provided not only by Kennedy, but also by Justices Blackmun, Souter, Stevens, and O'Connor in concurring opinions, had little to do with the technical apparatus of law and legal interpretation. Their reasons are almost entirely extralegal, and whatever their judicial merit, they can be grouped under four headings.

1. *Religion is divisive.* Justice Kennedy reasoned that the selection of a rabbi, rather than a clergyman from some other faith, carried "the potential for divisiveness." There was nothing in the official record to indicate that the custom of these prayers provoked any divisiveness among believers in the political community. This judicial theorem was derived neither from the facts offered by the particular case, nor from any text in the Constitution. Rather, it stands as a general supposition about religion. Indeed, in his concurring opinion, Justice Blackmun asserted: "Religion has not lost its power to engender divisiveness." As evidence, he cited an ACLU report that, along with the issue of the death penalty, school prayer "is the only issue that elicits death threats." Religion, it would seem, is not only potentially divisive, but potentially homicidal. The Court's insistent focus upon the term "potential" is revealing. Any number of different good and worthy human activities are potentially harmful to the civil community. Football rivalries, for example, can cause public disorder, and in extreme cases, a breakdown of amity between different groups of citizens. Yet no one would seriously argue that football ought to be privatized merely because of its "potential." Rather, we tend to reserve this kind of interdiction for either inherently bad activities, or for activities that, although good and worthy, are inherently dangerous. For instance, in tort law the use of certain kinds of drugs and mechanical devices is recognized as potentially harmful, and the law requires a higher level of responsibility and precaution on the part of manufacturers.

2. *Religion is coercive.* The justices in the *Lee* majority were well aware that these same kinds of prayer are made to convene every session of Congress. Why, then, should prayer be coercive in one setting but not in the other? Justice Kennedy reasoned that adolescents (in contrast to members of Congress) are particularly vulnerable to "peer pressure." Citing a number of social-psychological studies on teenage peer pressure, Kennedy wrote: "We do not address whether that choice is acceptable if the affected citizens are mature adults, but we think the State may not, consistent with the establishment clause, place primary and secondary school children in this position." Once again, there is not a shred of legal argument here. But it does provide a fascinating glimpse of yet another judicial theorem about matters religious, namely, that religion, at least in its public form, is peculiarly hazardous to the psyches of children. Like alcohol and tobacco, religion is something best left to the discretionary choices of adults. Presidential and congressional occasions of prayer can be tolerated, Justice Souter added, because they can be "ignored." Conveyed over an "impersonal medium" like radio and "directed at no one in particular," these exercises have no religious impact. Here Justice Souter followed Justice Brennan's remark in *Lynch v. Donnelly* (1984) that "In God We Trust" can be maintained on our coins because, by "rote repetition," such emblems have lost their "religious significance." In effect, so long as something materially religious no longer formally conveys religious messages— so long, that is, that the mind can remain entirely indifferent to its religious significance—religion can be tolerated in public things and places.

3. *Religion is not rational.* Justice Kennedy contended that one of the main problems with public prayer is that it drains secular events of their meaning. State-sponsored prayer suggests that "human achievements cannot be understood apart from their spiritual essence." Hence, the state wrongfully robs nonbelievers, and for that matter believers

themselves, of the ordinary meanings and values embedded in these transitional events of life—what he called "life's most significant occasions." Justice Souter amplified the point, saying that the separation of church and state requires the citizens to tolerate each other's religious idiosyncrasies. What is crucial in the eyes of one believer is apt to be "idiosyncratic" to another. Thus, religion consists of so many oddities, like Jewish dietary laws and Amish use of horse-drawn buggies. On this view, public prayer neither counts as one of the ordinary saliences of life, nor does it enrich them. Rather, the practice hurls the mind into a realm of subjective and cultural idiosyncrasies, a realm of either the suprarational or irrational, which tends to militate against the appreciation of ordinary values. Governmental sponsorship of prayer, averred Justice Blackmun, "transforms rational debate into theological decree." This is unbecoming to the mission of a public school in a democracy.

4. *Religion can mean whatever an individual wants it to mean.* Justice Souter maintained that the middle schools in Providence wrongfully endorsed "theistic religion." The Rabbi paraphrased the Bible, and in so doing he necessarily offended those who consider themselves religious, but not theistic. Religion "in general"—a rather wide net— must include the beliefs of those whose religion is either non-theistic or atheistic. This approach to the definition of religion would be farcical if it were applied to contract and probate law. But the main point to be noted here is that religion, at least for the purposes of First Amendment jurisprudence, can mean whatever an individual fancies— including beliefs and attitudes that have no connection to a deity. How government could ever establish or disestablish something this nebulous and subjective is a question left unanswered.

According to the dicta of the majority in *Lee v. Weisman*, the picture of religion is easily summarized. Religion is a potentially dangerous and harmful phenomenon. It is apt to engender divisiveness, even homicidal urges, in the political community. It threatens the psychological health and development of children. It tends to subvert the ordinary meanings and values of life. It is not rational, but rather subjective and idiosyncratic. It is contrary to the institutions of democracy. And whatever reality it has, it tends to elude even the most ordinary dictionary definitions.

If the majority's view is roughly correct, then perhaps it did not do the right legal thing (for there is no constitutional argument for its verdict), but it certainly did the right moral thing, because it helped the civil community to expurgate a potentially dangerous and irrational activity. This is a harsh and shocking estimation of religion. There is no sense of why religion should be a public good, nor, taken at its face, why religion should be something prized by individuals even at the private level. Indeed, were one to survey the Court's dicta about obscenity, he would find that obscenity is rarely described in terms as forbidding as is religion.

Of course, one can rummage around in Supreme Court dicta to prove almost any kind of proposition. The post-*Everson* Court's holdings on church-state issues typically run from fifty to seventy-five pages in length. Not unlike the *Congressional Record,* a miscellany of different facts and speculations are deposited in the text and notes of these official opinions. Since 1947, there have been thirty Supreme Court justices from an array of different denominational affiliations. While they have disagreed about particular church-state cases, and while many have complained that the jurisprudence of religion has become too complicated, the approach generally has been consistent with *Lee v. Weisman.* Consistent, that is, with these extralegal suppositions about the nature and value of religion. Of course, there have been justices who perceived religion differently. In *McCollum v. Board* (1948), Justice Reed filed a dissent warning that the Court was trying to separate religion and culture. In *Wisconsin v. Yoder* (1972), Chief Justice Burger tried to affirm something resembling the traditional value of religion. Moreover, some of the justices most inclined to portray religion in forbidding terms do from time to time say something to the contrary. Justice Douglas, for example, delivered the often cited dictum: "We are a religious people whose institutions suppose a Supreme Being" (*Zorach v. Clauson,* 1952). And in *Allegheny v. ACLU* (1989), Justice Kennedy faulted the Court for "an unjustified hostility toward religion." Nevertheless, the Court's record since *Everson* confirms the summary we sketched of *Lee v. Weisman.*

Further Dangers of Religion

Some of the key cases of the post-*Everson* Court illustrate the persistence of these ideas that religion is divisive, coercive, irrational, and something that eludes objective definition. For example, perhaps even more than *Everson,* the case of *McCollum v. Board* (1948) exemplified the new legal and social propositions of church-state jurisprudence. In Champaign, Illinois, an interdenominational association of Protestants, Catholics, and Jews obtained permission from the board of education to offer classes in religious instruction to public school children between fourth and ninth grades. No public monies were expended for the catechists. Only pupils whose parents signed permission cards were allowed to attend the weekly classes. Nonparticipating students were required to go elsewhere in the school building to pursue "secular study." The record showed no divisiveness among religious believers. If anything, the program seemed to be a model of ecumenism and religious amity.

Vashiti McCollum, whose child was enrolled in the public school, filed suit against the Champaign Board of Education, claiming that the program violated the establishment clause of the First Amendment. Although the Illinois Supreme Court ruled in favor of the program, the U.S. Supreme Court found it to be unconstitutional. Justice Black delivered the opinion of the Court. He opined that the program "affords sectarian groups an invaluable aid in that it helps to provide pupils for their religious classes through the State's compulsory public school machinery." According to Black, the offices of the state may never be used to aid religion. And for Black, it was clear that making it easier for ministers and rabbis to catechize their faithful counts as "aid."

The most interesting opinion in *McCollum*, however, was filed by Justice Frankfurter, who concurred with the majority. A harbinger of the future pattern of jurisprudence, Frankfurter's dictum represented a new way for the Court to call to mind certain theorems about religion that have no basis in either the text or history of the Constitution. Justice Frankfurter contended that the Champaign program "sharpens the consciousness of religious differences at least among some of the children committed to its care." And these are "precisely the consequences against which the Constitution was directed." "Good fences," he added, "make good neighbors." According to Frankfurter, the chief problem with the presence of even voluntary religious activities in public institutions is that it makes students aware of their differences along religious lines. In a word, religion is divisive. Its divisiveness stems not only from the fact that it causes overt conflict among believers. Rather, the divisiveness arises at the spiritual and psychological level. The very "consciousness of religious differences" alienates the citizens from their secular unity. Frankfurter was not just speaking about nonbelievers, who are made to feel like outsiders by the presence of religion in the schools. He was speaking generally, so as to include religious believers as well.

Thus he went on to opine that religion subverts a primary "symbol of secular unity." Designed to serve as perhaps the most powerful agency for promoting cohesion among a heterogeneous democratic people, the public school must keep scrupulously free from entanglement in the strife of sects. The preservation of the community from

divisive conflicts, of government from irreconcilable pressures by religious groups, of religion from censorship and coercion however subtly
exercised, requires strict confinement of the state to instruction other
than religious, leaving indoctrination in the faith of his choice to the
individual's church and home. Of course, this is not strictly a legal
proposition. Nothing in either the Constitution or in the 150 years of
previous case law (prior to 1947) would provide even the slightest
grounds for these notions. Indeed, Madison's famous *Federalist* 10 argued quite to the contrary: the Constitution does not have as its goal
the elimination of factions, whose deepest roots lie, Madison said, in
differences of property. Instead, the multiplicity of religious sects,
Madison contended, would tend to ameliorate rather than exacerbate
the harmful effects of religious faction, just as the multiplicity of prop-
ertied interests tends to inhibit a majority faction of, say, cotton-grow-
ers. The *Federalist Papers* are a monument to the proposition that strife
avoidance is not a principal goal of government, for that would require
the government to be built upon foundations contrary to human nature.

The notion that religion is not only peculiarly divisive but also
unbecoming to the mental and moral culture that ought to be fostered
in public schools resurfaced in particularly sharp form in *Lemon v.
Kurtzman* (1971). The case was important, among other reasons, because it provided the occasion for the Court's three-pronged "test" for
establishment clause cases. The case dealt with Pennsylvania and Rhode
Island statutes that provided state aid to church-related elementary
and secondary schools. The aid consisted of reimbursement for the
cost of teachers' salaries, textbooks, and instructional materials in specified secular subjects.

The Court asserted that to satisfy the First Amendment, a governmental practice must (1) reflect a clearly secular purpose, (2) have a
primary effect that neither advances nor inhibits religion, and (3) avoid
excessive entanglement. In explaining "excessive entanglement," Chief

Justice Burger argued that government must avoid intensifying "[p]olitical fragmentation and divisiveness on religious lines." Thus, while "potential" divisiveness had been an implicit standard in the Court's jurisprudence since *McCollum,* it now became an explicit "test," one still used by the Court.

With regard to divisiveness, Chief Justice Burger argued that while "political debate and division, however vigorous and even partisan, are normal and healthy manifestations of our democratic system of government . . . political division along religious lines was one of the principal evils against which the First Amendment was intended to protect." Even the "potential" for such division, he concluded, "is a threat to the normal political process." Perhaps the Chief Justice was the unintended victim of his own rhetoric here, but the argument he makes necessarily presumes that the division of citizens according to their religious sensibilities is an "evil"—at least for ordinary civil institutions. Note that Burger, like Frankfurter, did not say that religion *might* be divisive. He argued as though this is a settled truth, a fact about the real world, and one that makes the First Amendment intelligible.

In *Lemon,* Justices Douglas and Black supplied a clue to the reason why religion is dangerous. Referring to Catholic schools, they wrote: "The whole education of the child is filled with propaganda. That, of course, is the very purpose of such schools, the very reason for going to all of the work and expense of maintaining a dual school system. Their purpose is not so much to educate, but to indoctrinate and train, not to teach Scripture truths and Americanism, but to make loyal Roman Catholics. The children are regimented, and are told what to wear, what to do, and what to think." On this view, religious education is indeed contrary to the ideals and purposes of ordinary education. Justices Douglas and Black did not suppose that religious and secular education share common tasks. (An overlap of common tasks would provide grounds for believing that some aid to religious schools, at least in that part which concerns secular subjects, would be a common benefit). Rather, parochial education was regarded as a regime of closed-minded propaganda. Although Douglas and Black conceded that religious educators might be "good, zealous people," one is nevertheless struck by the fact that, on their characterization of the matter, it would be difficult to justify religious education even at the private level.

Interestingly, on the same day that *Lemon* was decided, the Court handed down a decision in a related case, *Tilton v. Richardson* (1971), which concerned the constitutionality of federal funding for Catholic colleges in Connecticut. In *Tilton* the Court decided that federal support for Catholic colleges did not violate the First Amendment. Trying to explain this apparent contradiction, Chief Justice Burger offered two observations. First, the Catholic colleges consist of students who are older, and therefore more immune to religious coercion. Second, the problem of divisiveness tends to be more acute in local primary and secondary schools than in colleges and universities. For these reasons, we can take a more relaxed view of the establishment clause. To the extent that religion is diluted, in other words, it can be admitted into the proximity of public institutions.

Earlier, in connection with *Lee v. Weisman,* we found Justice Blackmun warning that religion prompts homicidal urges. This is, of course, divisiveness in the highest degree. A similar conviction was expressed by Justice Stevens in his dissent in *Webster v. Reproductive Health Services* (1989). The "intensely divisive character of much of the national debate over the abortion issue," he asserted, "reflects the deeply held religious convictions of many participants in the debate." Of course, there is no reason to quarrel with Stevens's observation that the abortion issue is intensely divisive. Political parties, churches, professional organizations, and the Supreme Court itself are polarized over abortion. It is the very symbol of the so-called "culture wars." But Justice Stevens simply took it for granted that the divisiveness over abortion is a symptom of "religious convictions." Why should religious convictions prove so divisive? Justice Stevens wrote: "Indeed, I am persuaded [of] the absence of any secular purpose for the legislative declarations that life begins at conception and that conception occurs at fertilization...." Although Stevens himself seems to collapse issues of embryology into theology, his line of thought is clear. Religion does not follow the ordinary canons of rationality. Rather, it is an occult domain of value judgment forced upon public debate. Hence, like dietary laws and horse-drawn buggies, religious "reasons" for pro-life legislation represent the imposition on the public of arbitrary, idiosyncratic, and subjective beliefs. No wonder that abortion tends to arouse such implacable and furious emotions.

The notion that religion somehow defies ordinary canons of reason has frequently emerged in free exercise cases. In *Thomas v. Review Board* (1981), for example, Chief Justice Burger wrote for the majority of the Court in a case that concerned a Jehovah's Witness who left his job because his religious beliefs forbade making turrets for military tanks. When the State of Indiana denied him unemployment compensation, he contended this action violated his right to the free exercise of his religion. The Court found in favor of Mr. Thomas. Whether or not this particular decision was good jurisprudence, it is important to examine Burger's effort to wrestle with Thomas's inability to articulate with any clarity his "religious" beliefs as they affected his case. Burger wrote: "the resolution of that question is not to turn upon a judicial perception of the particular belief or practice in question; religious beliefs need not be acceptable, logical, consistent, or comprehensible to others in order to merit First Amendment protection."

There is some virtue to this assertion if Burger meant that the free exercise of religion is not protected because a court has determined what is reasonable in matters religious. But Burger's dictum is often cited to a quite different effect, namely, that religion need not be comprehensible to anyone other than the person making the claim that he or she is religious. Or as Professor Laurence Tribe has put it in reference to the *Thomas* decision, religion concerns "faculties beyond reason." It is one thing, however, to acknowledge the fact of religious and theological pluralism in a society; it is quite another to suggest that religion lacks objective, rationally ascertainable grounds; that it is somehow locked into a private, subjective, and idiosyncratic world of individual belief; and that it must necessarily elude any public standards of truth and falsity. If religion can mean virtually anything that an individual fancies, then religion can mean virtually anything, including beliefs that are seemingly unconnected to any commonsense definition of religion.

Yet this is precisely what the Court has said about religion. After Congress permitted religious exemptions from military service for pacifists who held religious beliefs "in relation to a Supreme Being," the Court declared in *United States v. Seeger* (1965) that one can qualify for religious exemption so long as the "belief . . . is sincere and meaningful and occupies a place in the life of its possessor parallel to that filled by the orthodox belief in God." Since religion does not require a belief in, or worship of, a deity, the law need only inquire into whether the belief or practice is held religiously; that is to say, with personal sincerity. It is entirely immaterial whether the individual conscience is bound by a personal, lawgiving God, or whether it is bound by the aesthetics of nature.

This view of religion has led to surprising and contradictory results in other cases. For example, in *Lynch v. Donnelly* (1984), the majority of the Court found that a nativity scene in Pawtucket, Rhode Island, was not religious because it amounted to nothing more than a "passive symbol" that could be construed in any number of ways according to the perceptions of the observer. Materially, of course, a nativity scene—consisting of the Christ child receiving the adoration of shepherds and kings—is religious. The armchair epistemologists on the Court had to presuppose that the formal meaning of religion is conferred by the observer. And so long as the material symbol does not necessarily trigger religious perceptions on the part of observers, it is not, for the purposes of First Amendment jurisprudence, an issue of religion. Yet in *Wallace v. Jaffree* (1985), a minute of silence in public schools was deemed religion, since the subjective intent of one of the Alabama legislators was to bring religion back into the schools. Here the material act was in no way religious, but it became so by dint of the subjective intent of the lawmakers.

Even more curious is the fact that the Court has, in large part, accepted Justice O'Connor's standard of the "objective observer." She has insisted that the Court must ascertain whether an "objective observer" would construe the state action as an endorsement of religion. The problem is that such an observer is already ruled out by the Court's presumption that religion stems only from private perceptions that are subjective and nonrational. Clearly, if a nativity scene need not count as religion, but a minute of silence must, there are no grounds for objective observers in matters religious.

In the District Court case *Smith v. Board* (1987), Judge Brevard Hand allowed secular humanism to be counted as religion, since it involves propositions about the nature and purpose of man, as well as about the origin and purpose of the universe. Dozens of expert witnesses testified, with some plausibility, that secular humanism functions sociologically and psychologically like a religion. Fifteen years earlier, Justice Douglas—no proponent of church-state entanglement—had insisted in *Wisconsin v. Yoder* that it is arbitrary to exclude someone like Henry David Thoreau from the category of religious belief. Judge Hand only followed the adage that what is good for the goose is good for the gander: if orthodox beliefs are to be excluded from civil life, then it would only seem fair to exclude heterodox ones. Of course, if this is taken literally, then almost every act of government, with the possible exception of its institution of a common standard of weights and measurements, involves establishment of religion. In *Lee v. Weisman,* Justice Kennedy proposed that religion amounts to the conviction that "there is an ethic and a morality which transcend human invention." This implies that any belief in objective principles of morality must necessarily count as a religion. In that case, the principled grounds for laws against murder, slavery, and confiscation of property without due process—not to mention protection of religious conscience itself— are nothing but religious in nature. If so, they should be forbidden by the First Amendment.

Much legal and conceptual chaos ensues from this arbitrary and whimsical view of religion. Imagine, by comparison, what would happen to criminal law if the doctrine of criminal intent were believed to have no ascertainable relation to objectively defined meanings of assault or larceny. Or what would become of the jurisprudence of free speech if the Court were unable to objectively classify the various species of speech—commercial, political, obscene, etc.—and then to determine the varying First Amendment protection each kind should receive. Whatever defies objective definition cannot be brought under ordinary canons of rationality, and in that case no rational law could be written or obeyed for the matter in question. Intentionally or unintentionally, the Court has taken the view that in religion there is only a night in which all cows are black.

Gerard Bradley has argued that "separation of Church and state," walled or otherwise, is a notion possible only in societies that (1) have clearly differentiated the sacred from the profane, where God's due and Caesar's are distinguished, (2) have a state in the Western sense that is clearly distinguished from society and culture, a concept of state that begins only with the sixteenth century, and (3) that organize religion into some concrete institution properly denoted a church." Bradley is surely correct about the historical and philosophical prerequisites of the establishment clause of the First Amendment. If church means "religion in general," and if religion can mean anything that an individual construes to be of ultimate importance, then there is nothing to establish or to disestablish. If conscience can mean whatever the individual sincerely believes, without reference to obligations rooted differently in divine or in human authority, there is no rational way to delimit the "free exercise of religion."

In short, the Court not only evinces an arbitrary and unnecessarily hostile approach to religion; it ultimately backs itself into the corner of having no subject to adjudicate. This is the price paid for depicting religion as something intractably idiosyncratic and subjective.

The Source of the Court's Perceptions

In sketching some of these judicial perceptions of religion in the post-*Everson* cases, we have not tried to determine whether any of them have legal merit or demerit. Rather, we have shown that they manifest an exceedingly skeptical and hostile view of religion. While we might doubt that their jurisprudence of religion has any consistent rhyme or reason, the dicta are remarkably consistent. They reflect a view of religion shaped by a legal mind totally dependent upon the patchwork of precedents and dicta of its own case law.

It would be foolish to suggest that law is not in large part an artificial world of human contrivance. Human laws seek to determine legal meanings and definitions, and are not necessarily the best place to look for real and primary definitions of reality. For instance, if one were to rely only upon probate law to understand the nature and value of relationships between parents and children, one would have a distorted picture of reality; rules of criminal procedure do not constitute the basic meanings of what is good or wicked in human acts. By the same token, First Amendment jurisprudence (even were it in a healthy condition) is not the best place to begin an inquiry into the nature and value of religion. Yet the contrivances of law are meant to serve reality. They are instruments of order, and as instruments of order they are worthless unless connected to the real world.

A legal proposition is a doctrinal formulation *of the law*. It is a doctrinal proposition, for example, that the Constitution forbids an establishment of religion. A social proposition, on the other hand, is a proposition about reality that is *brought to the law*. That religion is divisive and subjective is an example of a social proposition. All legal actions (making, administering, and adjudicating laws) involve both doctrinal and social propositions. Therefore, I am not suggesting that there is anything especially spurious about the adjudicative appeal to, and reliance upon, social propositions. Rather, I am highlighting the spurious nature of this particular set of social propositions. What is remarkable about the current judicial picture of religion is its lack of connection to primary legal texts, to history, or to the actual beliefs and practices of the people. Even its doctrinal propositions appear to be nothing but the social propositions of an élite class who (to give them the benefit of the doubt) have no sense of religion. Only someone who has no confidence in his grasp of the subject could seriously speak of "religion in general," or believe that the place of religion in society can be measured by an ACLU report on death threats allegedly arising from religionists, or that children are coerced if put in the vicinity of religious exercises, or that icons of Christ are not religious.

Although the judicial perceptions have little or nothing to do with a living sense of any practiced religion, they do generally reflect the biases of their social class. In *A Common Faith,* John Dewey insisted that the meaning of "religious" needs to be emancipated from the substantive term "religion." Dewey wrote that "religion . . . always signifies a special body of beliefs and practices having some kind of institutional organization, loose or tight. In contrast, the adjective 'religious' denotes nothing in the way of a specifiable entity, either institutional or as a system of beliefs. It does not denote anything to which one can point.... It denotes attitudes that can be taken toward every object and every proposed end or ideal." By reducing the value of religion to the values of religious attitude, Dewey hoped to retain what is prized in human experience without the "encumbrances" of "supernatural channels."

According to Dewey, so long as religious experience and perception are connected to beliefs in the supernatural, religion will prove harmful to the institutions of democracy because religion in its traditional guises (1) must swear allegiance to exclusive rather than to inclusive ideals, (2) abide by a doctrinal method that is "limited and private" rather than "open and public," and (3) adopt a stance toward social reality that is essentially punitive and divisive. Speaking of the tendency of religion to subvert the ordinary values of life, Dewey noted: "A body of beliefs and practices that are apart from the common and natural relations of mankind must, in the degree in which it is influential, weaken and sap the force of the possibilities inherent in such relations." This sounds like it was paraphrased by Justice Kennedy for his *Lee v. Weisman* opinion.

There is no indication that Justice Kennedy and his colleagues read John Dewey before drafting their opinions in *Lee v. Weisman*, but their presuppositions about religion are virtually indistinguishable from Dewey's. Dewey, to his credit, never disowned the fact that he was a cultured despiser of traditional religion. He never pretended that his point of view represented descriptive truths of what the American people believe about things religious. His was an abstract, philosophical approach to what he believed to be an enlightened attitude toward religion. The problem with the Court's approach is that it fails to acknowledge the philosophical presuppositions that animate it. The Court takes these presuppositions as the established and indubitable truths of social reality. To this extent, they are a matter of neither philosophy nor law. Rather, they are prejudices, which finally look like the worst features of what they themselves mean by "religion."

CHAPTER EIGHT

A Crisis of Legitimacy
(Including a Response to Critics)

I n *Planned Parenthood v. Casey* (1992), the Supreme Court made abortion the benchmark of its own legitimacy, and indeed the token of the American political covenant. To those who cannot agree with the proposition that individuals have a moral or constitutional right to kill the unborn, or that such a right defines the transgenerational covenant of the American political order, the Court urged acceptance out of respect for the rule of law. "If the Court's legitimacy should be undermined," the Court declared, "then so would the country be in its very ability to see itself through its constitutional ideals."

If the Court does not claim to act merely in its own name, but for the common good and the rule of law, how then should citizens regard the effort to link abortion with the legitimacy of the Court itself and thus, it would seem, with the legitimacy of our current political regime? We could put this in a different way by asking whether the Court—in laying down rules without authority to do so and then asking for obedience in the name of the common good—has acted *ultra vires,* beyond its constitutionally assigned powers. If so, its commands are not legitimate. The rule of law prohibits reallocation of shares of authority without the consent of the governed. Since the political common good depends on no branch of government taking more than its share of authority, obedience should not be given to an act that violates the foundation of the rule of law.

So put, we have only stated a principle. Does it apply to the actions of this Court? It seems to me that the situation is ambiguous and admits no clear answer. There is no doubt but we live today under an altered constitutional regime, where the rules are no longer supplied by a written document but by federal courts defining the powers of government ad hoc, through their own case law. This profound change from our previous order of government is often hidden by political and judicial rhetoric that gives honor to and even cites the written Constitution; yet, in contemporary theory and in practice, the document is really an authoritative occasion for, rather than a norm of, judicial interpretation. The changes have been further obscured by the fact that the new regime was not ratified by amendment or constitutional convention.

But this profound and confusing change does not necessarily make the new constitutional order illegitimate—at least not in the sense we are exploring here. It is plausible to argue that this new regime evolved over time with the tacit consent of the governed. Operationally speaking, every sector of government has acquiesced in the Court's understanding of its own powers and the powers of rival authorities. Though the elected representatives of the people may complain about particular judicial rulings and try to influence those rulings through judicial appointments and party platforms, none challenge the authority of the ruling principle itself. Our elected representatives do not merely comply with, but obey, the Court's understanding of the constitutional order, and they have tendered obedience for fifty years.

Thus, when the Court in *Casey* asks that its case law be given the obedience due to the Constitution, and when it insists that, above all, it must remain loyal to its own recently established precedents, it makes a reasonable request within the context of the new constitutional regime. In this new regime, judicial interpretation rules the text, according to the Court's perception of the common good and the changing needs of the polity. It can be pointed out that this is a reckless kind of polity—allowing the Court to define the nature and scope of political power on an ad hoc basis, without benefit of the debates of a legislative assembly or a constitutional convention, and without the contest of facts typical of an ordinary trial court. One would be very surprised indeed were it not to engender great injustices. For all of that, however, the Court does not necessarily act *ultra vires.*

But the issue of legitimacy can be examined from another point of view. Citizens can have a duty not to obey a law if it seriously injures the common good. And were such laws propounded as essential features of the constitutional order itself—which is to say, propounded as laws governing the making of any other laws—then we could reasonably ask about the legitimacy of that regime. Bearing in mind that we are speaking not of isolated statutes, but of authoritative renderings of the fundamental law, such laws would be laws (1) that deny protection to the weak and the vulnerable, especially in matters of life and death, and (2) that systematically remove the legal and political ability of the people to redress the situation. A polity that creates and upholds such laws is unworthy of loyalty.

The first thing to realize about our new regime is that the abortion right is not a unique or isolated feature of contemporary jurisprudence. The Court's own case law shows that in order to maintain the abortion right at the level of fundamental law, many other sectors of the states' legal order, at both statutory and common law, need to be altered: family law, marriage law, laws regulating the medical profession, and, as we now see with the recent circuit court decisions, criminal laws prohibiting private use of lethal force. The principle of *Casey* cannot leave the other institutions of the polity unaffected. Moreover, the Court's own case law shows that it is impossible to disempower political opponents of abortion without going on to disempower them politically on other issues as well. What is one's place in a political regime that regards abortion as defining of the constitutional covenant, that expands the principle to other institutions of both private and public law, and that politically disempowers opponents?

Three decisions reached by federal courts in the spring of 1996 reveal a pattern of fact that will allow us to take a broader view of the situation. These decisions exemplify both the inherently expansive nature of the new regime's abortion jurisprudence as well as its disempowerment of political opponents.

By statewide referendum in 1991, voters in the state of Washington had reaffirmed the provision of the criminal code that outlawed persons in its jurisdiction from "knowingly causing or aiding other persons in ending their lives." On March 6, 1996, the Ninth Circuit Court of Appeals ruled in *Compassion in Dying v. Washington* that the State of Washington is constitutionally powerless to prohibit physicians (its own licensees) from using lethal force to assist suicides. Seizing upon the infamous dictum of the abortion decision in *Casey*—"At the heart of liberty is the right to define one's own concept of existence, of meaning, of the universe, and of the mystery of human life"—Judge Stephen Reinhardt not only posited a "right to die," but also deemed the state's legislative motive cruel: "Not only is the state's interest in preventing such individuals from hastening their deaths of comparatively little weight, but its insistence on frustrating their wishes seems cruel indeed."

Meanwhile, in New York, the Second Circuit Court of Appeals ruled in *Quill v. Vacco* that while there is no "historic" right to die, the state of New York violates the equal protection clause of the Fourteenth Amendment with its prohibition against assisted suicide. By permitting patients to refuse treatment at the end of life, but not allowing physician-assisted suicide, the state unfairly treats similarly situated persons. The court brushed aside the distinction between letting die and killing. Although it was claimed in the press that the Second Circuit's opinion was more moderate because it did not posit a "right to die," both decisions reach the same result from the same principle.

Not surprisingly, in New York that principle was also the dictum in *Casey*. Judge Miner, writing for the majority in the Second Circuit, asked: "What concern prompts the state to interfere with a mentally competent patient's 'right to define [his] own concept of existence, of meaning, of the universe, and of the mystery of human life,' when the patient seeks to have drugs prescribed to end life during the final stages of a terminal illness?" Miner answers, "None." In other words, given two patients, each of whom can define the meaning of the universe, the state of New York violates equal protection when it allows the one to "define" himself by having treatment withdrawn while it forbids the other to "define" himself by requesting that a physician assist his suicide.

The third decision concerned a 1992 statewide referendum in which the voters in Colorado adopted an amendment, known as Amendment 2, to their constitution prohibiting laws that make homosexual orientation, conduct, and relationships the bases of special entitlements to minority status, quota preferences, and claims to discrimination. On May 20, 1996, in *Romer v. Evans*, the Supreme Court ruled that the amendment is totally without a rational basis, and is "born of animosity toward the class of persons affected." The Court declined to say whether its decision silently overturns *Bowers v. Hardwick* (1986), which upheld the State of Georgia's anti-sodomy law. Yet if Colorado's amendment has no basis other than animosity toward homosexuals, it is difficult to understand what rational grounds might exist for anti-sodomy laws, or, for that matter, laws restricting marriage to one man and one woman.

These decisions have two things in common. First, they expand individual liberty against traditional morals legislation. And second, they impugn the motives of legislators, which the Ninth Circuit found "cruel" and the Supreme Court found hateful. This is the pattern that we need to notice if we are to understand the legal and political mind of the new regime. This pattern did not begin, however, with the decisions of the spring of 1996.

Earlier in the century the Court aggressively protected individual rights of contract against the democratic process in the states. But after World War II, the Court began to insert itself into what James Madison called the "internal" objects of state governments, particularly the culture-forming institutions, including education, religion, marriage, and government's domestic control over matters of life and death. Reasoning that the people do not wish these things to be left to the ordinary legislative process, the Court incrementally created individual rights as immunities from the political ordering of these "internal" objects.

The Court's religion jurisprudence was especially important, and indeed was a kind of seedbed for the new regime. In 1947, the Court ruled that the establishment clause must be applied against the states, and that no establishment means no "promotion" of religion. In 1948, John Courtney Murray called the new religion jurisprudence "rigid, ruthless, sweeping," and insisted that the Court's doctrine "cannot be approved by the civic conscience." Murray was correct about the sweeping nature of the new doctrine; over the course of twenty years, religion was removed, bit by bit, from the civic order of state polities. Murray, however, did not live to see the next step. In 1971, nonestablishment came to mean that legislation could have no religious "purposes," even when the immediate matter and effect of the legislation is secular. Justice O'Connor would later add that such secular purposes must even be "sincere."

Thus, the Court prohibited public events that had been practiced in every jurisdiction since the founding of the nation. Then, to sustain its reasoning in the face of new litigation, the Court found itself having to bring ever new objects under its scrutiny, such as moments of silence and abstinence education. Indeed, as we saw in the last chapter, Justice Kennedy has gone so far as to maintain that the belief that "there is an ethic and a morality which transcend human invention" is itself religious. Ultimately, the Court had to interrogate the subjective motivations of legislators in order to detect the presence or absence of religion.

In a separate line of jurisprudence, the Court moved on to issues of sex, marriage, and abortion. In hindsight, we see that the new lifestyle rights were inherently expansive. In *Griswold v. Connecticut* (1965), the new right of privacy was meant to protect marriage, and was justified by reference to the "traditions and conscience of the people." In *Eisenstadt* (1972), however, the privacy right was expanded to cover any reproductive decision made by individuals. In *Roe* (1973), it included elective abortion. In *Carey* (1977), it included the right of teenagers to have access to contraceptives. In *Casey,* it mushroomed into an all-purpose right to define the meaning of the universe. The circuit courts now insist that it includes the liberty to contract a physician to assist one's death. What began as a judicial effort to stretch the Constitution to make it better reflect the "traditions and conscience of the people" quickly became the opposite—it became a reason for constitutionally invalidating those very traditions as the ground for public policies and laws.

This line of jurisprudence, for a time, steered clear of the motivational analysis used in religion cases. To be sure, the issue of religious motivations would, from time to time, emerge in a concurring or dissenting opinion, when members of the Court would speculate that state governments have no authentic secular purpose for laws restricting sexual conduct.

These two lines of jurisprudence have begun to coalesce. Judge Reinhardt of the Ninth Circuit acknowledges that judicial acceptance of physician-assisted suicide would cause "great distress" to people "with strong moral or religious convictions." The "or" is interesting, especially in the light of Justice Kennedy's virtual equation of religion with any ethics thought to "transcend human invention." Reinhardt warns, "They are not free, however, to force their views, their religious convictions, or their philosophies on all the other members of a democratic society, and to compel those whose values differ with theirs to die painful, protracted, and agonizing deaths." Laws prohibiting physician-assisted suicide, he concludes, do "injury" to some citizens for no other reason than "to satisfy the moral or religious precepts of a portion of the population." On this view, legislation informed by religion *or* by traditional morality expresses a malicious desire by some citizens to apply power against other citizens.

In this light, we can begin to understand the Court's decision in the case of Colorado's Amendment 2. Although in *Romer v. Evans* Justice Kennedy does not venture an opinion about the religious nature of animus against homosexuals, his decision depends heavily upon the attribution of motives. "Laws of the kind now before us," he writes, "raise the inevitable inference that the disadvantage imposed is born of animosity toward the class of persons affected." "If the constitutional conception of 'equal protection of the laws' means anything," he continues, "it must at the very least mean that a bare ... desire to harm a politically unpopular group cannot constitute a legitimate governmental interest." In other words, individual liberty is defined not merely by the kind of act or decision that one is free to engage in, but by immunity from a certain kind of motive or purpose on the part of the legislator.

This analysis of animus has been linked to equal protection before. In *Bray v. Alexandria Women's Clinic* (1993), the Court examined whether anti-abortion demonstrators could be held liable—under the Ku Klux Klan act of 1871 (amended in 1985)—of conspiring to deprive women of the equal protection of the laws by depriving women seeking abortions of their right to interstate travel. The *Bray* case is unlike *Romer* in dealing with private citizens' animus against a class. The two can be seen together, however, insofar as the definition of discriminatory purpose holds for both public or private agents. Discriminatory purpose, as defined in *Bray,* implies that the agent selects or reaffirms a particular course of action in part "because of" and not merely "in spite of" its adverse effects upon an identifiable group.

In *Bray,* it was proposed that women qualify as precisely such an "identifiable group." Justice O'Connor reasoned that the law must reach "conspiracies whose motivation is directly related to characteristics unique" to women. These characteristics are defined as "their ability to become pregnant and by their ability to terminate their pregnancies." For his part, Justice Stevens wrote, "When such an animus defends itself as opposition to conduct that a given class engages in exclusively or predominantly, we can't readily unmask it as the intent to discriminate against the class itself."

The proposition that pro-life demonstrators are liable to such discrimination was defeated in *Bray* by a single vote—Justice White was still on the bench. For our purpose, however, it is important to note the strong analogy to what the Court now accuses Coloradans of doing in adopting Amendment 2. When Justice Kennedy asserts that there is no rational basis for the amendment, and that the "inevitable inference" is that the action is "born of animosity toward the class of persons affected," he is saying, in judicial terms of art that the amendment was adopted "because of" and not merely "in spite of" its adverse effects upon an identifiable group. It is true, of course, that women have a federal right to have abortions while homosexuals do not (as yet) have a federal right to perform acts of sodomy. But the animus analysis reaches the same result, for a class is allegedly picked out and bullied in violation of the equal protection clause; whether the class is entitled to special judicial protection doesn't matter if the legislators or voters can be ascertained to have a suspect motive.

In sum, the political ability of the people to legislatively address common concerns in the terms of traditional morality must pass through a gauntlet of judge-made law in this new regime. If not disqualified on grounds of religion, legislation and other forms of public business may be disqualified on grounds of insufficiently "secular" motivation. And if not knocked down for that reason, it may be disqualified for failure to comport with what Gerard Bradley has called the "mega-right" of self-mystery definition posited in *Casey* (a right that now moves by analogy into physician-assisted suicide). And if not disqualified because of that, then it may be disqualified on grounds of motive to do injury, to discriminate, or to deny to persons equal protection of the laws.

These disqualifiers have been used alone and in concert to place public expressions of traditional morality outside the new political order. In fact, the Court may not need to invent a constitutionally protected right to die or to commit sodomy. Its current repertoire of nullification tests and devices are already sufficient to knock down prohibitory legislation on religious and equal protection grounds.

While it allows individuals to be self-governing, the federal judiciary's new constitutional order radically undercuts their ability to be self-governing in the political sense of the term. It excludes from the political process the objects of mutual deliberation that make political order desirable, indeed even possible. Desirable, because the culture-forming institutions of society cannot be sustained without common effort; there would be no need for politics were there not some important goods that require the deliberation, direction, and authority of the community. Possible, because once private individuals are allowed rights to use lethal force for vindicating justice in their own cause (as in abortion or euthanasia), it is difficult to see how even the most rudimentary foundations of the older political society—those which reserve the use of lethal force to public authority—still remain.

The new constitutional regime is a very bad regime. It withdraws protection from the weak and vulnerable, allowing the strong to define the status and rights of the weak; it privatizes matters that, in any legitimate political order, must be public in nature; it sets innumerable roadblocks to the rectification of the problem through mutual deliberation of citizens in legislative assemblies; and it has made what used to be its most loyal citizens—religious believers—enemies of the common good whenever their convictions touch upon public things. In 1994, the Court not only allowed the Racketeer Influenced and Corrupt Organizations (RICO) statutes to be applied against anti-abortion demonstrators, putting them in the same category with mobsters, but also allowed to stand a Florida law restricting the speech of pro-life, but not pro-choice, demonstrators in the vicinity of abortion clinics.

Unless the new constitutional order is profoundly reformed, citizens of rightly formed conscience will find themselves in a crisis. Insofar as private citizens have given tacit consent to the new regime, and thus allowed it to speak in their name, they face an unavoidable moral crisis. But the crisis falls even more immediately and heavily upon public officials, for the new regime orders them to do what they ought not to do, and not to do what they ought to do. They are ordered not to regard the unborn as having moral rights, and not to take those steps otherwise available to their offices to protect and remedy injustices against that class of persons. Soon, the same will be true with respect to the dying and infirm. Moreover, legislative, executive, and judicial officers in the states are ordered by the Court to prevent the application of laws and policies of citizens on no other ground than the citizen's moral or religious motivations.

It is late in the day, and our options have dwindled. Either right-minded citizens will have to disobey orders or perhaps relinquish offices of public authority, or the new constitutional rulers will have to be challenged and reformed. The first option leads inevitably either to withdrawal from politics or to civil disobedience. Since there is still a window of opportunity with regard to the second option, it would seem to be the responsible course. In order to adopt it, we must take three steps.

First, the people through their elected officials must withdraw whatever tacit consent has been given to the new constitutional order. Because the new regime was not erected by any ordinary process of amendment, referendum, or ratification, in principle the people still may alter it through their elected representatives. Perhaps the U.S. Congress will be able to invoke its powers under section five of the Fourteenth Amendment; perhaps Congress can use its powers under Article III to alter the Court's appellate jurisdiction. How this might be done must urgently be studied by those having experience and expertise in the actual institutions of government.

Second, issues like abortion, euthanasia, and gay marriage should not be treated as isolated from the broader constitutional crisis. Those who would try to play within the game imposed by the Court, in the hope of incrementally improving the situation issue-by-issue, actually deepen rather than mitigate the authority of the new order. Indeed, it tends to confirm the suspicion that citizens who hold conservative opinions about morals and religion lurch from issue to issue, trying to use the public order merely to win a point, if not to punish those who believe otherwise. Particular issues therefore need to be advanced for the purpose of prompting a constitutional crisis; and prompting the constitutional crisis is the responsible thing to do.

Third, of all the features of the new regime, the one that must be tackled first is the Court's motivational analysis, which first emerged in connection with religion, but which now spreads to other matters of legislation informed by substantive moral purposes. In effect, the Court makes it impossible to have anything other than a procedural common good as a motive or purpose for political activity. There is a real possibility that the moral and religious motivations of some citizens will become not only actionable at public law, through constitutional suits challenging legislation informed by such motives, but also actionable at private law. Unless the elected representatives of the people can compel the Court to refrain from invalidating political activity merely on the basis of the citizens' moral or religious motivation, the task of reform is blocked. Should that continue, the option remaining to right reason is the one traditionally used against despotic rule: civil disobedience.

A Response to Critics

The above was originally published as my contribution to the *First Things* symposium titled "A Crisis of Legitimacy," which appeared in November 1996. I explained why the Supreme Court has brought about a crisis of legitimacy, not just for the Court itself but for the entire constitutional order. I argued that this crisis is marked by two things: first, by a long train of court rulings that constitutionalize principles contrary to rightly formed conscience; and second, by a train of decisions that remove from the political order the ability of citizens to remedy the Court's errors. The citizens and their representatives in the political branches of government are required to obey, or at least comply with, rulings that express principles that are contrary to conscience, *and* they are required to believe that those rulings are the law of the Constitution, and must remain so short of an amendment. This double bind—an objectionable decision, then constitutionalized—is exactly what Abraham Lincoln objected to in the case of *Dred Scott v. Sandford:*[1] "Its language [is] equivalent to saying that [slavery] is embodied and so woven into that instrument that it cannot be detached without breaking the constitution itself."[2]

Many of our critics did not appreciate the aim of the symposium, which was not merely to quarrel with particular decisions of the courts, but to call attention to the double bind. As Lincoln understood the problem, no constitutional regime is undone by a stupid or even by an illegal use of power by a particular branch of government. Whether judges should be more or less "active" in their interpretation of the Constitution, indeed whether judges ought to be more or less considerate of traditional moral principles, are questions of politics and policy debates, as well as questions of law. They are not trivial issues, but neither do they threaten the regime. The regime is threatened or changed when specious principles, to use Lincoln's words, are "so woven" into the fundamental law that those principles cannot be dislodged without "breaking the constitution itself."[3]

In the *Weekly Standard,* David Brooks suggests that a "return to first principles is the antithesis of the Conservative Temper."[4] The *First Things* symposiasts, in giving "fealty to abstract ideals and beliefs," are tempted to favor them over the concrete conventions, pieties, and ongoing conversations that constitute society.[5] Mr. Brooks makes a Burkean point: a healthy polity, indeed, a polity in which political conversation is at all possible, does not constantly or lightly revert to abstract discussions of first principles.[6] Mr. Brooks, however, implicitly regards the symposium as trying to move (abruptly) disputes over policy to metaphysical, moral, and religious questions.[7]

In *Commentary,* Gertrude Himmelfarb makes a similar criticism. Questioning the legitimacy of *the regime,* Himmelfarb says, distracts from the humdrum of the ordinary political process where conservatives have won significant victories: "We have, in this respect at least, accomplished something like a major reform, if not a revolution. It has been confined largely to the arena of social policy and achieved through the normal workings of the political process. It has not even required any constitutional amendment, which makes it all the more commendable. Other areas, however—the culture, the media, academia, and, most notably, the judiciary—have resisted the conservative trend."[8] Himmelfarb suggests that the *First Things* symposiasts ignore the constraints of policy debates and allow their frustration over the state of *the culture* to spill over into questioning the legitimacy of *the regime*.[9] Arguing in the same vein, Midge Decter observes that the rhetoric of revolution—whether by the New Left or the 1994 Republican Congress—inexorably confronts the "stolidity and . . . contentment of the general populace" and the "sluggishness and obduracy of democratic society."[10]

Still other critics, again on the political Right, accuse the *First Things* editors and symposiasts of religious intemperance, and perhaps intolerance. Walter Berns asserts that the symposium confirms the opinion "that religious conservatives are extremists."[11] Francis Fukuyama suggests that by raising the issue of legitimacy of the regime, Christian conservatives are liable to be viewed as "a somewhat nutty and out-of-touch interest group."[12] For his part, Peter Berger goes further, alleging that the Religious Right has fixated upon and absolutized the issue of abortion, by suggesting "[it] seems to me . . . that for most of the First Things contributors, and for the magazine's editors, the driving concern has been not so much the power the courts have improperly assumed but rather what they have done with this power."[13] Interestingly, Berger agrees that the courts have usurped power, but insists that "[t]ime and again, the other two branches of government have usurped power in constitutionally dubious ways."[14] In other words, the symposiasts are not really concerned about the routine misdemeanor of usurpation of authority, but with the felony of the judicially imposed policy on the matter of abortion.

These critics make good points. For my part, I should not wish to dispute their wisdom. A healthy polity requires of its citizens patience and prudence in addressing the imperfections of government. In a democracy, all factions, including religious and other partisans of *First Things*, must learn how to be good losers. The virtues of civic life are distinct from the virtues of religious obedience. In any case, ordinary political conversation presupposes the legitimacy of the regime.

Yet these critics miss the most salient point of the symposium. It was not the editors or symposiasts of *First Things*, but the Supreme Court itself, in *Planned Parenthood v. Casey*,[15] that supplied the premises for the question of the legitimacy of the regime. For the Court self-consciously staked its own legitimacy, and indeed the legitimacy of the constitutional "covenant," on the principles that it discovered and applied in that case. The Court proposed a Lincolnian double-bind situation. Take away *Casey*, and the *First Things* symposium would be vulnerable to just the kind of criticisms made by Himmelfarb. If, however, we took the right measure of *Casey*, the charge of radicalism should be aimed at the Court, not at the symposium. So, it is necessary to return to *Casey*, and to reconsider the regime-threatening doctrine announced by the Court.

Before turning to *Casey*, two points are in order. First, I pick my words carefully when I say that a doctrine is "announced." The Court appears to understand that it was proposing something new. It evinced an unusual degree of candor and anxiety about the response of the polity to its handiwork in this case. Gerard Bradley has put the question in this way: "We need not know whether the doctrine of *Casey* is not yet law but a proposal—a judicially drafted bill—awaiting final approval."[16] Perhaps the Court will silently or explicitly relinquish its doctrine of the social contract in *Casey*. At this point in time, however, it will not do to interpret away the *Casey* doctrine as incautious dicta that reflect the Court's rather anxious response to a crisis. In the first place, all of the great cases where the Court has defined its own authority and the nature of the social contract[17] have been rendered in moments of crisis. In the second place, every student of American constitutional law knows that judicial dicta have a life of their own at law. Justice Brandeis's dictum in *Olmstead v. United States*, that the framers of the Constitution "conferred, as against the government, the right to be let alone—the most comprehensive of rights and the right most valued by civilized men,"[18] has become virtually a self-evident axiom of constitutional law. For good or ill, the interpreting community of constitutional law (judges, scholars, and activists) takes judicial dicta seriously. When one side dismisses an argument as mere dictum, everyone knows that this is a point of rhetoric. In the third place, the Court's dicta in *Casey* represent the most recent statement of its view of the social contract and the authority of the Court. To my knowledge, the majority of the Court has not repudiated the principles proposed in *Casey*.[19]

Second, it might be useful to define the word "regime," for our use of this word in the *First Things* symposium was criticized. The word "regime" is the translation into Latin *regimen* of the Greek word *politeía*—the constitution or form of the civic life. The *politeía* includes the ruling element or class (*políteuma*) and the common education (*paideía*).[20] The ancients did not distinguish as sharply the social and institutional facets of the *politeía*. The regime is more like the soul of a body politic, making it a political community (rather than a tribe, family, or economic corporation) and individuating it as a particular kind of political community (aristocratic rather than monarchical). This is not the place to speculate how the ancient meanings of *politeía* or *regimen* correspond to modern institutions. Here, it is enough for us to note that a regime changes when the ruling powers are reallocated. The change from a parliamentary democracy, where many individuals and groups hold ruling shares, to rule by a single party is a change of regimes. As I read it, in *Casey,* the Court announces precisely this kind of change in regime, and holds it out for approval or disapproval by the people. Moreover, the proposed change in the *políteuma* implies a profound change in the *paideía*—in the civic education respecting what or who is to be honored. In *Casey,* we catch a glimpse of that new *paideía:* the honoring of unbounded individual liberty and the superintendence of the judiciary in distributing the loaves and fishes of that right.

In *Planned Parenthood v. Casey,* the authors of the joint opinion write: "the reservations any of us may have in reaffirming the central holding of *Roe* are outweighed by the explication of individual liberty we have given combined with the force of stare decisis."[21] There are at least two grounds for their decision: first, a constitutional ground, which concerns the substantive due-process right of a woman to procure an abortion; and second, "a series of prudential and pragmatic considerations designed to test the consistency of overruling a prior decision with the ideal of the rule of law, and to gauge the respective costs of reaffirming and overruling a prior case."[22]

To complicate matters, in at least two places the triumvirate takes note of yet a third consideration: namely, the Court's legitimacy. The authors write that overruling *Roe v. Wade,*[23] "would *not only* reach an unjustifiable result under principles of stare decisis, *but* would seriously weaken the Court's capacity to exercise the judicial power."[24] Enumerating the grounds of their decision, the authors write: "After considering the fundamental constitutional questions resolved by *Roe,* principles of institutional integrity, and the rule of stare decisis, we are led to conclude this: the essential holding of *Roe v. Wade* should be retained and once again reaffirmed."[25]

This floating third principle—call it institutional integrity or authority—is the most important feature of *Casey*. We will return to it after considering the first two grounds of the decision.

Even on a cursory reading, one is perplexed by the fact that the answer given to the first question (whether there is a constitutionally protected right to procure an abortion) is at odds with the answer given to the question of stare decisis, for stare decisis is only intelligible if one has reason to suspect that the first issue was erroneously decided. But Justices O'Connor, Souter, and Kennedy vigorously defend, and indeed extend, the jurisprudence of individual rights running from *Griswold v. Connecticut*[26] through *Roe v. Wade*.[27] The authors of the joint opinion write: "It is a promise of the Constitution that there is a realm of personal liberty which the government may not enter."[28] Then, they rather crisply set forth the constitutional issue: "The underlying constitutional issue is whether the State can resolve these philosophic questions ... such ... that a woman lacks all choice in the matter, except perhaps in ... circumstances in which the pregnancy is itself a danger to her own life or health, or is the result of rape or incest."[29] Finally, after explicitly adopting the substantive due process method of privacy cases, they resolve the issue: "[a]t the heart of liberty is the right to define one's own concept of existence, of meaning, of the universe, and of the mystery of human life. Beliefs about these matters could not define the attributes of personhood were they formed under compulsion of the State."[30]

Why, then, go through the hand-wrenching of a stare decisis analysis? According to their own principles, a woman has a fundamental constitutional right to procure an abortion without undue burden. And this is only the species of a broader genus of liberty, gathered from the case law on matters of privacy and autonomy.[31] Thus, *Roe* does not stand to *Casey* in the fashion that *Plessy v. Ferguson*[32] stands to *Brown v. Board of Education*[33] or that *Lochner v. New York*[34] stands to *West Coast*

Hotel Co. v. Parrish.[35] In short, there is no need to explain why *Roe* was
not overturned if *Roe* was essentially correct on constitutional grounds.
Even more curious is the fact that, in the stare decisis section of the
opinion, the Court avers that for an entire generation abortion has
become a form of birth control, and that overturning *Roe* would dis-
turb the settled expectations of those who use abortion for that purpose.[36] But in the section devoted to the constitutional question—to
the issue of the rights of women—the Court does not make the fundamental right depend upon these contingent social facts. Rather, the
right is grounded in the very nature of the liberty at stake. There is no
reason to think that, were only a small fraction of women to use abortion for purposes of birth control, rather than some other means of
"self-definition," the Court could reverse *Roe* without undermining
a fundamental principle of the Constitution.

    What can we conclude from the Court's opinion? We might con-
clude that there was a difference of opinion among the triumvirate,
and they decided to include, on the one hand, the strongest argument
in favor of the constitutional right, and on the other, the strongest
argument in favor of stare decisis. The reason that I raise the incom-
patibility of the first and second grounds is to address those who would
diminish the problems presented by *Casey,* either by reducing the rights
analysis to mere dictum, or by so focusing upon the stare decisis analysis that the opinion is construed as a derogation from the principles of
Roe v. Wade. The true story is that the right is augmented and made less
dependent upon contingent social facts, *and* that stare decisis is invoked with respect to contingent social facts. One might suppose that
this conjunction of incompatibles reflects the dilemma of American
opinion on the subject of abortion.

    The most remarkable novelty of *Casey* is neither the alleged right
to invent the meaning of the universe nor the application of stare decisis
to the question of whether to overrule *Roe,* but rather the Court's

proposal that its own legitimacy is a principle for settling the dispute over abortion. After explaining the nature of the liberty right to be upheld, the Court states the following: "[I]t is necessary to understand the source of this Court's authority, the conditions necessary for its preservation, and its relationship to the country's understanding of itself as a constitutional Republic."[37] At this juncture, the Court begins to develop a position that is without precedent in our constitutional history: "The Court's power lies . . . in its legitimacy, a product of substance and perception that shows itself in the people's acceptance of the Judiciary as fit to determine what the Nation's law means and to declare what it demands."[38]

Were an executive officer to define his power in this fashion, we might suspect it was Mussolini. It is a doctrine not merely of supremacy in law, but of what I shall call *exemplarism*.[39] An organ of government is legitimate insofar as it is able to speak the voice of the whole people, and insofar as the people are able to hear their own voice in it.

Consider the following declarations of the triumvirate in *Casey*:

> To all those who will be so tested by following, the Court implicitly undertakes to remain steadfast, lest in the end a price be paid for nothing. . . . So, indeed, must be the character of a Nation of people who aspire to live according to the rule of law. Their belief in themselves as such a people is not readily separable from their understanding of the Court invested with the authority to decide their constitutional cases and *speak before all others* for their constitutional ideals. If the Court's legitimacy should be undermined, then, so would the country be in its very ability to see itself through its constitutional ideals. The Court's concern with legitimacy is not for the sake of the Court but for the sake of the Nation to which it is responsible. . . .

Where, in the performance of its judicial
duties, the Court decides a case in such a way as to resolve the sort
of intensely divisive controversy reflected in *Roe* and those rare, com-
parable cases, its decision has a dimension that the resolution of the
normal case does not carry. It is the dimension present whenever the
Court's interpretation of the Constitution calls the contending sides
of a national controversy to end their national division by accepting
a *common mandate* rooted in the Constitution.[40]

The metaphor of roots or rooting is interesting because the triumvirate goes on to say that "[t]he *root* of American governmental
power is revealed most clearly in the instance of the power
conferred by the Constitution upon the Judiciary of the United
States and specifically upon this Court."[41]

The meaning conveyed by this language is unmistakable. The root
of the ruling power is revealed most clearly in the judiciary. The judiciary is not a co-equal branch, but a branch that enjoys some legitimate claim to more fully exemplify the "root." This notion is given
further weight by the Court's insistence that it does not merely decide
the case, but issues a "common mandate." Thus, the Court in *Casey*
speaks beyond the parties to the case to the entire nation, and argues
that the people could not understand themselves as a political or constitutional entity except through the rulings of the Court. As Professor
Bradley puts it, the Court announces: "We will be your Court, and you
will be our people."[42]

It is important to distinguish this bid to change the *políteuma* from
previous expressions of judicial authority. Let us take two cases that
are defining moments of Article III powers, *Marbury v. Madison*[43] and
Cooper v. Aaron.[44] In the first, the Court defined its power in reference
to other branches of the U.S. government;[45] in the second, it defined

its power in reference to state governments.[46] I do not intend to examine these decisions at the level of detail they deserve. Rather, I wish to contrast them with *Casey* in order to show that *Casey* certainly appears to cross a threshold that had not been crossed before.

Notice that the *Casey* Court does not merely reiterate the important, but relatively modest, point about judicial review made by Justice Marshall in *Marbury v. Madison:*

> Those who apply the rule to particular cases, must of necessity expound and interpret that rule. If two laws conflict with each other, the courts must decide on the operation of each.
>
> So, if a law be in opposition to the constitution; if both the law and the constitution apply to a particular case, so that the court must either decide that case conformably to the law, disregarding the constitution; or conformably to the constitution, disregarding the law, the court must determine which of these conflicting rules governs the case. This is of the very essence of judicial duty.[47]

Justice Marshall makes no reference to the legitimacy of the Court's power beyond the written Constitution. He makes no assertion of judicial authority beyond the case at hand. No doubt, Justice Marshall's understanding of judicial authority implicitly contains the idea of the Court policing the boundaries of the people's conversation through the institutions of the U.S. government. For all of that, however, Justice Marshall's articulation of the principle of judicial review does not hint at a doctrine of judicial exemplarism. Marshall refused to issue a writ of mandamus delivering a governmental post to Mr. Marbury; yet he did not issue a "common mandate" to the people.

In *Dred Scott,* the Court tried to make a bid to issue a mandate to the entire body politic on the subject of slavery. That bid was clearly and decisively rejected by Lincoln in his First Inaugural Address:

I do not forget the position, assumed by some, that constitutional questions are to be decided by the Supreme Court; nor do I deny that such decisions must be binding in any case, upon the parties to a suit, as to the object of that suit, while they are also entitled to very high respect and consideration, in all parallel cases, by all other departments of the government. And while it is obviously possible that such decision may be erroneous in any given case, still the evil effect following it, being limited to that particular case, with the chance that it may be over-ruled and never become a precedent for other cases, can better be borne than could the evils of a different practice.

At the same time the candid citizen must confess that if the policy of the government, upon vital questions affecting the *whole people,* is to be irrevocably fixed by decisions of the Supreme Court, the instant they are made in ordinary litigation between parties, in personal actions, the people will have ceased, to be their own rulers, having, to that extent, practically resigned their government into the hands of that eminent tribunal.[48]

The key in this passage is Lincoln's phrase—"questions, affecting the whole people." He denied that the whole of the common good is exemplified and governed by the Article III judicial power. He understood that were the Court's authority to exemplify and reach the whole of the common good, it would be a change of regimes—indeed, a change as startling and novel as the effort by Justice Taney to declare that an unbounded natural right of slavery exists in, and was intended by, the Constitution.

If we turn to *Cooper v. Aaron,* we find some incautious remarks about judicial authority, which, if not qualified, would amount to a new doctrine of judicial supremacy. Immediately after *Brown,* a school board in Little Rock, Arkansas, was delaying implementation of desegregation, and the governor of Arkansas threatened to use National Guard units to block desegregation of schools. After citing *Marbury v. Madison,* Chief Justice Warren wrote:

> It follows that the interpretation of the Fourteenth Amendment enunciated by this Court in the Brown case is the supreme law of the land, and Art. VI of the Constitution makes it of binding effect on the States "any Thing in the Constitution or Laws of any State to the Contrary notwithstanding." Every state legislator and executive and judicial officer is solemnly committed by oath taken pursuant to Art. VI, cl. 3, "to support this Constitution" . . . . No state legislator or executive or judicial officer can war against the Constitution without violating his undertaking to support it.[49]

Responsible constitutional scholars are aware that these sentences cannot stand without qualification because, so far, they conflate the Constitution and the Court's occasional case law. If *Cooper* is read in a flat-footed way, the Constitution is nothing more nor less than the status quo of the Court's interpretation—an idea that would hardly reassure minorities.

Although *Cooper* seems to cross a threshold into a novel doctrine of constitutional order, it can be grabbed by its coattails and brought back. The main holding in *Cooper* is that state authorities cannot unilaterally nullify rights won in a federal court under the Fourteenth Amendment. At stake here is not the exclusive supremacy of the judiciary, but of the federal government in matters reached by the Fourteenth Amendment. In his concurring opinion, Justice Frankfurter seemed to realize that the remark about judicial supremacy had to be put in such a context: "Every act of government may be challenged by an appeal to law, as finally pronounced by this Court. Even this Court has the last say only for a time. Being composed of fallible men, it may err. But revision of its errors must be by orderly process of law. The Court may be asked to reconsider its decisions, and this has been done

successfully again and again throughout our history. Or, what this
Court has deemed its duty to decide may be changed by legislation,
as it often has been, and, on occasion, by constitutional amendment."[50]

Looking at it from Justice Frankfurter's perspective, *Cooper* is not
an apt precedent or analogue for the doctrine spelled out in *Casey*.
First, there is no root-and-branch metaphor identifying the people's
grant of power with the judiciary. Second, although desegregation was
a national controversy, the Court in *Cooper* does not address itself to
the entire nation, but rather to state officials in Arkansas who were
attempting to nullify rights won in a federal court. Third, in light of
Justice Frankfurter's concurring opinion, other governmental actors
are not bound by their Article VI oath to conflate the Constitution
with the voice of the Court in a particular case. Rather, they are required to correct a judicial error through an orderly process of law. In
sum, despite two sentences that seem to conflate the Constitution with
the case law, *Cooper* on the whole preserves the ideal that our constitutional order consists of many ruling shares, and many voices. Although *Cooper* does represent an aggressive policing of boundaries by
Article III courts, it does not change the *políteuma*.

Such cannot be said for *Casey*. In no more than a stray dictum or
two, the Court claims to have settled a national controversy, and asks
for the obedience of the nation precisely on the ground of the Court's
competence to do so: "Their belief in themselves as such a people is
not readily separable from their understanding of the Court invested
with the authority to decide their constitutional cases and *speak before
all others* for their constitutional ideals. If the Court's legitimacy should
be undermined, then, so would the country be in its very ability to see
itself through its constitutional ideals. The Court's concern with legitimacy is not for the sake of the Court, but for the sake of the Nation
to which it is responsible."[51] Plainly, the Court here goes beyond the
judicial duty to speak the law in the case at hand; it claims to speak the

constitutional ideals, and to be the primary voice in that regard. Had Lincoln been faced with that doctrine of judicial supremacy and exemplarism in connection with *Dred Scott,* he could not have taken his Article VI oath; or, he could have taken the oath only on the condition of rejecting the Court's view of its authority.

If we take Lincoln's perspective, the *First Things* symposium raises exactly the right questions with regard to *Casey.* For us, as for Lincoln, there are two issues. First, there is the question of whether a right is protected by the fundamental law of the Constitution; second, there is the question of the scope of the Court's jurisdiction over that question. In *Casey,* the Court declares an unbounded right of liberty, and it declares its own plenary authority to exemplify the voice of the people—so much so, that were the Court resisted the people would lose their regime, their *politeía.*[52]

No one knows how far the present Court is committed to this new doctrine, or even whether it perceives it as a new doctrine; it can be only a matter of speculation whether the Court has considered the implications of *Casey.* On its face, however, this is a regime-changing doctrine. Whereas the Court once invoked the Constitution to protect rights and ruling shares against the will of transient majorities, *Casey* claims to speak for a supermajority of the entire people—it speaks for the collective will, or at least the "thoughtful part."[53] (One can only imagine the status of the unthoughtful part with regard to its share in the common good.) If this expression of power were put in the mouth of an executive officer of government, or in the mouth of a French-style Committee for Public Safety, we would see it for what it is: the reduction of the *políteuma* to one voice. Between the declaration of the Court and the common good, no place remains for the operation of public reason except in obedience to the Court. To the extent that this radical reconfiguration of the regime goes unchecked, the Court will continue to shut down any ruling voice other than its own. To the extent that other branches and departments of government comply with, or tacitly approve, the doctrine of judicial supremacy and exemplarism, the regime changes. And with each tacit approval, season after season, a new *paideía* inexorably emerges: To honor what the Court honors, and to honor it precisely because the Court so demands.

Take, for example, the *Boerne v. Flores*[54] case. The Court contended that the Religious Freedom Restoration Act[55] (RFRA) was a usurpation of power by Congress.[56] In this decision, the Court abstained from the exemplarist language of *Casey,* but the reduction of ruling voices to that of the Court is evident. Five decades ago, the Court (not Congress) incorporated the religion clauses of the First Amendment against the states. In its evolving jurisprudence of religious liberty, the Court generally took an expansive view of free exercise. State laws that impaired the free exercise of religion were held to a high standard of scrutiny. Free exercise of religion was protected not merely by an anti-discrimination principle, but by the positive principle that the people's discharge of their religious duties (prayer and good works) should not be significantly impaired, even when the law is one of general applicability neutral on its face with respect to religion. States had to show compelling interest and narrowly tailored means.

In the *Employment Division v. Smith*[57] ruling, the Court changed its own standard of review, reducing the free exercise clause to an anti-discrimination principle.[58] Despite severe impairment of the people's religious practices, states only need to show that they did not discriminate against the religion so affected. In response, by a virtually unanimous vote, Congress enacted RFRA, which was signed by the President in 1993.[59] In *Boerne,* the Court ruled RFRA unconstitutional on the ground that Congress's authority to enforce the Fourteenth Amendment extends only to those rights whose scope have been defined by the Supreme Court. In other words, the protections guaranteed by the

Fourteenth Amendment are no more and no less than what the Court decrees in its occasional case law—even when the case law changes from term to term, and when those changes embody completely contrary principles. Framed only a decade after *Dred Scott,* the enforcement clauses of the three Civil War amendments were intended to prevent the Court from hijacking the amendments.

Suppose the Supreme Court were to rule that re-segregation of schools comports with the equal protection clause of the Fourteenth Amendment. Then suppose that Congress tries to remedy that mistake, by passing a law pursuant to its section-five powers—a law that in effect restores the higher standard articulated by the Court itself. According to the framework set out in *Boerne,* Congress would be usurping authority. At any given moment, the Constitution is coincident with the Court's pronouncements.

Seen against the background of *Casey,* the Court in *Boerne* has swatted down perhaps the only remaining power capable of checking abuses of judicial power. The *Boerne* holding allows the Court to act unilaterally and to render important clauses of the Constitution immune from the conversation of other branches and departments of government. Justice Kennedy makes it look like Congress is defining its own powers when it tries to hold the Court to the Court's own standard in previous cases. After citing Justice Marshall in *Marbury,* Justice Kennedy concludes:

> When the political branches of the Government act against the background of a judicial interpretation of the Constitution already issued, it must be understood that in later cases and controversies the Court will treat its precedents with the respect due them under settled principles, including *stare decisis,* and contrary expectations must be disappointed. RFRA was designed to control cases and controversies, such as the one before us; but as the provisions of the federal

statute here invoked are beyond congressional authority, it is this Court's precedent, not RFRA, which must control.[60]

The upshot is that, while the Court is free to change its case law at will, and thus to make the Constitution a mere by-product of its shifting opinions, the other branches and departments must submit to the case law as though it were the Constitution. This is not Justice Marshall's understanding of judicial review. It is the *Casey* doctrine. And that doctrine takes us beyond both the interminable scholarly disputes about the historical origin and scope of judicial review, and routine concerns about one branch of government exercising too much authority with respect to this or that particular issue of the moment.

It is true, of course, that the Supreme Court has not yet disallowed the people's right under Article V to amend the Constitution. But amendment is virtually the only route left for correcting a judicial error. This situation follows logically from *Casey*. For in its understanding of itself as the root of governmental power, the Court presumes that it holds a plenary grant of authority to speak in the name of the entire polity—a presumption that can only be gainsaid by amendment. All other constitutional voices are silenced. The polity must submit to the Court's definition of its power, or the polity has to commit itself to a never-ending plebiscite. Indeed, a constant plebiscite tacitly admits the claims made by the Court about its own authority. Either way, we find ourselves approaching something like "the end of democracy."[61] (Once again, with respect to critics like David Brooks,[62] it is necessary to understand how it has come to pass that the table of civic conversation is being reduced to abstract discussion of the first principles of a regime.)

One of the lessons of this century, which nearly everyone claims to have learned, is that unlimited executive force in human government is dangerous. Throughout the civilized world in the 1920s and

1930s, people became dissatisfied and contemptuous of legislatures and parliaments. In Spain, Italy, Germany, Russia, Japan, and even to some extent in the United States (during the Great Depression), people wanted public conflicts and crises to be resolved by strong executive action. The multi-voiced, polycentric model of political authority was abandoned in favor of exemplarism. Executive powers were thought to exemplify the common good, not to mention the "thoughtful part."[63] After World War I, the civilized part of the world beat its breast with so many mea culpae, and resolved never again to retreat from the civil conversation of constitutional democracy, and never again to hand over power to unbounded executives. Interestingly, even during the Cold War, Americans vigilantly guarded against executive power that would arrogate to itself the right to be the only voice and the only power that speaks for the people.

But the very generation that learned the lesson about the hard despotism of unbounded executive power failed to learn the lesson about the soft despotism of courts. In the case of contemporary America—and, increasingly, in both Canada and Europe as well—courts, rather than executive officers, claim to be the final and exclusive voice of the people. Courts tell us when to stop talking and when to obey. The emerging doctrine of judicial supremacy and exemplarism is alien to our institutions; it has a very bad track record when expressed through executive organs of government; and it makes the fundamental law a theater of constant dispute over authority and first principles of the regime.

CHAPTER NINE

Dignitatis Humanae, Religious Liberty, and Ecclesiastical Self-Government

W hen Pope John XXIII convened the Second Vatican Council in 1962, most observers understood that the Council would need to address the issue of religious liberty in the civil sphere. Early drafts of a statement on relations between Church and state were included in a schema on the Church.[1] At the close of the First Session of the Council, the subject was moved over to the schema on ecumenism. Finally, at the Third Session in the fall of 1964, after some 380 amendments, the schema on religious liberty had become an independent document. It was not so clear, however, whether to undertake a general reconsideration of principles or whether to confine its work to a policy statement. All of these questions—where to place the statement, what title to give it, the range of its content and mode of treatment—reflect the troubled history of Church and state in the modern period.

A century earlier, at the First Vatican Council (1869–1870), the question of the Church's liberty and authority *ad intra* was taken up, and, to some extent, resolved. The Council affirmed papal jurisdiction over the whole Church.[2] Such affirmation was deemed necesary be-cause many of the European states asserted that local churches enjoyed civil liberty only in union with the state, and that the state had power to superintend the offices and properties of the Church. The new governments born and reborn in the revolutions of the nineteenth century seized ecclesiastical properties, abolished monasteries and religious orders, liquidated or took over seminaries and parochial schools, controlled the flow of communication between Rome and dioceses, and, in many instances, asserted the right to veto, nominate, and even appoint ecclesiastical authorities. The new states used older ecclesiological doctrines of the supremacy of the local or national church vis-à-vis Rome. In France, for instance, this was called Gallicanism; in Germany, Febronianism; in Austria, Josephetism; in Italy, Riccism.[3] The ecclesiologies of the *ancien régime* were restored in the late eighteenth and nineteenth century to express the power of the new nation states.

Consequently, issues of ecclesiology were deeply interwoven in the mélange of disputes between the Church and the states. Vatican I rejected root and branch the ecclesiology of Gallicanism. In so doing, the Council resolved a narrow but important part of the problem of the Church's authority and liberty—at least *ad intra*. Vatican I's basic proposition concerned whether the liberty of the Church must be answered in terms of its unity, and whether the unity of the Church required communion with the Bishop of Rome. In short, Vatican I concluded that Catholic bishops were not functionaries of the state or of national churches.

Pastor Aeternus, issued on July 18, 1870, infuriated the European powers. The Austrian government promptly cancelled its concordat with Rome, claiming that the papacy after July 19, 1870, was not the same government with which it had negotiated. In Prussia, Bismarck initiated the infamous *Kulturkampf,* during which time (1873–1887) more than half the Catholic hierarchy in Prussia were imprisoned for refusing to comply with laws giving the state power over the ordinary government of the Church. Although the immediate effect of Vatican

I was to exacerbate the suspicion, and sometimes the outright bellig-
erence, of the European states toward the Church, the Council saved
the Church's internal structure one generation before the European
powers committed a kind of international and cultural suicide in the
trenches of World War I.

At Vatican I, some theologians and bishops lobbied for a conciliar
statement that would specifically address the Church-state problem,
perhaps even going so far as to doctrinalize various papal decrees against
the new states. The Syllabus of Errors, issued in conjunction with the
encyclical *Quanta Cura* (1864),[4] listed erroneous propositions, many
of which concerned matters of civil governance. In the first month of
the Council, a draft of *De Ecclesia Dei* was leaked to the German press.[5]
Of special interest were its five chapters and twenty-one canons on
Church and state.[6] From the standpoint of the late twentieth century,
the material in these chapters and canons would be regarded as
unproblematic. For example, Chapter X declares the Church a "perfect society" having its own public law (completed in the 1917 and
1983 Codes of Canon Law). Chapter XIII insists that God is the author of both ecclesiastical and political societies, that they co-exist with
their own respective spheres of law, that they ought to mutually help
each other, and that the state should respect the rights of the Church.
Chapter XIV rejects the idea that political morality consists only of
principles of utility and public opinion and that rights of religion depend
upon political expedience. Chapter XV enumerates rights of the Church
in matters of education, seminaries, religious orders, and property. The
canons, too, would be familiar to anyone who has read *Dignitatis
Humanae*. For example, the canons reject the proposition that "[a]ll
rights among men are derived from the political State, and there is no
authority but what is communicated by it" (can. 19); that "[t]he supreme rule of conscience for public and social actions lies in the law
of the political State, or in the public opinion of men: (can. 20); that "it

belongs to the Civil Power, by virtue of its supreme authority to judge
and decree in matters of religion" (can. 21). Given the taut emotions
besetting the relationship between the papacy and the European governments at that time (highlighted in 1870 when the Pope lost his
jurisdiction over the city of Rome and declared himself a prisoner in
the Vatican), cooler judgment prevailed. There would be no conciliar
decree or declaration on Church and state.[7]

From 1870 until the end of World War II, the problem of the
Church's liberty *ad extra* was pursued in two ways. First, popes issued
encyclicals and other directives on the Church's relation to civil governments. Leo XIII (1878–1903) wrote some eighty-five encyclicals,
more than thirty of which dealt in one way or another with civil
government and the Church's relationship to it. While some of the
Leonine encyclicals would not outlast the particular occasion or problem they addressed, others were masterpieces of political theology that
would transcend the era.[8] Second, through the diplomatic instrument
of concordats,[9] the Church attempted to protect its liberty country by
country. Most famous was the 1801 Concordat with Napoleon, which
lasted until 1905. Several dozen other concordats were signed with
European and South American regimes.

The most striking thing about this period is that although the
Church was equipped on the one hand with philosophical and theological doctrines on the relationship between Church and the states
(in the abstract), and on the other with an ad hoc diplomatic policy
realized via concordats, the Church lacked a middle-level policy bringing together the speculative and diplomatic poles. During the nineteenth century, the Congregation for Extraordinary Ecclesiastical Affairs, first brought into being during the French Revolution, became
part of the popes' "kitchen" cabinet. The title of this curial department
conveys a sense of that era. Although it can be labeled the era of Catholic intransigence—against the revolutions, against confiscation of

Church properties, against usurpation of the papal states, and indeed against modernity itself—a more apt characterization is the era of emergency. As political Christendom crumbled under the revolutions of the nineteenth century and then vanished altogether in the wars of the twentieth century, the situation was politically so volatile as to defy the development of a single policy on the part of the Church.

The Church's contemporary doctrine of religious liberty began in the 1940s, during the pontificate of Pope Pius XII (1939–1958). First, as a Vatican diplomat and Secretary of State, and then as pope during the Second World War and its aftermath, Pius XII demonstrated a keen interest in precisely the issues—theoretical and practical—necessary to develop an articulated papal position on Church and state. His Christmas addresses in 1942 and 1944 represented a significant breakthrough in the Roman estimation of the modern states. It was Pius XII who abandoned the older Roman policy of intransigence toward modern democratic governments, and who began the process of making the necessary distinctions for shaping a new approach to Church-state relations. In this regard, Pius XII can be credited with two things. First, he did not speak as though the Church were still situated within political Christendom. Second, he took as normative the democratic regimes' self-understanding of the nature and scope of their authority: namely, as governments legally limited by constitutions and morally limited by a commitment to human rights.[10] Though Pius XII was critical of certain aspects of democratic government, his concerns were expressed in the manner of an internal, rather than a merely external, criticism. Contemporary teaching on Church and state unfolds in terms that are recognizably Pian.[11]

The Second Vatican Council

The Second Vatican Council addressed the issue of the Church's liberty, both *ad intra* and *ad extra*. With respect to the former, the most important sources for examination are the Constitution on the Church (*Lumen Gentium*, 1964) and the Decree on the Office of Bishops (*Christus Dominus*, 1965). As for the latter, the main sources are the Constitution on the Church in the Modern World (*Gaudium et Spes*, 1965) and the Declaration on Religious Liberty (*Dignitatis Humanae*, 1965).

Dignitatis Humanae ("*DH*" or "Declaration") is the text that will serve as the anchor of my exposition and analysis. The reason is easily explained. *DH* attempts to supply what had been missing for two centuries, namely, a "middle level" position that unifies principle and policy. Before I turn to *DH*, it is necessary to describe the relevant details of the Declaration during and after the Council.

At the ninth public session of Vatican Council II, on December 7, 1965, Pope Paul VI promulgated the Declaration on Religious Liberty. There were more *Non placet* votes registered for *DH* than for any other document approved by the Council.[12] Since 1965, the far Left and Right have been in heated agreement that this pamphlet-sized document augers a revolution. Archbishop Lefebvre, for example, refused to sign it, and would eventually lead a schismatic movement based in part on his displeasure with *DH*.[13] Even those who are not interested in radicalizing *DH* have tended to make claims on its behalf that extend beyond what the document actually says.[14]

In order to properly interpret *DH*, one should remember that it is a "middle level" approach to the cluster of problems and issues summarized under the rubric "religious liberty." It is not a complete exercise in either the theory or the practice of Church-state relations. The relationship between Church and state, and more broadly between religion and society, is an enormous subject, thrown across a vast historical, social, philosophical, and theological canvas. In order to understand *DH*, one must delineate the range of problems that were put on the table of the Council. Compared with the great conciliar constitutions (e.g., *Lumen Gentium* and *Gaudium et Spes*), where the Council broadly spoke its mind and supplied exceedingly rich contexts for taking stock of things, *DH* is very short, terse, and anything but loquacious.[15]

Situating the Issues

At the Council, the subject of religious liberty was considered and debated in light of three different models of how the Church might be situated vis-à-vis temporal authorities. The models were not merely abstract, for each had a historical track record.

The first model is that of political Christendom. Since the eighth century, the Catholic Church was wedded to Western society in the form of a single, though differentiated, *corpus mysticum*. Today, many speak of a theologico-political, or Church-state, "problem." For centuries, however, Church and state was a single body, internally differentiated by two authorities, each of which was thought to share in Christ's *triplex munus* of priest, prophet, and king. The king participated in Christ's rule *pedes in terra* (feet on earth), while the episcopal authority imaged Christ's rule *caput in caelo* (head in heaven). As Ernst Kantorowicz noted in *The King's Two Bodies,* nearly a millennium of Church-state relations in the West was conducted within a model that is scarcely imaginable to the contemporary mind.[16] Today one rarely thinks of the state as a body, much less a body shared with the Church. Although the organic model governing the relationship between Church and state underwent many permutations, it nonetheless persisted in one form or another into the nineteenth century. At each step along the way, the language of self-governance changed, for both the Church and states, according to new notions of what it meant to be a juridical and moral person or *self*.[17] Despite the variety and permutations of the model, Leo XIII generally summarized it in *Immortale Dei* with the phrase *Fuit aliquando tempus:* "There was once a time when States were governed by the philosophy of the Gospel."[18]

This is not the forum to detail this complicated, fascinating, and often troubled history. Although this model was for the most part practically obsolete by the time of the Second Vatican Council, it was not entirely defunct. A scattering of countries still gave special recognition to Catholicism, either by way of constitutional law or concordat. Moreover, centuries of Church teaching were developed within the orbit of this model, including the papal encyclicals of the nineteenth century. Although recent popes never taught that harmonious relations between the Church and civil government require special assistance and recognition of the true religion by the state, such was the ideal. This ideal was rooted in two points of theology. First, the obligation to recognize and serve the truth of religion is not restricted to individuals. Societies, as well as the individual, bear an obligation to perform acts that satisfy the virtue of religion. Of course, precisely how societies are to do so, without usurping the functions of the Church, has been a complicated and controverted issue from the beginning of political Christendom in the West. Second, the kingship of Christ is both spiritual and temporal. It would be a contradiction of fundamental Christology to believe that Christ's reign is only spiritual.

Undoubtedly there were bishops and theologians who wanted this model to be the crucible of *DH,* and thus vindicate either the Left or the Right on matters of Church doctrine, the modern revolutions, and on the general situation of the Church in modernity. Most bishops wanted a useful "middle level" statement that would change the emphasis of the Church's teaching without contradicting fundamental theology. *DH* adopted a carefully calculated silence on establishment of religion, at least insofar as it was understood according to the older model.

The second model can be called the neutralist or separationist regime, according to which the Church enjoys a negative liberty vis-à-vis civil authority. What is most important is the ground of the negative liberty. It is one thing to say that a government constitutionally, by positive law, lacks authority over matters religious (e.g., "Congress shall make no law respecting an establishment of religion . . . ."); it is quite another thing to assert that government on principled grounds must remain neutral on religion as such. Both are capable of generating a kind of negative liberty. The latter example, however, has more far-reaching implications. The neutralist regime can imply: (1) a radical privatization of religion—at its most extreme refusing to recognize the moral and juridical status of religious bodies; (2) a reduction of the moral and juridical status of the Church to that of other private associations; and (3) a denial that civil authority has any participation in the veridical order of truth.

Although the bishops were not experts in political philosophy, they were most likely not unfamiliar with the general lines of the neutralist regime. Furthermore, whereas the bishops remained mostly silent about political Christendom, they were careful to frame the civil right of religious liberty in such a way that it did not imply either a theoretical or practical endorsement of neutralism.

The third model has already been mentioned. This is where the status and liberty of the Church is conflated with the status and liberty of the state itself. In modern times, it goes back to the Peace of Augsburg (1555), which effected a settlement of religious conflict in Germany on the basis of the formula *cuius regio, eius religio* ("whoever rules, his religion"). Far from being a flimsy legal device for a temporary *modus vivendi* in Germany, *cuius regio* established itself as a fundamental doctrine of state during the age of absolutism. In Catholic nations, *cuius regio* often vested itself in the titles and claims of ancient Christendom (e.g., "the Most Christian Prince," "Monarch, by the Grace of God"),

when princes were sworn to a quite different ideal of service to the
Church. It was not always easy to distinguish where *cuius regio* meant
princely service and protection of the Church according to the first
model, and where it amounted to a thinly disguised hijacking of the
Church by the temporal authority. It was in the interest of the regalist
party to obfuscate and to make the new doctrine look like the old one.
For the bishops at the Second Vatican Council, this model was well
known. Not only had it bedeviled Church-state relations in Europe
for three centuries, but it reappeared in the communist states after
World War II in the form of puppet churches. Interestingly, when the
Archbishop of Krakow died in 1962, the Polish government vetoed
seven candidates before agreeing to Karol Wojtyla, who proved to be
problematic for them after his election as pope in 1978. The communist state's exercise of the traditional right of the *placet* had nothing to
do with political theology, but it showed clearly enough the perdurance
of the *cuius regio* doctrine. Bishop Wojtyla of Krakow became a major
player on the committee that drafted *DH*.

Interpreting the Silence about Establishment

In *DH* §1, the reader finds a clear statement of the scope of the
Declaration: "So while this religious freedom which men demand in
fulfilling their obligations to worship God has to do with freedom
from coercion in civil society, it leaves intact the traditional Catholic
teaching on the moral duty of individuals and societies towards the
true religion and the one Church of Christ."

It might prove surprising, if not frustrating, that *DH* puts to one
side theoretical treatment of the issues that directly touch, in American
terms, upon establishment of religion. Instead, *DH* treats the civil liberties required for the protection and fulfillment of man's duty to
worship God. Undoubtedly, the discussion of religious liberty will have
implications for establishment of religion. One implication is men-

tioned, very briefly, at *DH* §6. In circumstances where one religion is given "special civil recognition," the rights of other citizens and religious communities should be "recognized and respected . . . ."

A reader might reasonably say: After all these centuries of church and society constituting a kind of *corpus mysticum,* and after all the various and sundry establishments of religion, it hardly seems possible that the "official" reckoning with this history would be reduced to the disclaimer in §1, regarding what the Council leaves untouched, and the rather terse sentence of §6 on the need for the state to respect the rights of minorities in situations where the Church is privileged in the constitution. The correct response is that it is not possible because *DH* does not undertake such a reckoning. For the Second Vatican Council, it was quite enough to tackle the problem of the religious civil liberties of individuals, communities, and the Church Herself.

In addition to the fact that the drafters of *DH* could not agree on how to formulate and resolve every problem, other reasons can be given for their decision to emphasize religious liberty rather than the establishment or disestablishment of religion. First, it would have taken a Herculean effort to sort through 1,500 years of history for the purpose of identifying which governmental expressions of Catholicism, or for that matter, of religion, were good, merely acceptable, or unacceptable. Second, by the 1960s the most pressing problems facing the Church were how to induce secularist regimes to respect freedom of religion and how to use the Church's moral and spiritual resources to support constitutionally limited government in the wake of the world wars. Third, although it might come as a surprise to many American jurisprudents, the Catholic Church did not, and does not, believe that disestablishment is a principle superior to free exercise.

Finally, it should be noted that both Vatican II and John Paul II addressed the need for a theology of social liberty, especially in regard to the laity and sacralization of culture. *Gaudium et Spes*[19] §43 invites

the laity "to impress the divine law on the affairs of the earthly city."
("*lex divina in civitatis terrenae vita inscribatur*"). The *Decree on Laity,
Apostolicam actuositatem,* similarly notes at §7 that "[t]he whole Church
must work vigorously in order that men may become capable of rec-
tifying the distortion of the temporal order and directing it to God
through Christ." *The Catechism of the Catholic Church* asserts that "[t]he
social duty of Christians is to respect and awaken in each man the love
of the true and the good. It requires them to make known the worship
of the one true religion which subsists in the Catholic and apostolic
Church.... Thus, the Church shows forth the kingship of Christ over
all creation and in particular over human societies."[20]

In a certain respect, this theological reflection has just begun. One
can see why, in 1965, it would have been precipitous to force *DH* to
attempt to resolve the issue of how religious liberty and confession of
religious truth on the part of civil society might be synthesized in a
distinctly contemporary mode—one in which democratic institutions
prevail, where civil liberties of all are duly honored, and where
christianization or rechristianization has progressed to the point that
the essence of the Gospel has worked its way into a fully public mani-
festation. *DH* does not rule it out, but by the same token it does not
bring it into view as a pressing problem. Just as *DH* does not revisit all
of the past problems, it refuses to project its teaching, by way of hy-
pothesis, into the distant future.

DH therefore declares: (1) that the Church ought to be free to be
about its business, which includes the obligation of the laity to sacralize
culture, (2) that everyone has the duty and therefore the right to freely
fulfill their obligation to worship God, and (3) that this right ought to
be given constitutional expression. I use the term "everyone" because
DH §6 insists that the duty to respect involves "individual citizens,
social groups, civil authorities, the Church and other religious communities." I take this to mean that, whatever relationship might obtain

between the Church and civil society, and regardless of what the state does or does not do, everyone must respect liberty against external coercion in matters religious. That includes the imaginary scenario of a culture successfully evangelized. The Church declares itself to be a claimant and a supporter of this order of liberty, both with respect to the duties of the state and the wider and deeper order of human society.

Thus, the Council adopted a centrist position. It identified the principles proximate to the relevant subject (immunity of individuals and religious communities from external coercion), it drew a conclusion in the practical order (constitutional recognition of the principles), it took note of a few possible implications (what must obtain in states that give special recognition to Catholicism), and remained discreetly silent about the rest, especially about governmental exemplifications of religious truth. This silence can be fairly interpreted as meaning that the Church does not rest its case for liberty on the confessing state. It would be a mistake to make *DH* say anything more, or less. One might ask whether *DH* is completely silent, however, on the posture of government toward truth. The answer is no.

Rejection of Liberal Neutrality

The first part of *DH* (§§2–8), entitled *Libertas religiosae ratio generalis,* treats religious liberty according to the general principle of human dignity. The dignitarian position is developed in terms of natural law.[21] In explicating the *ratio generalis,* the Council had to distinguish its position from what I have called the liberal model. The liberal model can generate a negative liberty in the civil order in either the natural law or liberal paradigm. First, it could be argued that the individual enjoys by natural right a self-expressive autonomy, untethered to any antecedent obligation. This kind of liberal dignitarian position exists in recent U.S. constitutional law, specifically in privacy and free-exercise case law.[22] *DH* §2, however, asserts that "the right to religious freedom has its foundation not in the subjective attitude of the person, but in his very nature." This "nature" is not known exclusively from thin considerations, denuded from every theological and religious source. Second, it could also be argued that government is incapable of making judgments on matters religious. In his Memorial and Remonstrance, for example, James Madison insisted that "Religion is wholly exempt from its cognizance."[23] *DH* §§5–6, on the other hand, contend that government has an obligation to promote the free exercise of religion.

DH §3 states that man has been made to participate in divine governance. The Eternal Law sweetly [*suaviter*] disposes man to fulfill his duty to know and to assent to the truth. Such reference to Wisdom 8:1 has a long history in Catholic theology. It was one of St. Thomas's favorite biblical texts for describing divine governance.[24] In recent times, popes have cited the passage in order to admonish governments to heed the divine exemplar (*Mit Brennender Sorge* and *Summi Pontificatus*, for example).[25] Before the state imposes its laws and sanctions, men are already moved by God through the causality of their own nature to seek and adhere to religious truth. Religious obligation is a principle antecedent to human custom and positive law. Thus, *DH* does not proffer a merely anthropocentric doctrine of conscience: "It is through his conscience that man sees and recognizes the demands of the divine law."[26]

Therefore, the right of religious liberty is situated in something more than a mere faculty of liberty. Conscience is the mediation of a discourse between man and God. *DH* §3 appeals to St. Thomas's discussion of divine authority over the *actus interior*, the interior act of human judgment and conscience, insisting at §2 that "[a]cts of this kind cannot be commanded or forbidden by any merely human authority." Coercion of conscience, then, violates human dignity *and* divine right (§3): "[T]o deny man the free exercise of religion in society, when the just requirements of public order are observed, is to do an injustice to the human person and to the very order established by God for men."

Thus, *DH* goes on to say that limits on religious liberty, as regards the *actus exterior,* have to be derived from that same order. The passage just cited uses the phrase: "when the just requirements of public order are observed." As various drafts of *DH* were debated, Bishop Karol Wojtyla of Krakow made a crucial intervention, asking that *DH* §7 make clear that when the state limits liberty, it do so *ordini morali objectivo conformes*—"in conformity with the objective moral order."[27] In Catholic parlance, this means in accordance with natural law. The qualification was necessary for two reasons. First, the qualification emphasizes that external limits on freedom are not drawn from principles completely alien to those which ground religious liberty itself. The common good and individual conscience are not located in separate orders of moral truth. Second, the qualification was necessary in order to make clear to the communist states that "public order" cannot be a pretext for overriding basic moral principles.[28]

Negative liberty is therefore developed by *DH* in terms of the substantive obligation of individuals to pursue, assent to, and to order their lives according to, religious truth. Because the principle expresses an obligation, it cannot be reduced either to individual liberty or to governmental incompetence. When government recognizes the right of religious liberty, it is not respecting an empty liberty. Moreover, *DH* contends that the absence of human authority over the interior act of conscience requires government not only to respect the psychological dimension of the individual, but also the jurisdiction of God. Thus, natural law creates a norm for what constitutes an *ultra vires* act on the part of government.

Positively, government, "the purpose of which is the case of the common good in the temporal order, must recognize and look with favor on the religious life of citizens." However, "if [the government] presumes to control or restrict religious activity it must be said to have exceeded the limits of its power" (§3). Here, then, is the proposition. Government should actively promote, but not usurp, religious acts. While *DH* does not try to provide a list of policies that would comport with religious liberty, *DH* §§5–6 explicitly mention facilitating the right of parents to have their children educated religiously.

DH advocates a robust policy of "accommodation" not dissimilar to *Zorach v. Clauson*[29] and *Wisconsin v. Yoder.*[30] Yet, by way of comparison, these two decisions are not entirely apt because both are set within the context of the Supreme Court's neutralist/separationist doctrine.[31] Since *Everson v. Board of Education,*[32] the Court has held that the establishment clause forbids government at any level from aiding and promoting religion—not just preferential aid to a particular denomination or religion, but aid to religion in general. In *Lemon v. Kurtzman,*[33] the prohibition on preferential aid was expanded to include the intention and motivation of legislators, who are constitutionally bound to have "secular" intentions.[34] The Court interprets Madison to mean that government must not "cognize" matters religious—not just to refrain from imposing its jurisdiction *over* religion, but to make no judgments according to dictates of religion.

Over the fifty-plus-year career of separationist jurisprudence, the free exercise clause has become like an appendix that cannot do any useful work; correlatively, when it works, it conflicts with the establishment clause.[35] The core problem is the separationist logic. Because free exercise of religion seems to favor rights of religion (in contrast to, say, free exercise of sport),[36] American courts seem increasingly more comfortable reducing specifically religious claims to those of free speech or free expression. By making one government duty reside in the establishment clause and another reside in protection of free speech, the Court does not have to balance two facets of religion in public life. The price paid for this bifurcation of religious issues is that, rather than enjoying a substantive right to religious liberty, citizens enjoy an all-purpose right to free speech, which cannot be limited by restraint as to content, religious or otherwise.[37] In effect, religious liberty is rendered completely subordinate to a doctrine of disestablishment. Religious liberty can therefore materialize only by migrating to another sector of the First Amendment—usually freedom of speech.

This is not the place to consider the confusions and dead-ends of American First Amendment jurisprudence vis-à-vis religious liberty. What matters, though, is that DH does not create such confusion. Of course, this is easier said than done, because DH commences, for the most part, from concrete matters of policy where conflicts inevitably arise. Even so, it is important to note that DH does not embody a separationist or neutralist logic.

The second point to be made is that, on the issue of the competence of government in DH §3, the second schema, the *Declaratio prior*, said that the "State is not qualified [*ineptam esse*] to make judgments of truth in religious matters." After vigorous debate, this sentence was abandoned in the penultimate draft. And for good reason. First, it might have been construed to mean that government lacks even the epistemic warrant to judge that religion is good, thus undercutting the argument of DH itself; second, it could obscure the responsibilities of government on mixed matters, such as marriage and abortion; third, it almost certainly would have favored the neutralist and indifferentist doctrines that DH otherwise took such great pains to avoid. While it is true that it does not provide a detailed map of the acceptable range of government's cognizance of religion, DH does not remove government altogether from the veridical order—that is, the order of truth—in matters religious.[38]

Rejection of Cuius Regio

DH is unusually loquacious about an important problem: the freedom of the Church. The most critical passage is found in §13:

> Among those things which pertain to the good of the Church and indeed to the good of society here on earth, things which must everywhere and at all times be safeguarded and defended from all harm, the most outstanding surely is that the Church enjoy that freedom of action which her responsibility for the salvation of men requires. This is a sacred liberty with which the only-begotten Son of God endowed the Church, which he purchased with his blood. Indeed it belongs so intimately to the Church that to attack it is to oppose the will of God. The freedom of the Church is the fundamental principle governing relations between the Church and public authorities and the whole civil order.
>
> As the spirited authority appointed by Christ the Lord, with the duty imposed by divine command, of going into the whole world and preaching the Gospel to every creature, the Church claims freedom for herself in human society and before every public authority. The Church also claims freedom for herself as a society of men with the right to live in civil society in accordance with the demands of the Christian faith. . . .
>
> Ecclesiastical authorities have been insistent in claiming this independence in society. At the same time the Christian faithful, in common with the rest of men, have the civil right of freedom from interference in leading their lives according to their consciences. A harmony exists therefore between the freedom of the Church and the religious freedom which must be recognized as the right of all men and all communities and must be sanctioned by constitutional law.

Whereas *DH* proceeds cautiously on other questions, the wording here at §13 is decisive: "the most outstanding surely is that the Church enjoy that freedom of action which her responsibility for the salvation of men requires." Such freedom is called "sacred" [*libertas sacra est*] because it is endowed by Christ. Accordingly, the Council speaks without qualification of a "fundamental principle" (*principium fundamentale*) in the relation between the Church and governments—one that cannot be unseated by considerations of "prudence," whether those considerations be introduced by the Church or by the state. In reaching this fundamental principle, it was crucial to distinguish it from the general right of religious liberty grounded in human dignity. The Church's "sacred liberty" stems from divine mandate directly, rather than via secondary causality. This is why *DH* §13 speaks of a *concordia* but not a conflation of the two titles to freedom.

Unlike the question of whether the state should somehow manifest or exemplify the claims of the one true Church—a question that *DH* declined to treat, even by way of historical survey—*DH* does indeed treat the obverse of that question. *DH* rules out the regalist doctrines that would make the Church an organ of the state. This is the problem that has haunted the modern history of Church-state relations (mostly, but not exclusively, in Europe). Wilhelm Emmanuel von Ketteler, Bishop of Mainz, whose thoughts on this subject were influential during the pontificates of Pius IX and Leo XIII, took sober measure of the *cuius regio* ideology.[39] While giving due honor to the monarchies of old, Bishop von Ketteler contended that *cuius regio* was "nothing more than destructive idolatry."[40] Rather than looking to Rome for a model of independent spiritual authority, the nations wanted to revive the powers of the ancient Caesars. According to Seneca, Nero said: "Have I of all mortals found favour with Heaven and been chosen to serve on Earth as vicar of the gods? I am the arbiter of life and death for the nations . . . ."[41] Hence, von Ketteler's accusation that monarchy at that time amounted to little more than "pagan ultramontanism."[42]

This history is indisputably the background of DH §13, though the totalitarian regimes of eastern Europe and Asia were likely in the forefront of the drafters' minds.[43] DH §13 recites practically verbatim important sentences of Leo XIII's letter, *Officio Sancissimo,* to the Church in Bavaria. Bavaria experienced what was called a "covert *Kulterkampf.*"[44] Pope Leo wrote: "Of the rights of the Church that it is Our duty everywhere and always to maintain and defend against all injustice, the first is certainly that of enjoying the full freedom of action she may need in working for the salvation of souls. This is a divine liberty, having its author the only Son of God, Who, by shedding of blood, gave birth to the Church . . . ."[45] As one noted commentator pointed out, the phrase "freedom of the Church" occurs more than one hundred times in the Leonine corpus.[46]

The Church's formulation of precisely what it rejected in the *cuius regio* doctrine was considerably sharpened in the century preceding Vatican II. As noted earlier, Vatican I announced that the corporate unity of the Church does not consist of a federation of autonomous local units. During the 1860s, Camillo Tarquini developed a canonical position that the Church is a *societas perfecta,* having the ends and powers characteristic of a political community in its own right.[47] Leo XIII frequently reiterated Tarquini's claim. While the Church's authority cannot be reduced to the same proximate source as the authority of other human communities,[48] and while its ultimate end transcends that of the state, its constitution nevertheless resembles that of a civil community. After the Second World War, Pius XII gave two important allocutions on the theme of the Church as a *societas perfecta.*[49] Although the idea of the Church as a juridical and moral person was not especially new, the emphasis placed upon the point represented a change of sensibilities since the era of political Christendom. In the modern world, the problem was not so much the establishment of Church by the state, but rather its differentiation from the state.[50] What was most important was that the Church could be differentiated without reducing itself to the status of other private associations. In other words, religious liberty considered only in the light of the *ratio generalis* would misrepresent what the Church claimed for her own liberty.

DH §13, therefore, should be read alongside the Vatican II decree on bishops, *Christus Dominus,* issued five weeks before *DH. Christus Dominus* §20 states: "Since the apostolic office of bishops was instituted by Christ the Lord and is directed to a spiritual and supernatural end, the sacred Ecumenical Council asserts that the competent ecclesiastical authority has the proper, special, and, as of right, exclusive power to appoint and install bishops." The finishing touch was made in the 1983 *Codex Iuris Canonici,* which stated that: "[N]o rights or privileges of election, appointment, presentation or designation of Bishops are conceded to civil authorities."[51]

Critics of *DH* have complained that §13, despite its Leonine credentials, derogates from the tradition of the Church. Although *DH* clearly states the obligation of the state not to absorb the Church, or to regard the Church merely as one private party among others, *DH* §13 does not speak of the state's obligation (ideally) to confess the true religion. Archbishop Lefebvre, for one, protested that the line "*Libertas Ecclesiae est principium fundamentale*" was wrong because the issue was not merely the state's duty to the Church, but its duty to "recognize the social royalty of Our Lord Jesus Christ."[52] A complete response to this objection entails a patient and thorough survey of where the conciliar documents take up the social ramifications of Christ as priest, prophet, and king. Here, it will suffice to reiterate a point made earlier, namely that *DH* §1 put the issue of corporate obligations to confess the truth to one side. Instead, the bishops investigated the narrower issue of the civil liberty of human persons in matters religious, and subsequently addressed the question of the liberty and mission of the Church.

Still others have objected that the Church has claimed the wrong principle, even for Herself. Michael Davies, for example, noted that "Pope Paul VI made it clear that he certainly interpreted *Dignitatis humanae* as meaning that freedom *alone* for the Church can be considered normal in principle."[53] Mr. Davies referred to Pope Paul VI's homily at the close of Vatican II on December 8, 1965. On this occasion, the message (*Aux Governants*) was read by Achille Cardinal Lienart of Lille, France. Davies is perplexed by the sentence, "[s]he asks of you only liberty, the liberty to believe and to preach her faith, the freedom to love her God and serve Him, the freedom to live and to bring to men her message of life."[54] Davies perhaps was misled by John Courtney Murray, who quoted the same sentence in support of his personal thesis that *DH* renounces all special privileges and establishments for the Church, and that her claim is freedom, nothing more.[55]

In this case, Murray was wrong. In the first place, Murray, who usually counseled narrow and focused readings of the issues under review, here tried to make *DH* (after the fact of its promulgation) resolve something that it expressly said it would not take up. In the second place, a doctrinal reading of "nothing more" cannot be supported by *DH,* which not only asks the state to preserve liberty within the context of a "just . . . public order," but also asks the temporal authorities to appreciate that, according to the Church's own understanding, its liberty is grounded in a divine mandate. Recall the opening words of *DH* §13: "Among those things which pertain to the good of the Church and indeed to the good of society here on earth, . . . the most outstanding surely is that the Church enjoy the freedom of action . . . ." Indeed, *DH* insists that the Church's liberty derives first from Christ (hence, the *principium fundamentale*), and also (*etiam*) from her character as a society of men.

After the Council, Murray voiced a different opinion: "This unique theological title, however, cannot be urged in political society and against government. The mandate of Christ to His Church is formally a truth of the transcendent order in which the authority of the Church is exercised and her life as a community is lived. Therefore it is not subject, or even accessible, to judgment by secular powers as regards its truth or falsity."[56] It must be noted, however, that this was Murray's opinion, which in my view is contradicted by *DH* and *Gaudium et Spes*.

In the third place, the sentence that perplexes Davies is taken out of context. Here is the text of *Aux Governants* read by Achille Cardinal Lienart:

> We proclaim publicly: We do honor to your authority and your sovereignty, we respect your office, we recognize your just laws, we esteem those who make them and those who apply them. But we have a sacrosanct word to speak to you and it is this: Only God is great. God alone is the beginning and the end. God alone is the source of your authority and the foundation of your laws. Your task is to be in the world the promoters of order and peace among men. But never forget this: It is God, the living and true God, who is the Father of men. And it is Christ, His eternal Son, who came to make this known to us and to teach us that we are all brothers. He it is who is the great artisan of order and peace on earth, for He it is who guides human history and who alone can incline hearts to renounce those evil passions which beget war and misfortune. It is He who blesses the bread of the human race, who sanctifies its work and its suffering, who gives it those joys which you can never give it, and strengthens it in those sufferings which you cannot console. In your earthly and temporal city, God constructs mysteriously His spiritual and eternal city, His Church. And what does this Church ask of you after close

to 2,000 years of experiences of all kinds in her relations with you, the powers of the earth? What does the Church ask of you today? She tells you in one of the major documents of this council. She asks of you only liberty, the liberty to believe and to preach her faith, the freedom to love her God and serve Him, the freedom to live and to bring to men her message of life. Do not fear her. She is made after the image of her Master, whose mysterious action does not interfere with your prerogatives but heals everything human of its fatal weakness, transfigures it and fills it with hope, truth and beauty. Allow Christ to exercise His purifying action on society. Do not crucify Him anew. This would be a sacrilege for He is the Son of God. This would be suicide for He is the Son of man. And we, His humble ministers, allow us to spread everywhere without hindrance the Gospel of peace on which we have meditated during this council. Of it, your peoples will be the first beneficiaries, since the Church forms for you loyal citizens, friends of social peace and progress.[57]

As the text makes clear, Paul VI was not suggesting that the Church's liberty consists *only* of a negative freedom, which is to be discussed (*ad extra*) *only* in procedural terms. Paul VI does not ask the states to establish or even to privilege Catholicism; rather, he asks them to respect its sanctifying mission and power in society.[58]

Conclusion

In sum, my conclusion is as follows. First, the beginning of wisdom in reading *DH* is to respect its silences. It should not be read as a treatise on establishment of religion. As discussed, the silence of *DH* on this matter evinces prudence that should not be dismissed as a mere pragmatic resignation in the face of disagreement. Moreover, establishment and disestablishment of religion mean different things, depending on the particular legal culture. As noted in connection with American jurisprudence, *DH's* position on religious liberty would probably count as favoring the establishment of religion. Second, we should pay attention to those issues that *DH* does settle. *DH* §§2–8 advance a principled argument for religious liberty, grounded not in subjective disposition or in empty liberty, but in man's nature. Moreover, religious liberty is not subordinated, as it is in American law, to a neutralist doctrine of disestablishment. How the notion of "the objective moral order" would permit the state, in particular cases, to limit the right is not described in any detail. Finally, *DH* §13 certainly puts to rest any notion of establishment drawn from the *cuius regio* tradition, where the Church is established "in" the state.

Having observed the precise points and limits of *DH,* three general considerations can be concluded.

First, *DH* provides, at least in principle, a way to correct the concordat policy that so hampered the Church prior to World War II. As noted earlier, after 1789, the Church attempted to protect its liberties by cutting the best deal it could, country by country. *DH* provides a framework that effectively integrates principle with policy and diplomacy, and it does so in language readily identifiable to states. To be sure, the principles of moral and constitutional liberties are not uncontested. There exist significant differences among states and international bodies about the interpretation and application of moral or human rights. The Church experiences continuing crises in Africa and Asia, where both individual and corporate religious liberty remain unprotected. The Chinese government, for instance, recently ordained bishops for its state-approved church, showing that the *cuius regio* doctrine is not completely dead. In Sudan, there is terrible persecution of Catholics. Certain factions in India reject the idea that the Church is free to evangelize and incorporate converts. The main point is that *DH* spells out clearly enough what the Church expects in whatever country it finds itself, and not merely by way of a Chinese, Sudanese, or Indian policy. While all of this does not eliminate the need for diplomacy, it mitigates the *ad hoc* policies that so limited the Church in the era of concordats.

Second, *DH* does not make a new case for the liberty of the Church. It does, however, recognize that the Church's claim for its own liberty must be complemented with a claim for the liberty of others. Such a policy is necessary for the Church's credibility and consistency. Provided that one avoids extreme interpretations, such as conflating the two distinct titles to liberty, *DH* is rightly credited as a major development in the way the Church situates itself in the political world. The liberty of the Church does not require political hegemony. On balance, *DH* much better serves the liberty and mission of the Church, which now comprises more than one billion Catholics, including adherents in missionary lands where the Church's greatest external problem is the lack of constitutionally protected civil liberty.

Third, *DH* represents a broader spirit of detachment from the problem of the state. Historically, the Catholic Church has been wedded to many different kinds of political societies. It has tried to achieve some measure of concord with ancient emperors (pagan and Christian), tribal chieftains, kings, leagues of cities, absolute monarchs, colonial governments, revolutionary governments, and, during the last century, constitutional democracies. This history is a kind of double-edged sword. On the one hand, whenever the concord was deep and long-lived, the Church became dependent upon a political culture. The Church, naturally enough, mourned the demise of its own twin. On the other hand, the long and varied history gives the Church a certain psychological and spiritual advantage. Having seen so many different regimes come and go, the Church can cultivate a spirit of detachment.

Detachment has always been understood, of course, from a theological standpoint. The Church, after all, is *in* but not *of* the world. In every generation, the Church has asserted that she is a society not only different than, but independent of, the state. In the post–1789 world, the Church was forced to learn (or relearn) how to distance its affairs from the state. Gradually, after much trial and error, the Roman Church saw how to interpret and adapt itself to this distance between Church and the state; namely, to a position that is not a twin of the Church, but recognizes, respects, and protects civil liberties. In the documents of Vatican II, and in the work of the present papal magisterium, the state is an instrumental good whose purpose is to protect the flourishing of societies other than the state itself. The twentieth century was a dreadful school in which everyone, including the Church, had to learn how to demystify the state. *DH* takes a rather sober view of the powers of the state. Not only does it have nothing to say about the temporal powers reflecting *imago dei,* but nothing about the notion of *two swords.* Rather, the theological language is reserved chiefly for the Church, family, culture, and nations.[59] Although it must at this point remain a matter of speculation, the Church's position today is all the more timely because the nation-states of the post-Napoleonic world are undergoing a profound transformation. No one is quite sure what will remain of them in this era of globalization.

CHAPTER TEN

Technology and the Demise of Liberalism

Having accepted the Stillman Chair of Catholic Studies at Harvard, Christopher Dawson arrived in New York City on September 30, 1958. He summarized his impression of the new world in this way:

> No one from the Old World can land at New York without being immediately impressed by this spectacle of gigantic material power. ...There is nothing like it in Europe or I think anywhere else. It seems to mark the coming of a new age and a new civilization. . . . But viewed in the perspective of history it is a very strange and surprising thing. The ancient Egyptians built pyramids that were even greater than the skyscrapers of New York, in terms of the human effort expended, but they were for the tombs of God-Kings. The relatively poverty stricken peoples of medieval Europe erected vast cathedrals and abbeys, but these were the expression of their common faith and their hopes for eternity. But to-day we build temples greater than the Egyptian pyramids or the Gothic Cathedrals and they are dedicated to toothpaste or chewing gum or anything that anyone wants. . . ."[1]

One might suspect that these were merely the grumpy remarks of an Englishman who was born in 1889 in a twelfth-century Welsh castle. But Dawson was only preparing his audience for a far more serious evaluation of the culture. Modern technology, he went on to say, is a "Frankenstein" that increases governmental power and decreases individual liberty.[2] Of course, this was a time in which Americans thought rather well of themselves. But Dawson contended that the ideology of the Cold War distracts our attention from the fact that the democracies and the totalitarian regimes converge in at least one important respect: namely, that they are planned societies, organized around technology, and governed by technocratic elites.[3] Dawson concluded by insisting that "the ultimate issue for modern civilization" is the recovery of a humanism sufficient to withstand "the disintegrating and dehumanizing influences of technology."[4]

It would be a mistake to attribute Dawson's remarks about technology to his aristocratic dislike of Gotham and to his even deeper antipathy for the managerial class. I say that it would be a mistake, because such remarks were not mere *obiter dicta*. In fact, Dawson's criticism of the technological society is one of the most persistent themes in his books and lectures. From his first published work, *Progress and Religion* (1929), to the lectures given during the twilight of his career in America, he was emphatic in his judgment that the chief enemy of culture is not liberalism or the other secular religions of progress but technology. The secular religions of progress that arose during the eighteenth and nineteenth centuries expressed an older humanistic culture going back at least to the Renaissance. These ideologies defined progress in humane terms. They envisioned perfections that belong or ought to belong to individuals: for example, enlightenment, benevolence, justice, and rights. In Dawson's estimation, however, liberalism was a transitory and relatively brief phase of culture, lasting less than a century. It was a mere bit player on a stage controlled by larger forces that measured progress in terms of an array of tools, not the least of which are the methods of the managerial class. This class represented to Dawson what St. Paul meant when he spoke of the "Cosmocrats of the Dark Eon"—that is, of rational powers that make use of things below reason to conquer and rule the world of man.

I must admit that in previous readings of Dawson's work, I was not persuaded by the critical, if not apocalyptic, remarks he made about technology. But the thesis that technology is the basis of secular culture, and that liberalism was but a transitory phrase en route to technocracy, was argued so forcefully, from the beginning to the end of his career, that we ought to take stock of what he had to say.

In this chapter I will revisit Dawson's thought on this subject. First, I will give a Dawsonian definition of liberalism. In particular, I want to mention why Dawson thought that liberalism was a humane culture, and why we should fear, rather than gloat over, its demise. Second, I will discuss his thesis that technology is the real basis of secular culture, that liberalism failed to control technology by failing to assign to the machine some end beyond a merely materialistic idea of progress and well-being. Third, I will take one technology as a case in point illustrating Dawson's thesis.

Rush Limbaugh notwithstanding, there is no precise definition of liberalism, either in ordinary speech or in professional scholarship. Liberalism can denote institutions and cultural practices, as well as ideas and theories about those institutions and practices. In the nineteenth century, especially in the Anglophone world, liberalism first denoted a set of ideas about how the legal system ought to be reformed, particularly the system of criminal law. Liberals like Jeremy Bentham and John Stuart Mill argued that the penal code should reflect enlightened principles of social utility rather than the moral taboos and passions of public opinion. Reform of the penal system was the pivotal idea for a broad-ranging set of reforms concerning child labor, mandatory education, women's suffrage, and economic markets. In all of these areas, and in many more, the liberal called first for legal and then for full-scale institutional reforms that separated the coercive force of law from the customary notions of morality. The liberal believed that the individual, emancipated from the public force of religion and custom, is the engine of cultural, economic, and even religious creativity. (No doubt Pope Pius IX had all of this in mind when he declared in 1854 that it is "an error to believe that the Roman pontiff can or should reconcile himself to, and agree with, progress, liberalism and modern civilizations.")[5]

It would be impossible to give a definition that captures (at a proper level of detail and complexity) all of the different aspects and phases of liberalism. Rather than define it, I will cite a single passage from John Stuart Mill's *On Liberty* (1859). Mill wrote that:

> There is always need of persons not only to discover new truths and point out when what were once truths are true no longer, but also to commence new practices and set the example of more enlightened conduct and better taste and sense in human life. This cannot well be gainsaid by anybody who does not believe that the world has already attained perfection in all its ways and practices. It is true that this benefit is not capable of being rendered by everybody alike; there are but few persons, in comparison with the whole of mankind, whose experiments, if adopted by others, would be likely to be any improvement on established practice. But these few are the salt of the earth; without them, human life would become a stagnant pool. Not only is it they who introduce good things which did not before exist; it is they who keep the life in those which already exist ....There is only too great a tendency in the best beliefs and practices to degenerate into the mechanical; and unless there were a succes-

sion of persons whose ever-recurring originality prevents the grounds
of those beliefs and practices from becoming merely traditional . . .
there would be no reason why civilization should not die out. . . .[6]

Mill went on to add the following thought: "The progressive
principle . . . whether as the love of liberty or of improvement, is
antagonistic to the sway of custom, involving at least emancipation
from that yoke; and the contest between the two constitutes the chief
interest of the history of mankind. . . ."[7] "Europe is, in my judgment,
wholly indebted to this plurality of paths for its progressive and many-
sided development."[8]

This, I propose, is the genuine article. Liberalism was not a theory
of democracy. Liberals of all stripes, from Mill to Tocqueville, feared
the leveling effects of democracy, egalitarianism, and mass public opinion. Nor should liberalism be equated with the rationalism of the
Enlightenment, for liberals championed the spontaneous genius, who
more resembled the artist than the scientist or the philosopher. In this
regard, it should be recalled that liberalism arose during the period of
Romanticism. Nor should liberalism be equated with the scientific
rationality of the industrial revolution, for liberals also feared the alli-
ance between democratic opinion and the machine. Indeed, in *On
Liberty* the machine is almost always the metaphor for the anti-liberal
principle.

The idea of the free market of economic exchange was actually a
small piece of a much larger metaphor of the free market of ideas, of
what Mill called "experiments in living." For the liberal, the state and
its rule of law had the limited role of providing only the skeletal structure of procedures that facilitate the liberty of individuals. Liberals
contended that the state should not have the role of central planning
or management. Adam Smith, for example, observed that the legislator
"seems to imagine that he can arrange the different members of a great

society with as much ease as the hand arranges the different pieces
upon a chessboard. He does not consider that . . . in the great chessboard of human society, every single piece has a principle of motion
of its own. . . .'"[9] It was a chief tenet of the liberal creed that society must
defer to this individual "principle of motion." The liberal believed that
any social order worth living in will emerge in unplanned ways, as a
result of individual creativity.

Of course, liberals devoted themselves to a plethora of reform
movements that used coercive power to change the law. But, at least in
theory, these reforms were not supposed to dictate, from on high, the
results of individual liberty; rather, they were meant to remove cultural
and societal impediments to liberty.

Liberalism was truly a new and awesome idea of how culture ought
to be reproduced. It was to be reproduced, not by custom and habit,
not by central management, but pell-mell, by spontaneous individual
choices. For the liberal, individual liberty is the goose that lays the
golden egg. Of course, liberalism never was purely embodied in any
nation or political party—and history clearly teaches that the liberals
could not resist using governmental power to make the goose lay the
egg. But here we are speaking of liberalism as an ideal; and, as an ideal
that captured the imagination of the educated classes of the West, it
was different from other secular religions of progress (for example,
Marxism) precisely because it eschewed the idea that progress is dependent on the coercive apparatus of Caesar.

Dawson was very respectful of liberalism. In a number of his books,
he depicted it as a secularized version of Augustine's doctrine of the
two cities. In the *City of God,* St. Augustine depicts two cities. On the
one hand, there is the *civitas terrena,* which because of self-love is
always dying and therefore cannot be an agent of progress. At best, the
earthly city can maintain a kind of external order of justice. On the

other hand, there is the *civitas Dei,* temporally embodied in the Church. This city, bound together by charity rather than coercion, is the agent of progress. As Dawson writes, Augustine's theology deprived "the state of its aura of divinity," and "for all its unworldliness, first made possible the ideal of a social order resting on the free personality."[10] Again, to quote Dawson: "It is only in Western Europe that the whole pattern of culture is to be found in a continuous succession and alternation of free spiritual movements; so that every century of Western history shows a change in the balance of cultural elements, and the appearance of some new spiritual force which creates new ideas and institutions and produces a further movement of social change."[11]

Of course, this sounds very similar to the passage we read earlier from Mill's *On Liberty.*[12] The liberal vision of history and culture, Dawson explained, took over from Christendom not only its universalism, its sense of a spiritual purpose higher than the state, but also its dualism— although now it is the church that is "the liberal equivalent of the powers of darkness, while the children of this world have become the children of light."[13] Dawson called liberalism a "sublimated Christianity"[14]—a humanitarian Christianity, relieved of the burdens of the supernatural and ecclesial authority. But he argued that liberalism was not relieved of the archetypal pattern of Western culture; it only changed the dramatic cast of the story.

It should be emphasized that Dawson did not begrudge liberalism its virtues.

- It advocated limited government and taught that nothing of lasting value can take place behind the back, as it were, of the moral effort of the free individual.[15]
- Despite its more or less explicit doctrine of individualism, liberal culture embodied a kind of humanitarian idealism.[16] Cruel penal

codes were reformed, famine and disease were combated, education was mandated.[17]

• Despite its doctrine of emancipation from custom, in the golden age of liberalism (Victorian England and America at the turn of the century), the family thrived as an independent social unit. Though sentimentalized and privatized, the family was at least somewhat protected from the forces of government and the market.[18]

• It developed a system of economic markets, which Dawson said was a "vast cooperative effort" requiring "a very high degree of social discipline and organization."[19]

• Moreover, like the older pattern of Christendom, liberal culture was transnational, transethnic and transracial. Like the Christian missionaries of the sixteenth and seventeenth centuries, who took the religious seed of European culture to all the continents, liberalism also had international aspirations. The domestic reforms of liberal culture were exported internationally.

Thus, Dawson dreaded the passing of liberal culture, for its demise deprived the West of a cultural pattern that had persisted for nearly two millennia. In *The Judgement of the Nations,* he wrote that "Christians have no reason to look on the defeat of this spirit with complacency or indifference . . . [for] these [liberal] ideas are not empty abstractions. They are the foundations of human life; and when they are undermined, the whole edifice of civilization is dissolved. . . ."[20]

According to Dawson, liberalism was "transitional and impermanent," lasting for less than a century.[21] What took its place was what Dawson called "the planned society,"[22] which aspires to reproduce culture by means of technology. Technological order, he claimed, is "now the real basis of secular culture."[23] The only thing it shares with liberalism is faith in a progress that is merely temporal and this-worldly. In all other relevant respects, the new order is the opposite of liberalism. Where liberals had faith in individual liberty and creativity, the technological order bespeaks necessity and uniformity; where liberals wanted to break the monopoly of the state, the technological order guarantees that only the state can mobilize the forces necessary for basic human undertakings. But the most important point is that liberal culture was still humanistic; despite liberal ideas, most people continued to live in the fashion of what C. S. Lewis called "old Western man." Real secularism, according to Dawson, could not emerge until technology made it possible for most people to live without the ideals and practices of the older Western order. Modern science changed the way that the educated class conceived of the world; but technology changed the way people lived.

Now, it must be said that by technology Dawson did not mean science, which is simply the effort to understand the natural environment. Nor did he mean merely the tools of applied science, for example, steam engines, computers, and so on. Rather, he meant the systematic application of tools to culture, especially to those areas of culture which had always been reproduced by humanistic activity, for example, sexual intercourse, family, religion, and economic exchange. In short, by technology, Dawson meant the practice(s) of treating culture in the same way that the tool treats the natural environment. And this is simply another way of saying that the tool is no longer an instrument but rather the measure of the human world.

Modern technologies are not only "labor-saving" devices. A labor-saving device, like an automated farm implement or a piston, replaces repetitive human acts. But most distinctive of contemporary technology is the replacement of the human act, or of what the scholastic philosophers called the *actus humanus*. The machine reorganizes and to some extent supplants the world of human action, in the moral sense of the term.[24] Hence, the policy of mutual assured destruction supplants diplomacy; the contraceptive pill supplants chastity; the cinema supplants recreation, especially prayer; managerial and propaganda techniques replace older practices and virtues of loyalty, and so on. Therefore, it is important to understand that Dawson's criticism of technology is not aimed at the tool per se. His criticism has nothing to do with the older and, in our context, misleading notion of "labor-saving" devices. Rather, it is aimed at a new cultural pattern in which tools are either deliberately designed to replace the human act or at least have the unintended effect of making the human act unnecessary or subordinate to the machine. Of course, Dawson did not live to see the emergence of "virtual-reality" technology, but he would have recognized it as part (perhaps the culminating part) of the continuum of technologies that he had in mind.

Consider, for example, the following remark written in 1870 by a British officer in the Indian Civil Service: "Railways are opening the eyes of the people who are within reach of them. . . . They teach them that time is worth money, and induce them to economise that which they had been in the habit of slighting and wasting; they teach them that speed attained is time, and therefore money, saved or made . . . . Above all, they induce in them habits of self-dependence, causing them to act for themselves promptly and not lean on others."[25] What is most striking about this statement is that the machine is regarded as the proximate cause of the liberal virtues; habits of self-dependence are the effect of the application of a technology. The benighted peoples of the subcontinent are to be civilized, not by reading Cicero, not by conversion to the Church of England, not even by adopting the liberal faith, but by receiving the discipline of trains and clocks. The machine is both the exemplar and the proximate cause of individual and cultural perfection.

The quote is also interesting because it supports Dawson's notion that liberalism was unable to impart liberal culture to non-Western peoples. (I cannot think of a single non-Western culture that was liberalized in the nineteenth or twentieth century.) Rather, the liberal imparted to these peoples Western technology: principally, military and managerial techniques, as well as the technologies of mass culture, especially those related to the entertainment industry and to propaganda.

It is worth mentioning that John Dewey's most popular book, *Reconstruction in Philosophy* (1920), was based upon his lectures in Tokyo, Peking, and Nanking. Dewey preached abroad what he preached at home: namely, that the main purpose of the human mind is not truth but praxis; we think not so much to know but to change our environment, especially the human environment. Above all, Dewey taught that we must have the audacity to think and to act beyond the limits of traditional habits and customs. Yet, as Americans discovered in 1941, the Japanese did not become liberals; rather, they became armed to the teeth. And even after we imposed a liberal constitution on Japan after the war, it was a mere legal template laid over a modern technological society. In fact, postwar Japan was the first industrial society to sponsor abortion and contraception. Dawson believed that liberalism weakened the immune systems of traditional cultures; and indeed history itself testifies to the fact that rather than moving from Confucianism to liberalism, they moved straightaway to the ideal of the social engineer. They became modernized and adopted the economic, social, and military imperatives of the machine.

Today, across all of the different political cultures, technology is required for the state's administration, for its military security, its propaganda, its markets, indeed for its very legitimacy. Governments rise and fall on the basis of their success in supplying the population with the technological means to achieve temporal happiness. The older liberal ideals of limited government, individual creativity, and of an autonomous private sphere more or less immune from centralized planning are violated whenever the technological imperative dictates otherwise.

In this respect, liberalism everywhere failed to hold the line. It did not control the erosion of local liberty by nation-states, but rather on its cultural watch the individual became dependent on government in ways that would have been unimaginable by despots of the old regime; local liberty became nothing more than a euphemism for a different sector of the nation-state's administration. It did not check the ideology of planned economies; rather, in what may be the cruelest irony of all for the liberal, the term liberalism became synonymous with the state-managed economy (in all of the Western democracies today, the "liberal" party stands for a state-managed economy). It did not succeed in its cultural mission of creating societies based upon freedom and persuasion but rather succumbed to the militarization of the state and to the creation of new police powers and systems of surveillance.

Dawson held that liberal culture paved the way for the technological order by separating the private and the public spheres, leaving the latter defenseless against the new technologies.[26] It was the ideal, and, to some extent, the practice, of liberalism to prohibit the state from acting for substantive moral and religious ends. The public sector was enlisted to facilitate what seemed, at first, to be relatively noncontroversial, even "neutral" ends: for example, security from enemies abroad and material well-being at home. These ends do not seem to dictate to the individual any particular version of the good life. Left to his own private discretion, the individual seemed to remain his own "principle of motion."

It is easy to understand why the liberal would regard technological order as something that leaves liberal values intact. Technology is not an ideology or a religion; it is not a person or even an institution.

Nor does it have any inherent cultural properties; for we see that technology can be transferred from culture to culture, working just as well in Cambodia as in Cleveland. But, of course, modern technology is not neutral. In *The Judgement of the Nations,* Dawson explained that "the spiritual elements in the Liberal culture were not strong enough to control the immense forces which had been released by the progress of the applied sciences and the new economic techniques. The advent of the machine, which was in a sense the result of the liberal culture, proved fatal to the liberal values and ideals, and ultimately to the social types which had been the creators and bearers of the culture."[27] The new technological order exacted as its first price the liberal, who it made obsolete (the Hillary Clintons of this world only pronounce a humanitarian benediction over the work of the social engineer); but the technological order exacted as its ultimate price the traditional humanistic culture, of which the liberal was bearer. By 1942, Dawson concluded that this transition was complete and, for any foreseeable future, irreversible.

There are a myriad of examples that could be cited to illustrate why this conviction about the neutrality of technology is mistaken. But I will give one specific example, which happens to be one that Dawson himself discussed in an essay entitled "The Patriarchal Family in History" (1933): namely, the problem of contraception. I will focus on contraception for three reasons: (1) quite apart from any issues of moral theology (and I have no intention here of engaging in any moral homiletics on the subject), contraception is a civilizational issue because it bears upon the basic cell of society, the family; (2) contraception provides an especially vivid example of how a technology can completely reorganize a cultural order, from its system of justice, to its economic markets, to its religious institutions; (3) it is a case in point for how liberalism does not define or control but only rationalizes technology; by rationalize, I mean that liberal rhetoric only hands out permission slips, as it were, for bringing the individual under the dominion of technology.

Contraception has a long history, which I cannot rehearse in detail in this chapter. But I will pick up the story during the golden age of liberalism, which in this country would be the late nineteenth century. In the last decade of that century, the Massachusetts legislature passed an anti-contraceptive statute, which read, in part, as follows: "Whoever sells, lends, gives away an instrument or other article intended to be used for self-abuse, or any drug, medicine, instrument or article whatever for the prevention of conception or for causing unlawful abortion, or advertises the same, or writes, prints, or causes to be written or printed a card, circular, book, pamphlet, advertisement or notice of any kind stating when, where, how, of whome or by what means such articles can be purchased, obtained, or manufactured or makes any such article shall be punished. . ." (Mass. c. 272, §21). In 1917, this statute was interpreted by the Massachusetts Supreme Court in *Commonwealth v. Allison* (1917): "[Its] plain purpose is to protect purity, to preserve chastity, to encourage continence and self restraint, to defend the sanctity of the home, and thus to engender in the State and nation a virile and virtuous race of men and women."

Such statutes were passed by several state legislatures, consisting for the most part of secularized Protestants. Anti-contraceptive laws were but one facet of a larger reform movement that tried to protect the family, and women in particular, from the disintegrating forces of industrialization and the mass market. For example, laws were passed that held industry to higher standards with respect to female employees—precisely because they were mothers or prospective mothers. The Mann Act (1910) made it a felony to transport or to aid the transport of a woman in interstate commerce for the purpose of "debauchery."

The point I want to make is that even during the heyday of laissez faire, the principle was well established, and often followed, that technology ought to be subordinated to society's moral interest in the family. With respect to contraceptives, it was a matter of common sense that, if widely distributed, they would undermine the principal cell of society. Writing in 1933, Dawson did not find it necessary to invoke any specifically Christian, much less Catholic, principles when he said that contraception "must lead inevitably to a social decadence far more rapid and more universal than that which brought about the disintegration of ancient civilization."[28] The patriarchal family, he noted, "requires chastity and self-sacrifice on the part of the wife and obedience and discipline on the part of the children, while even the father himself has to assume a heavy burden of responsibility and submit his personal feelings to the interests of the family.... [F]or these very reasons the patriarchal family is a much more efficient organ of cultural life. It is no longer limited to its primary sexual and reproductive functions. It becomes the dynamic principle of society and the source of social continuity."[29]

In 1930, Anglicans broke ranks with nearly the whole of Christian tradition with a declaration at the Lambeth Conference that permitted use of contraceptives by married couples for grave reasons. Though the Anglicans greatly weakened the moral case against contraceptives, the Lambeth statement was exceedingly "conservative" and cautious by our standards today. The fact remained that, until the 1960s, no one claimed fundamental rights to have contraceptive sex; nor did anyone seriously challenge the authority of the state to pass morals legislation of this sort.

What changed? Was society more liberal in the 1960s than it was at the turn of the century? The change took place primarily because of a technological advance. The progesterone pill was developed in the late 1950s and shortly thereafter was marketed in the United States.

The technological characteristic of the pill was crucial: orally administered, requiring no surgical procedure, it was seemingly a pill alongside other pills. Significantly, it was marketed as a birth-control pill rather than as a contraceptive. In a technological society, the word "control" signifies a responsible act. And because it was not a barrier method, even Catholic physicians argued that the pill was not a contraceptive.

Although barrier methods of contraception had been known about for decades, it was only after the introduction of the progesterone pill that there was any significant movement for a reform of the law. In 1965, in *Griswold v. Connecticut,* the Court found anti-contraceptive laws to be unconstitutional. In fact, the Court went so far as to invent a new, fundamental right of privacy. But what was especially interesting about the case is that, although this new right was justified in the name of individual liberty and marital privacy, it actually emancipated manufacturers and physicians. The Connecticut statute had not only prohibited the use of contraceptives, but had made criminally liable "[a]ny person who assists, abets, counsels, causes, hires or commands another to [use contraceptives]. . . ." The litigant in the case was not a married couple, suing over governmental intrusion into the sacred precincts of the bedroom; rather, the appellant, Dr. Buxton, was a professor at the Yale Medical School who also served as medical director for Planned Parenthood. In other words, the rhetoric of individual liberty was mere window dressing for the liberty of the manufacturers and purveyors of the pill, who allied themselves with the managerial class. This became undeniably clear in a 1977 case, *Carey v. Population Services,* when the state of New York's ban on the distribution of contraceptives to minors was challenged and found unconstitutional. Here, the Court said that "[r]estrictions on the distribution of contraceptives clearly burden the freedom to make such [reproductive] decisions." Thus, what began rhetorically as a solemn right of married couples against the state became in reality a right of social engineers to accustom minors to the new standards of technological hygiene.

In *Roe v. Wade,* of course, the Court extended the right of privacy to abortion. Once again, it is interesting that the Court used the rhetoric of individual liberty to make more palatable a decision addressed chiefly to the technological elites, which in this case were medical professionals. Before writing his opinion, Justice Blackmun visited the Mayo Clinic, where he learned that anti-abortion legislation only had the goal of protecting women from incompetent medical procedures. Thus, the emergence of safe abortion procedures removed the rationale of those laws. The moral and legal orders, in other words, are to be defined by the efficiency of modern medicine. Indeed, the trimester scheme, which defined legal personhood in terms of "viability," did not really designate ontological properties of the fetus so much as to align fetal development with a medical schedule. (It is tantamount to the idea that someone riding on Metro-North is a traveler not by dint of being on the train, but by virtue of whether he gets off at Pelham or New Rochelle.)

In *Roe,* Justice Blackmun spoke in almost sacred terms, not of the woman's liberty, but of her relationship to the physician. But even more to the point was the companion case, *Doe v. Bolton* (1973), which effectively secured a right to abortion on demand by defining the idea of maternal health so broadly as to justify virtually all third-trimester abortions. In the *Doe* case, the Court struck down any criteria other than the individual physician's "best clinical judgment" as the standard for undertaking the abortion procedure. *Roe* and *Doe* did not directly emancipate women but rather emancipated their physicians—first from the police powers of state governments and then from their own hospitals and peer-review boards. In the name of individual liberty, the multi-million-dollar industry of the clinic was brought into being.

Twenty years later, in *Planned Parenthood v. Casey* (1992), the Court reconsidered the constitutionality of *Roe*. Admitting that the decision had dubious constitutional credentials, the Court was remarkably candid about why it cannot be overturned:

> Abortion is customarily chosen as an unplanned response to the consequence of unplanned activity or to the failure of conventional birth control. . . . For two decades of economic and social developments, people have organized their intimate relationships and made choices that define their views of themselves and their places in society, in reliance on the availability of abortion in the event that contraception should fail. The ability of women to participate equally in the economic and social life of the Nation has been facilitated by their ability to control their reproductive lives.

The key is the word "unplanned," for it indicates that human activity is to be regarded in the same fashion as impersonal nature. Like lightning, floods, and tumors, the event of pregnancy follows a line of causality independent of a truly human act; hence, it needs to be brought under the control of a technology. The Court frankly admitted not only that abortion is practiced for the most part as ex post facto birth control, but that the practice has become a necessity.

In other words, the increments of legal emancipation track the increments of technology, and the increments of technology are recast as kinds of social necessity. In order to make room for what was, in itself, a relatively small part of the pharmacological revolution, the entire legal and moral order of the polity was changed: (1) the Bill of Rights was reinterpreted, to make what was once homicide at criminal law a fundamental right at constitutional law; (2) all common law pertaining to the responsibility of husbands over wives and children was summarily struck down; (3) divorce laws were changed; (4) professional associations of physicians and lawyers changed their by-laws to condemn any opposition to this continuum of technologies; (5) churches changed their moral theologies to accommodate the separation of sex and procreation; (6) public school curricula changed, and indeed new cabinet offices invented for the purpose of habituating even prepubescent children to the use of contraceptive technology; (7) even a conservative writer like George Will, who authored the book *Statecraft as Soulcraft,* now recommends Norplant patches as a remedy for the breakdown of the family in the inner city.

No culture would permit its basic institutions and practices to be so dramatically changed simply by the dictate of individual liberty or, for that matter, as a rationalization for sexual pleasure; the remarkably rapid nature of these changes can be understood only if we realize that the technological order is regarded as a necessity. And, as the ancient legal dictum put it, "necessity knows no law."

I am not so naïve as to suggest that this one little device, swallowed with a glass of water, is the efficient cause of all of these troubles. The pill was received in the post–World War II suburbs, in which an array of technologies (chiefly the automobile) made possible a form of family life functionally independent of paternal authority. But the pill does give an especially vivid example of how the humane elements of a culture are reinterpreted to render technology immune from the direction of any higher principle. Even justice turns out to be the right of individuals to have equal access to the technology. The separation of sex from procreation, and the separation of procreation from the social roles and social virtues of motherhood, are not the result of feminism; rather, feminism is the result of these increments of technology. (The same can be said for homosexual parents. It is not merely coincidental that cultural and legal approbation of the homosexualist family followed after the contraceptive pill, and after the development of the in-vitro technologies that reproduce human life independent of any particular social form.)

Edmund Burke wrote that "[t]o complain of the age we live in, to murmur at the present possessors of power, to lament the past, to conceive extravagant hopes of the future, are the common dispositions of the greatest part of mankind.... Such complaints and humours have existed in all times; yet as times have not been alike, true political sagacity manifests itself in distinguishing that complaint which only characterizes the general infirmity of human nature, from those which are symptoms of the particular distemperature of our own air and season."[30] As a historian of culture, Dawson tried to provide this discernment. He insisted that "[t]he problem that faces us today is, therefore, not so much the result of an intellectual revolt against the traditional Christian morality; it is due to the inherent contradictions of an abnormal state of culture."[31] The late George Grant said that technology is the "ontology of the age."[32] Although Dawson himself never used these exact words, they convey his fully considered judgment of the state of modern society.

The modern religions of progress, including liberalism, were religiously heterodox expressions of the older Christian and humanistic culture. Liberalism could be understood in older, more familiar categories. Technologism, however, is something brand new. In the face of the technological society, the culture-forming mission of Christianity will have to begin from scratch—but begin at a much lower level than did the missionaries of the Dark Ages, who brought the vestiges of high Roman culture to the barbarian peoples of northern Europe. The Venerable Bede and St. Boniface, however, did not have to teach those Celtic and Gothic peoples the rudiments of culture itself. It was a dark age, but it was dark, Dawson said, "with the honest night of barbarism."[33] The terrifying thing about modern barbarism is that it is not only more culturally primitive than barbarians of old, but it is immeasurably more powerful, prosperous, and ruthless.[34]

Born in the waning Victorian liberal culture, Dawson lived to see its demise. By the end of his career, Dawson seemed to understand that the new culture is something for which there is no history, for it has no precedent. Perhaps the verdict is still out on the Islamic states, which are attempting to preserve a traditional religious culture even while embracing the necessities of modern technology. But everywhere else, traditional cultures have folded under the technological order. Even the Catholic Church, which has longer experience than any institution in dealing with bad governments, with human frailty, with heretics and ideologues of every stripe, nevertheless seems deeply perplexed at how to deal with a people who are convinced that their everyday well-being depends upon the technological order—on what the encyclical *Veritatis splendor* calls the "all-intrusive culture."[35]

St. Boniface instructed the pagans not to worship a tree, for which he was martyred. But what is the proper address to the technological society? To give up the contraceptives but keep the microwaves? To use machines in moderation? The difficulty in even formulating the issue accurately indicates the perplexing nature of the problem. Abstractly considered, most technologies are not in themselves designed for morally wicked ends; the distinction between proper and improper use is always relevant. But we are not speaking abstractly. Rather, we have investigated the problem of an ensemble of technologies with their corresponding cultural habits. Whereas the moralist will examine human choices one by one, focusing upon the particular act, the cultural historian is interested in cultural habits and institutions, for these trace out the actual and imaginative bounds of men and women as social beings. It is in this latter respect that the problem of modern technology is something more than the moral problem of individual choices. As any parent who has tried to discipline the television-watching habits of his children can attest, the moral effort of picking and choosing when and where to "plug in" does not adequately represent the full nature of the problem. George Grant has correctly pointed out that we cannot understand the novelty of our technological society until we appreciate the extent to which it is a "package deal."[36]

Dawson was on the right track when he called our attention to the dominion of technology and why it has changed the nature of our world. As a cultural historian, Dawson understood that the core of a culture is found once we locate the thing that the culture would never relinquish or even imagine itself relinquishing. I submit that in our case that core is not individual liberty, or sex, and certainly not religion. It is not even the machine. Rather, it is the machine insofar as it promises an activity superior to the human act.

CHAPTER ELEVEN

Reasons for Civil Society

In *Man and the State* (1951), Jacques Maritain argued that the political "madness" of twentieth-century Europe can be traced to the fact that modern democracies had never truly renounced the ideology of "substantialism"[1]—the myth "that the state is the people personified."[2] The so-called "absolutist" regimes of the sixteenth and seventeenth centuries claimed absolute sovereignty on the basis of a theological myth, the divine right of kings; the new regimes claimed the same powers, but now as a donation of the people themselves. For Maritain these different myths generated the same result: a conception of the state regarded *not* as a relatively higher power within a network of authorities constituting the body politic, but rather as a separate and transcendent power entitled to act upon the body politic. At the end of World War II, Maritain felt that it was time to admit that one despotism had been exchanged for the other. Insofar as ideologies compete to produce a separate and transcendent state, history teaches that non-democratic ideologies can produce such a state more effectively. In a famous sentence at the conclusion of chapter 3 of *Man and the State,* Maritain asserted: "The two concepts of Sovereignty and Absolutism have been forged together on the same anvil. They must be scrapped together."[3]

Maritain's alternative is an instrumentalist conception of the state. By this, he certainly did not mean that the political common good is a merely instrumental good; rather, he meant that the apparatus of public law is an instrument serving the rights and liberties of various societies, which, together, form a whole that cannot be equated with the state. In Maritain's view, the postwar repair of the nations—achieving a "pluralistically organized body politic"[4]—requires us to say both yes and no to the modern political experiment. No, to the concept of absolute sovereignty; yes, to the eighteenth-century Enlightenment's notion of inalienable rights—viz., rights that cannot be transferred to the state.[5]

I will emphasize in this final chapter that Maritain's critique of substantialism represents an important moment in the history of Catholic political theory. He was by no means the only Catholic thinker to move in this direction.[6] In the late 1940s, the idea of the "juridical state," distinct from the body politic, was advanced by John Courtney Murray. Pope Pius XII, too, moved the Church in this same direction. In his Christmas addresses of 1944, he asserted that democracy "appears to be a postulate of nature imposed by reason itself,"[7] chiefly because it can serve as a check upon despotism. The Pope did not use the word "instrumental," but in context it is clear that he and Maritain were advocating the same position. Democracy can be recommended insofar as it checks the despotism of the state, *and* (here is the crucial qualification) insofar as social unity does not model itself on this instrument. Social unity, Pius warned, always must be regarded as an intrinsic perfection of human beings. The state is an instrument of different modes of solidarity; it is neither the substance nor the exemplar of society. Hence, by convergent lines of argument, Catholic thinkers decisively shifted away from solidarist (or exemplarist) conceptions of the state in favor of solidarist conceptions of the body politic. This change of perspective would prevail at Vatican II. In *Gaudium et Spes,* for example, we read: "As for public authority, it is not its function to determine the character of the civilization, but rather to establish the conditions and to use the means which are capable of fostering the life of culture. . . ."[8] "The political community exists, consequently, for the sake of the common good, in which it finds its full justification and significance, and the source of its inherent legitimacy. Indeed, the common good embraces the sum of those conditions of the social life whereby men, families, and associations more adequately and readily may attain their own perfection."[9]

To really appreciate the importance and novelty of this move away from solidarist conceptions of the state to solidarist conceptions of civil society it would be necessary to understand how long it took for the modern (post-1789) Church to come to this insight. From 1789 to 1939, Roman authorities understood perfectly well the despotic and even totalitarian impulses of the new regimes. They also understood that the doctrine of royal absolutism had produced its mirror image in the revolutionary regimes. Papal encyclicals usually defended the rights of society against the states born in the revolutions. Even so, theologians like Bishop von Ketteler, and popes from Pius IX to Pius XI, were unwilling to completely abandon what then was called a corporativist conception of the state. For one thing, their imaginations were still informed by the sacral model of kingship, and it would take the Great War to make that model practically obsolete.[10] The more important reason, however, was the one mentioned by Pius XII in his 1944 Christmas address: they feared that once the state was depicted in instrumentalist terms, the other organs of society would inevitably follow suit. In other words, they feared that the liberal state, even in its most favorable depiction as an instrument rather than the substance of the common good, would produce atomism and instrumentalism in every other sector of society. The disaster of World War II made it necessary to reconsider. Maritain's work deeply influenced this reconsideration of the nature of the state. Today, one can discern the stamp of his mind on the encyclicals of John Paul II, who, if anything, expounds the instrumentalist conception of the state more aggressively than did Maritain himself.

If the theory of the instrumental state represents a decisive adaptation of Catholic thought to the best of liberal tradition, what sense are we to make of the rest of the liberal tradition, which does tend to view civil society in terms similar to the state? As von Ketteler asserted in the mid-nineteenth century, "The associations that modern liberalism sponsors . . . are mechanical assemblages of people who are thrown together merely for some superficial, utilitarian end."[11]

A perusal of current literature on civil society would indicate well enough that this problem has not been entirely put to rest. Take, for example, Ernest Gellner's *Conditions of Liberty: Civil Society and Its Rivals.* Gellner sets out to explain (for a central and eastern European audience) what makes polities of the West so much more successful than their rivals in the East. He insists that the correct answer is not democracy or capitalism—nor even a constitutional scheme of legally protected individual liberties—but rather the "miracle of Civil Society."[12] "Civil society," as Gellner defines it, "is that set of diverse non–governmental institutions which is strong enough to counterbalance the state and, while not preventing the state from fulfilling its role of keeper of the peace and arbitrator between major interests, can nevertheless prevent it from dominating and atomizing the rest of society."[13]

We notice that Gellner's definition focuses our attention on the instrumental function and value of civil society. It checks the powers of the state and of the extended family. This view is traceable to Montesquieu, who held that liberty is found only in moderate governments, "where power must check power by the arrangement of things."[14] Intermediate powers (*pouvoirs intermédiaires*), especially in aristocratic societies, contribute to the scheme of power checking power.

Tocqueville, who more than anyone else set the terms of discussion about civil society, perhaps was more appreciative than Montesquieu of the intrinsic value of free, non-governmental institutions.[15] Yet his famous discussion of intermediate associations in *Democracy in America* is framed almost entirely in the terms of how they remedy the destructive consequences of modern democracy, especially its bent toward centralization and uniformity. Tocqueville never fully transcends the instrumentalist conception of civil society.

The problem with the instrumentalist depiction of civil society is that it leaves few options for defending civil society other than showing that useful goods, including liberty, are more efficiently produced and distributed by non-governmental agents. As Gellner says, civil society is the "social residue left when the state is subtracted."[16] So, if there are socially useful goods better achieved in the private sector, it becomes necessary either to give power-checking-power reasons or cost-benefit reasons for why we ought to subtract from the state's power. We are all familiar with such policy arguments: e.g., that education is better attained if parents have more options for where to send their children to school, or that security for the elderly is best effected through private investment than by state mandated social security. The author of a recent book titled *More Guns, Less Crime* goes so far as to argue that citizens ought to be able to carry concealed weapons because private citizens, acting in self-defense, kill three times as many criminals each year as are killed by the police.[17] In an ingenious new book, *Membership and Morals,* Nancy Rosenblum advances the escape valve model of civil society, once again in reference to the state.[18] A pluralism of private associations, including those which are incongruent with ideals of liberal democracy, are useful, she explains, because they let off the steam of illiberal impulses.

The main problem with the policy-oriented view of civil society is what it leaves out of the picture. The power-checking-power and economistic reasons typically leave out of the picture the intrinsic perfections that make solidarity worth undertaking for its own sake.

Let us briefly consider a thirteenth-century treatise that may be the first, or at least one of the first, systematic defenses of civil society. Medieval thinkers, of course, had no single linguistic equivalent for our terms "civil society." Theologians like Thomas Aquinas used variations on the word *societas: societas oeconomica, societas politica, societas privata, societas publica, societas saecularis,* and so forth. But they did understand the value of free associations not reducible to the family or the state. The case in point is *Contra impugnantes,* Thomas's apologetic for the Dominican vocation.[19] First, allow me to say a few words about *Contra impugnantes,* and then I will show why it is relevant to modern Catholic social and political theory.

In the year 1256, Thomas and Bonaventure were summoned to the court of Pope Alexander IV to defend the newly formed mendicant orders. William of Saint-Amour, a doctor of the Sorbonne, charged that the "double spirit" of action and contemplation embodied by mendicants was a novel way of life that perverted the principles of both civil and ecclesiastical society. In *De periculis novissimorum temporum* ("The perils of these most novel [or, last] times," 1256), William of Saint-Amour launched a number of criticisms toward the mendicants. The mendicants, he asserted:

- violate the principle of a society of contemplatives by seeking to act on others rather than being purely receptive of divine grace;
- violate civil and ecclesiastical jurisdictional authority by moving from place to place, unlike secular and monastic clergy;
- violate the virtue of humility by acquiring and communicating learning in universities;
- violate monastic order by refusing to engage in manual labor;
- violate principles of justice by dispensing wisdom for alms;

- violate principles of familial order by recruiting young men and women.

Thomas's response comes down to us in the *Opusculum* titled *Contra impugnantes,* written in 1256 and probably summarized orally for the Pope in that same year. Here, I will outline the main thrust of his response. Thomas contends that the "active life" consists of more than political rule and mercantile pursuits.[20] Granted that religious are neither magistrates or businessmen, they are "active" in other ways, including the communication of knowledge and wisdom by teaching and preaching. The active life, generically understood, is the communication of gifts. In this, all agents imitate God. Strictly speaking, there is no such thing as a society that is in every respect receptive. Although *societas* is an analogous term, every society, he argues, is constituted by "communications"[21] whereby goods are given and received. In Thomas's works, every analogous use of the word *societas* is mirrored by uses of the word *communicatio: communicatio oeconomica, communicatio spiritualis, communicatio civilis,* and so forth. The word *communicatio* simply means making something common, one rational agent participating in the life of another. Society, for Thomas, is not a thing, but an activity.

The multiplicity of vocations and skills whereby men engage in different common projects for the benefit of all society, Thomas argues, is grounded "primarily in Divine Providence, and, secondarily, in natural causes whereby certain men are disposed to the performance of certain functions in preference to others."[22] Thus, he argues for a "right" of men to associate for good works across classes and states of life: "any person who is competent to perform some special function, has a right to be admitted to the society of those who are selected for the exercise of that function." That Dominicans would sit and teach in schools alongside the laity and the youth was a point of scandal in the controversy. It seemed that the fixed order of social classes was being jumbled. But, Thomas contended: "an association of study is a society, established with the object of teaching and learning; and as not only laymen, but also religious, have a right to teach and to learn, there can be no doubt that, both these classes may lawfully unite in one society."[23]

Therefore, to prevent free men and women from associating for the purpose of communicating gifts is contrary to the natural law. It is tantamount to denying to rational agents the perfection proper to their nature, and denying to the commonweal goods it would not enjoy were it not for free associations. To the argument that the active-contemplative would no longer possess the fruit of his contemplation, Thomas points out that the giving of knowledge does not deplete the gift possessed by the giver. The contemplative is not less graced when he preaches what he receives from God; nor is the teacher less learned when he communicates knowledge to the student; nor is anyone less "free" by virtue of imparting a gift to another. Thomas here quotes Augustine's *De doctrina christiana:* "Everything that is not lessened by being imparted, is not, if it be possessed without being communicated, possessed as it ought to be possessed."[24]

But what about authority? Isn't it depleted if multiplied? This, in fact, was one of the major fears of local church authorities about Dominicans taking the fruit of contemplation into universities and pulpits. Thomas answers that this charge makes sense if authority is thought to consist only in the power to make laws. The free society of mendicants does nothing of the sort, for Dominicans do not usurp the authority of magistrates or bishops, but rather enjoy authority that naturally supervenes upon doing a job well. Interestingly, Thomas mounts an argument against the creation of monopolies in the academic professoriate.[25] Indeed, he even makes cost-benefit arguments in behalf of mendicant teachers and preachers. Mendicants work for the social good, taking only freely given alms: they make no effort to legally compel compensation for their efforts; rather, they only argue at law for the right to receive those donations freely given to them.[26]

Though this is a rather compact summary of Thomas's argument, nonetheless we can draw into view a picture of the kind of he society has in mind. It is a society constituted by a voluntary reciprocal action for the common good; a society that multiplies associational authorities without usurping the authority properly belonging to lawmaking authorities (ecclesiastical and civil). But it is also a society distinguished from the more sedentary pattern of rights, obligations, and classes that characterizes the family and extended kinship. Thomas's argument for voluntary societies must be sharply distinguished from the premodern understanding of the "ancient constitution." Based upon charters, customs, and local privileges, the ancient constitution preserved plural authorities, and it had considerable resources for resisting centralization—but it was essentially conservative. As in the *Magna Carta,* the prince was forbidden to make incursions into those spheres of aristocratic liberty and authority where he had never been before. In effect, the prince was forbidden to introduce novel forms and applications of authority. Thomas's argument for liberty is of an entirely different sort, for he argues for the invention of new forms of associational liberty despite the claims of vested privilege and class. And as I have mentioned, he claims "rights" not only for the corporate mission of the mendicants, but also for individuals.

With remarkable clarity and prescience, Thomas saw what was at stake in the charges that mendicants travel too much, refuse manual labor, and recruit the young. Let us examine and briefly comment on each of these three charges before moving back to the main point of this chapter.

Mendicants are unlike secular clergy, who are bound to their diocese, and unlike monks, who are bound by a vow of stability to their monastery. They understood that *societas* cannot be absolutely con-

strained to such places and boundaries. The body politic of Christendom
was international, and the good of that body politic transcended the
relatively static conditions of feudal order. The diocesan clergy and
monks reduplicated feudal order in their respective organizations. The
mendicants broke free of that feudal order not only by mobility—
their portable authority, as it were—but also by refusing to be bound
to the monastic practice of manual labor. The effort of critics to keep
religious in a single place, under the drudgery of manual labor, was
nothing less than an effort to block the introduction of new social
forms in society. Here, of course, the "form" was evangelical. It concerned purely voluntary societies brought into being neither by commerce, nor by positive law, nor by matrimonial procreation, but by free
response to grace. Such societies of gift-givers do not cancel out legal
or paternal authority, but by the same token neither are they reducible
to it. As Thomas understood in his own case, the bid to prevent Dominicans from recruiting the young was motivated by the desire to
shield authority from novelty, from freedom, and ultimately from grace.

It might seem to be a long stretch from medieval societies of
mendicants, living in voluntary poverty, to modern issues of civil society. But it isn't, really. In *Rerum Novarum* (1891), Pope Leo XIII's
argument for the rights of association by laborers relies directly on
Contra impugnantes.[27] Some scholars have suggested that Pope Leo
borrowed the language of "rights" from John Locke.[28] Perhaps there is
some truth to this interpretation with respect to Leo's understanding
of property rights. The main argument in *Rerum Novarum,* however, is
not from the right of property but the right of association. As for the
rights of private association, Leo's use of rights language is drawn directly from Thomas's *Contra impugnantes.*

In *Centesimus Annus,* written both to celebrate the centennial of
Rerum Novarum and the collapse of communism in eastern Europe,
Pope John Paul II continues this line of argument. He refers to "inter-

mediate communities [that] exercise primary functions and give life
to specific networks of solidarity."[29]

> When man does not recognize in himself and in others the value and
> grandeur of the human person, he effectively deprives himself of the
> possibility of benefiting from his humanity and of entering into that
> relationship of solidarity and communion with others for which God
> created him. Indeed, it is through the free gift of self that one truly
> finds oneself. This gift is made possible by the human person's essen-
> tial "capacity for transcendence"....As a person, one can give oneself
> to another person or to other persons, and ultimately to God, who
> is the author of our being and who alone can fully accept our gift. A
> person is alienated if he refuses to transcend himself and to live the
> experience of self-giving and of the formation of an authentic hu-
> man community oriented towards his final destiny, which is God. A
> society is alienated if its forms of social organization, production and
> consumption make it more difficult to offer this gift of self and to
> establish this solidarity between people.[30]

Perhaps it would not be entirely misleading to say that there has
been a laicization of the idea of society as *communicatio*—a laicization
already begun in *Rerum Novarum* when Leo XIII took the defense of
mendicant liberty as a model for a defense of the rights of workers to
organize. This laicization is especially necessary in societies where so
many things are mediated by free choice, and where the primary model
of free choice is drawn from economic markets. In this kind of society,
it is necessary to provide something more than merely instrumental
reasons for free, social order. Indeed, it becomes necessary to give reasons for what is *perfected,* rather than merely *maximized,* by free choice.
The modern mind has little trouble understanding what is maximized
by a zone of free society, that is, by a zone of freedom that is not reducible to the law of the state. Gellner, for example, will propose that

this zone of liberty constitutes a check upon the power of the state, which, in turn, gives rise to economic associations, which, in turn, maximize productivity, which, to close the circle, immunize society against the overweening administrative ambitions of state power. But what is perfected in this process? Or to put the question slightly differently, what would be missing from the world if the state were to be the primary agent in charge of bringing about social goods? Except to say that life would be suffocating, and our private choices reduced in scope, Gellner does not tell us.

Taking Isaiah Berlin's celebrated distinction between positive and negative liberty in "Two Concepts of Liberty," we can frame the question in this way.[31] Liberalism has triumphed in Catholic political theory insofar as the state is no longer considered the end, substance, or exemplar of positive liberty (freedom *for*). There is an entirely appropriate way to express liberty in negative terms (freedom *from*) vis-à-vis the state. But how do we understand the liberty of society itself?

I read the work of the present papal magisterium as an effort to answer that question. The question is not whether it is useful to enjoy "private" liberties insofar as they are distinguished from the power of the state. Since the collapse of the communist experiment, the argument from utility has been won. The question today is what to do with liberty and how to understand it on something more than the grounds offered by economists.

Solidarity is an inherently complex notion.[32] To provide only a short list, in contemporary papal encyclicals solidarity can mean: (1) common material *things,* which are subject to distributive justice; (2) sociological or economic *states of affairs,* such as technological and economic interdependence; (3) *personal attitudes,* dispositions, or virtues with regard to what is, or should be, common; (4) *activities,* in the sense of teamwork and collaboration toward common ends; (5) loving *communion* between persons, where the communion is the very goal of action.

If we examine recent encyclicals, we discover three main foci for the terms "solidarity" or "common good." Undoubtedly, there are others. But these three can be gathered easily from the texts.

First, the common good can consist of goods realized in individuals, which are called "common" by virtue of a common species. For example, human beings share a common humanity, even though there is no "humanity" existing independently of individuals, nor a "humanity" distributed to persons. This ontological perfection is only "in" individuals; so, from individuals we gather the predicate that is common.

By virtue of our common humanity, three notions arise: (1) common status, in the sense that no person is more or less human than another; (2) common ontological perfections, such as health, knowledge, and religious devotion; (3) common utilities, such as money, food, and technology. Each of these can be the ground of moral and legal rights; each can express a reason for solidarity. In *Sollicitudo Rei Socialis,* the "virtue" of solidarity is described (initially) as the willingness to make a moral response to common goods as we have just described them: "It is above all a question of interdependence, sensed as a system determining relationships in the contemporary world in its economic, cultural, political and religious elements, and accepted as a moral category. When interdependence becomes recognized in this way, the correlative response as a moral and social attitude, as a 'virtue,' is solidarity."[33]

Thus, when John Paul II speaks of "solidarity towards society's weakest members,"[34] he emphasizes our common humanity, which prohibits us from cutting corners in the distribution of legal rights and economic resources. When, in *Pacem in Terris,* John XXIII speaks of "the requirements of universal common goods,"[35] and when *Gaudium et Spes* refers to one person depending on another "in needful solidarity,"[36] the common utilities are being emphasized.

I place these three diverse notions of "common" into one set, because they are either properties realized in individuals (e.g., human, life, knowledge, health), or useful goods (food, computers, health care plans) that are made common by virtue of a just order of distribution.[37] If we restrict ourselves to this first set of meanings, we shall understand that we are all human, and that there are cords of interdependence in realizing our perfections. We conduct most of our debates about civil society at this level, for here we engage the persistent issues in public policy, including the characteristically instrumental problems about how best to distribute and nurture fundamental human goods and utilities. Here, too, in the Anglo-American world, we typically consider the question of where the agency of the state ought to begin and end.

The second set of meanings for solidarity and common good can be described generally as *common activities.* The notions of "collaboration," "cooperation," the "spirit of creative initiative," and the "expanding chain of solidarity" express, in different ways, and at different levels, common goods as common activities. Depending on the particular encyclical, the idea of solidarity as common activities is applied to domestic political order, international relations, the initiatives of intermediate societies, and economic life. In *Centesimus Annus,* John Paul II emphasizes that the market represents not only the good of things to be distributed, but also the good of reciprocal actions:

> By means of his work a person commits himself, not only for his own sake but also for others and with others. Each person collaborates in the work of others and for their good. One works in order to provide for the needs of one's family, one's community, one's nation, and ultimately all humanity. Moreover, a person collaborates in

the work of his fellow employees, as well as in the work of suppliers and in the customers' use of goods, in a progressively expanding chain of solidarity.[38]

Here, our main focus is not given to the external good to be commonly distributed, but rather goods inherent to activity. It raises the issue of subsidiarity. If the common good is constituted by the common activity, then whenever "higher" powers intervene in such a way that the common activity is supplanted, or whenever the result of common activity is achieved behind the back, as it were, of the collaborative activity itself, the distinctive good of society is lost. Take, for example, the common activities that go into the work of an orchestra. Every part needs to be harmonized with the others in order to produce the desired result. If the good being aimed at were simply the external result, however, then there is no reason, other than aesthetic preference, why a computer-generated concerto wouldn't suffice. But we all know that common activity constitutes part of the good being aimed at.

The point is that where collaboration is not an inherent, but a merely useful good, the grounds for subsidiarity are greatly weakened. Except on contingent grounds of efficiency, there is no good reason why the state should do everything, or by the same token, do nothing. Therefore, it seems that a truly useful concept of subsidiarity depends upon a concept of solidarity that preserves the intrinsic value of collaborative activity. Without that value, discussion about subsidiarity easily becomes, as in our American policy debates over "federalism," an issue of magnitudes concerning money and power.

Suppose, for example, that a policy expert could show that "welfare" is most efficiently delivered by subcontracting the work to a private firm. In this case, care of the indigent is neither by the state nor by civil society. Would we be missing anything by commissioning others to do this work? The same question can be asked with respect to a wide array of collaborative activities. For example, why shouldn't parent's subcontract acts of parenting to someone else? If solidarity were restricted to the first set of notions (common nature, perfections, and utilities) we could satisfy (hypothetically) the requirements of the common good by adopting whatever policies most efficiently distribute the useful goods. The fact that we do not engage common activities is neither here nor there, except perhaps as a matter of individual preference. It is only when we identify goods of common activities that we can discover a principled limit to the power of the state as well as to the subcontracting (or "outsourcing") mentality characteristic of markets.

At this juncture it is appropriate to introduce John Paul II's understanding of the "subjectivity" of society. In *Centesimus,* he refers to the subjectivity of society in terms of "structures of participation and shared responsibility."[39] He writes, "the social nature of man is not completely fulfilled in the State, but is realized in various intermediary groups, beginning with the family and including economic, social, political and cultural groups which stem from human nature itself and have their own autonomy, always with a view to the common good. This is what I have called the 'subjectivity' of society which, together with the subjectivity of the individual, was canceled out by 'Real Socialism.'"[40] Notice that the argument against socialism is not chiefly an argument about its inefficiency: viz., that the common good, as a just distribution of resources, was not met. Rather, what was "canceled out" was the common good(s) constituted by free, collaborative agents.

The expressions "subjectivity of society" and "expanding chain of solidarity" often sit adjacent to yet another idea of common good. Earlier, I quoted John Paul II's rather flat definition of the virtue of solidarity as a certain moral attitude taken toward interdependence. Now, consider the following definition, which crops up two sections later in *Sollicitudo:*

Solidarity is undoubtedly a Christian virtue. In what has been said so far it has been possible to identify many points of contact between solidarity and charity, which is the distinguishing mark of Christ's disciples. . . . Beyond human and natural bonds, already so close and strong, there is discerned in the light of faith a new model of the unity of the human race, which must ultimately inspire our solidarity. This supreme model of unity, which is a reflection of the intimate life of God, one God in three Persons, is what we Christians mean by the word "communion."[41]

We see that a distinct notion has been added to the idea of the common good, namely the common good as *communion*. Marriage, for example, is a useful good insofar as married people can use their relationship as a means for the distribution of goods and services (for themselves, for their children, and for wider society). Marriage can also be viewed as a common good constituted by collaborative activities and mutual deliberation. Philosophers and jurisprudents have taken care to notice how marriage, in this regard, exemplifies the political principles of regimes. In the 1878 polygamy case, Chief Justice Waite observed: "In fact, according as monogamous or polygamous marriages are allowed, do we find the principles on which the government of the people, to a greater or less extent, rests."[42] Beyond these aspects of a common good, however, marriage aims at communion of the spouses. This communion is a special form of the love of friendship because it uniquely requires a one-flesh unity. In Catholic theology, it also a sign and instrument of the union of Christ and the Church.[43]

The encyclicals and conciliar documents speak of "spiritual unity," or "interior unity," or "communion" typically in reference to marriage, eucharistic fellowship, and baptism, through which the individual is grafted into the body of Christ. The "civilization of love" includes all of these diverse notions of common good, and not just the theological one. But the theological concept of communion is the main model for what the papacy means by the proposition that man is inherently social.

Maritain's generation had to win the argument about the nature of the state. It represented a long overdue reckoning with the Anglo-American experiment. Now that Catholic thought has been liberated from any temptation to sacralize or substantialize the state, attention can, and must, be given to the pressing issue of society itself.

So long as we restrict our attention to the external dimension of liberty, liberalism and Catholic social thought can agree that the state has a certain instrumental role serving social pluralism. But when we turn toward the internal dimension of this pluralism, when we turn to the reasons for civil society, these two traditions are not always congruent. Let us return to Gellner's understanding of the "miracle" of civil society.

Gellner insists that it is not enough merely to subtract the power of the state. For once we subtract the power of the state, we can be trapped in a suffocating world of social forms and norms. Islamic nations, for example, have rather weak states, but a strong *Umma* (way of life) that pervades society. In the more fully mature societies of the West, civil society is also valued because it emancipates us from the familial and religious powers that can command our obedience and allegiance. Here, Gellner diverges from Tocqueville's conception of civil society as "intermediate" or "secondary" powers.[44] For Gellner, civil society constitutes a zone of immunity from these secondary (or intermediate) commanding powers. The "miracle" of civil society is the liberty of individuals to freely choose their identities, careers, and associations.

Because civil society is not a sphere of ruling powers of any sort, it must be understood on the model of the economic market.[45] Market order arises not from the commands of the state, but from the choices and preferences of free agents; at the same time, a commercial society will tend to weaken fixed social forms and norms. Thus, the "miracle" of civil society is what Gellner calls the "modular man": "The moral order has not committed itself either to a set of prescribed roles and relations, or to a set of practices. The same goes for knowledge: conviction can change, without any stigma of apostasy. Yet these highly specific, unsanctified, *instrumental*, revocable links or bonds are effective. The associations of modular man can be effective without being rigid."[46]

Gellner's account is intended to be both descriptive and normative. This is the way civil society functions in the societies of the West, and this is precisely the order of liberty that liberals ought to defend. One can admit that the modeling of civil society upon the order of the market has enormous appeal. As the French social theorist Pierre Manent has pointed out, "Liberalism eroded social commands and individual will. But it also has a remedy for that erosion. Amid the discrediting of every norm, it retains one: competitiveness. This is one of the principal reasons that liberalism has come back into favor. Everyone in liberal society shrinks at the prospect of giving or receiving a genuine order, since nothing seems to justify commands or obedience. Competition therefore remains the only acceptable candidate for social regulation, since the norm it offers is immanent to social activity. It is imposed on no one, it implies no dogmatism."[47]

While liberals valued civil society principally for instrumental reasons, Catholic social thought emphasized the intrinsic value of social forms like the family, the private school, churches, and labor unions. And, Catholic social thought has always been suspicious of the market model of social pluralism. Though Catholic thinkers certainly defended the economic market against socialism, they remained wary of any effort to make society itself conform to a market. What Gellner celebrates as the "modular man" represents very nearly the opposite of the social pluralism defended in Catholic social thought and teaching.

Notes

CHAPTER ONE: NATURAL LAW AND CATHOLIC MORAL THEOLOGY

* A version of this chapter first appeared in *Preserving Grace: Protestants, Catholics, and Natural Law*, ed. Michael Cromartie (Grand Rapids, Mich.: William B. Eerdmans Publishing Co. & Ethics and Public Policy Center), 1997), 1–30. A different version was published as "Veritatis Splendor and the Theology of Natural Law," in *Veritatis Splendor and the Renewal of Moral Theology*, ed. J. A. DiNoia, O.P. and Romanus Cessario, O.P. (Princeton, N.J.: Scepter, 1999), 97–127.

1. Yves R. Simon, *The Tradition of Natural Law: A Philosopher's Reflections*, ed. Vukan Kuic, intro. Russell Hittinger (New York: Fordham University Press, 1992 reprint, orig. 1965), 5.

2. Thanks to Steve Long, Robert Tuttle, and Keith Pavlischek, who made useful suggestions and criticisms of earlier drafts of this chapter.

3. *Church Dog.*, II/1, §36.

4. *Adv. Judaeos*, cap. 2 (PL 2-2, 599, 600), *quasi matrix omnium praeceptorum Dei. . . . non scriptam, quae naturaliter intelligebatur.*

5. A millennium later, Thomas Aquinas would also refer to the time between the Fall and the Law as the time of the law of nature, when God left men to what little they could glean from the original law in order to curb their pride (*Summa Theologiae* I-II, q. 98, a. 6; for the most part I rely throughout this book upon the translation by the Fathers of the Dominican Province [New York: Benzinger Brothers, 1947–48], with a few minor alterations of my own). As for who knew and abided by the natural law, Thomas says the patriarchs, who were men of faith. Commenting on the figurative meaning of the sacrifices in the Jewish ceremonies, Thomas tries to draw together the phases of revelation in Christology:

> The figurative cause is that the bread signifies Christ Who is the *panes vivus* [living bread]. . . . He was indeed an ear of corn, as it were, during the state of the law of nature, and in the faith of the patriarchs; he was like flour in the doctrine of the Law of the prophets; and he was like perfect bread after he had taken human nature; baked in the fire, that is, formed by the Holy Spirit in the oven of the virginal womb; baked again in a pan by the toils which he suffered in the world; and consumed by fire on the cross as on a gridiron. (*S.t.* I-II, q. 102, a. 3, ad 12)

For Thomas's estimation of Abraham, see note 20.

6. Gregory of Nyssa, *The Life of Moses,* trans., intro., and notes by Abraham J. Malherbe and Everett Ferguson (New York: Paulist Press, 1978), II §§215–16.

7. Note the similarity to Thomas's formulation of the first precept of law in *S.t.* I-II, 94.2—*Bonum est faciendum et prosequendum, et malum vitandum,* the good is to be done and pursued, and evil resisted. Thomas calls it the *primum praeceptum legis,* the first precept of law.

8. Regarding debates *ad extra,* the patristic theologians tend to worry about rival Jewish or Gnostic accounts of divine governance. Gnostics asserted that the "law" in Gn 2:17 was a dietary (and hence a positive) law of the Demiurge, the same deity that shows up later in Jewish scriptures giving more positive (and usually dietary) laws. Against the rabbis, Christian apologists contended not only that there is a law after the Mosaic law, but that the *lex nova* restores a law antecedent to Sinai.

9. *per primam Dei gratiam, id est per legem naturae.* Council of Arles (A.D. 473), Denzinger-Hünermann (Les Éditions du Cerf, Paris, 1997), §336.

10. *Instit. Justin.* I.2.

11. Ibid., I.2.3.

12. Ibid., IV.18.4.

13. *Decretum Gratiani* I.D.I., can. 3, 4.

14. *S.t.* I-II, q. 91.

15. The new *Catechism of the Catholic Church* gathers all law together under the rubric "moral law," the various species designating modes of divine pedagogy (*CCC* §§1950–52).

16. *S.t.* I-II, q. 91, a. 2, ad 1.

17. It is an understandable but regrettable mistake to focus exclusively on *S.t.* I-II, q. 94. Here, indeed, Thomas speaks of natural law in terms of what is first in the mind and first in nature (viz. the intellect's adherence to indemonstrable human goods). He makes no reference to God. But in q. 94 he is not defining the natural law; the *ratio formalis*—what it is, and what makes it law—is discussed in qq. 91 and 93. Question 94 takes up the *ratio materialis*: natural law as an effect in the creature.

18. *S.t.* I-II, q. 93, a. 2.

19. *S.t.* I-II, q. 90, a. 4, ad 1.

20. In II Rom., lectio 3 (§§ 215–16), St. Thomas notes that unless we distinguish between the two classes of gentiles, Rom 2:14 would be open to a Pelagian reading of these two words *naturaliter* and *faciunt.* In *S.t.* III, 1.6, St. Thomas contends that the election of Abraham and the dispensation of the law to Moses presupposed the restoration of knowledge of the sovereign of the natural law: "He was pleased to choose Abraham as a standard of the restored knowledge of God and of holy living."

21. *S.t.* I, q. 1, a. 1.

22. *S.t.* II-II, q. 94, a. 1.

23. Thomas Aquinas, *Collationes in Decem Praeceptis,* I, line 27, édition critique avec introduction et notes par Jean-Pierre Torrell, in *Revue des sciences philosophiques et théologiques* 69 (1985): 5–40, 227–63.

24. *S.t.* I-II, q. 97, a. 1, ad 1.

25. *S.t.* I-II, q. 89, a. 6.

26. *S.t.* I–II, q. 98, a. 6.

27. Thomas Hobbes, *De Homine*, X.5.

28. *Flumina honestatis redeunt ad mare iuris naturalis, quod ita processit, ut quod in primo homine pene perditum est, in lege mosayca relevaretur, in evagelio perficeretur, in moribus decoraretur.* Johannes Faventinus, *Summa*, British Museum, MS Royal 9 E. vii, fol. 2, c. 2. Cited in Gaines Post, *Studies in Medieval Legal Thought* (Princeton, N.J.: Princeton University Press, 1964), 524.

29. For example, Leo XIII's *Diuturnum,* issued on June 29, 1881, three months after the assassination of the Russian czar Alexander II, who was killed on the very day that he signed a new liberal constitution, directly criticizes the secular ideologies of natural law.

30. Maurice Cardinal Roy, "Occasion of the Tenth Anniversary of the Encyclical *Pacem in Terris*" (April 11,1973), no. 128, in Joseph Gremillion, *The Gospel of Peace and Justice* (New York: Orbis Books, 1976), 557.

31. *Pacem in Terris* (1963), §1.

32. Yves Simon was a conspicuous exception. He worried that the problem of natural law in our times is not so much the need to defend the idea against its cultured critics, but rather to prevent it from being ensconced in ideologies formed under the practical pressure of responding to the various intellectual and institutional felonies of modern life.

> Our time has witnessed a new birth of belief in natural law concomitantly with the success of existentialism, which represents the most thorough criticism of natural law ever voiced by philosophers. Against such powers of destruction we feel the need for an ideology of natural law. The current interest in this subject certainly expresses an aspiration of our society at a time when the foundations of common life and of just relations are subjected to radical threats. No matter how sound these aspirations may be, they are quite likely to distort philosophic treatments. For a number of years we have been witnessing a tendency, in teachers and preachers, to assume that natural law decides, with the universality proper to the necessity of essences, incomparably more issues than it is actually able to decide. There is a tendency to treat in terms of natural law questions which call for treatment in terms of prudence. It should be clear that any concession to this tendency is bound promptly to cause disappointment and skepticism. (Simon, *The Tradition of Natural Law,* 23)

33. Joseph Cardinal Bernardin, "Seeking a Common Ground on Human Rights," *Depaul Law Review* 36 (1987): 159–65.

34. *Evangelium Vitae,* §18.

35. Ibid.

36. Servais Pinckaers, O.P., *The Sources of Christian Ethics,* trans. Sr. Mary Thomas Noble, O.P. (Washington, D.C.: The Catholic University of America Press, 1995), 298–99.

37. Josef Fuchs, *Moral Demands and Personal Obligations,* trans. Brian McNeil (Washington, D.C.: Georgetown University Press, 1993), 100.

38. Ibid., 55.

39. The majority of Paul VI's Commission for the Study of Problems of the Family, Population, and Birth Rate issued a report urging that the Church change its teaching on contraception. The majority report can be found in *The Tablet* (April 22,

1967), 449–54; the minority, or conservative, case in *The Tablet* (April 29, 1967), 478–85; and the progressive "Argument for Reform" in *The Tablet* (May 6, 1967), 510–13. In the "Argument for Reform," signed by Joseph Fuchs, S.J., of the Gregorian University, it is asserted that "the concept of natural law, as it is found in traditional discussion of this question is insufficient; for the gifts of nature are considered to be immediately the expression of the will of God, preventing man, also a creature of God, from being understood as called to receive material nature and to perfect its potentiality" (511). Put to one side Fuchs's attribution of voluntarism to the tradition (that created order proceeds from the divine will rather than the divine intellect). The crux of this position is that natural law is nothing other than the "gifts of nature," including human dominion itself. There is no indication that there is anything here in the order of law; in fact, it is suggested that the order of law begins in human prudence. A more telling passage in this regard asserts that "God has left man in the hands of his own counsel. To take his own or another's life is a sin not because life is under the exclusive dominion of God but because it is contrary to right reason unless there is question of a good or higher order. It is licit to sacrifice a life for the good of the community" (511). The authors of the majority report at least had the honesty to state their theological premise clearly. They reasoned that although the sources of human life are from created nature, the rules for the choice and administration of that natural value fall to human jurisdiction. Although the progressives castigate the traditional understanding of natural law as a kind of biologism, on their own account the natural law can be nothing other than pre-moral biological order that awaits a specifically moral norm. This is exactly the position that Cardinal Roy (above, note 30) adopted as the interpretation of *Pacem in Terris*.

40. Fuchs, *Moral Demands*, 39.
41. The encyclical says, "Deep within his conscience man discovers a law which he has not laid upon himself but which he must obey. Its voice, ever calling him to love and to do what is good and to avoid evil, tells him inwardly at the right moment: do this, shun that. For man has in his heart a law inscribed by God. His dignity lies in observing this law, and by it he will be judged. His conscience is man's most secret core, and his sanctuary. There he is alone with God whose voice echoes in his depths" (*Gaudium et Spes*, §16).
42. Fuchs, *Moral Demands*, 157.
43. Ibid., 40.
44. *Veritatis Splendor*, §4.
45. The subtitle reads: *De Fundamentis Doctrinae Moralis Ecclesiae*, "Concerning the Foundations of the Church's Moral Teaching."
46. *Veritatis Splendor*, §4.
47. Ibid., §37.
48. Ibid., §40.
49. Ibid., §74.
50. Ibid.
51. Ibid., §29.
52. John Calvin, *Institutes of the Christian Religion*, trans. John Allen, 2 vols. (Philadelphia: Presbyterian Board of Christian Education, 1936), I, ii.1, 270.

53. *Veritatis Splendor,* §11.

54. Ibid., §13.

55. Ibid., §9. See Karol Wojtyla: "For 'a religious man' means not so much 'one who is capable of religious experiences' (as is generally supposed) as above all 'one who is just to God the Creator'" (Karol Wojtyla, *Love and Responsibility,* trans. H. T. Willetts [San Francisco: Ignatius Press, 1981], 223).

56. Georges Cottier, O.P., "Morality of a human act depends primarily on object chosen by will" (*L'Osservatore Romano* no. 6 [February 9, 1994]: 11).

57. E.g., in *Laborem Exercens* and *Evangelium Vitae.*

58. *Veritatis Splendor,* §36.

59. Ibid., §41.

60. In scholastic parlance, the human reason is a measuring measure (*mensura mensurans*) only insofar as it is first a measured measure (*mensura mensurata*).

61. "Others speak, and rightly so, of theonomy, or participated theonomy, since man's free obedience to God's law effectively implies that human reason and human will participate in God's wisdom and providence" (*Veritatis Splendor,* §41).

62. *Veritatis Splendor,* §2.

63. Ibid., §§12, 46.

64. Ibid., §38.

65. Ibid., §58.

66. "The judgment of conscience does not establish the law; rather it bears witness to the authority of the natural law and of the practical reason with reference to the supreme good, whose attractiveness the human person perceives and whose commandments he accepts" (Ibid., §60).

67. Ibid., §45.

68. In the *London Tablet* Bernard Haring rejected the papal encyclical *Veritatis Splendor,* basing his objection (in part) on a right of conscience grounded in natural law. See *National Catholic Reporter,* November 5, 1993.

69. *Veritatis Splendor,* §86.

70. Ibid., §103.

71. *Church Dog.* II/I, § 36, "Ethics as a Task of the Doctrine of God," 527.

72. On the new catechism, see note 15.

73. John Courtney Murray, S.J., *We Hold These Truths* (New York: Image Book edition, 1964), 53.

74. Sen. Joseph Biden, "Law and Natural Law," *Washington Post,* September 8, 1991. Senator Biden, it may be recalled, voted against the confirmation of Robert Bork because, among other reasons, Bork expressly rejected judicial uses of natural law. Against Bork, Biden declared: "I have certain inalienable rights because I exist."

CHAPTER TWO: NATURAL LAW AS "LAW"

* A version of this chapter appeared in the *American Journal of Jurisprudence* 39 (1994): 1–32.

1. *Summa Theologiae* I-II, 91.2: *Et talis participatio legis aeternae in rationali creatura lex naturalis dicitur.*

2. "These dictates of Reason, men used to call by the name of Lawes; but improperly: for they are but Conclusions, or Theorems concerning what conduceth to the conser-

vation and defence of themselves; whereas Law, properly is the word of him, that by right hath command over others. But yet if we consider the same Theoremes, as delivered in the word of God, that by right commandeth all things; then are they properly called Lawes." *Leviathan*, I.xv. John Austin observes: "The whole or a portion of the laws set by God to men is frequently styled the law of nature, or natural law: being, in truth, the only natural law of which it is possible to speak without a metaphor. . ." (*The Province of Jurisprudence Determined* (1832), Lecture I, 10).

3. The natural law discussion covers §§35–64.

4. *Adv. Judaeos*, cap. 2 (PL 2-2, 599, 600), *quasi matrix omnium praeceptorum Dei . . . non scriptam, quae naturaliter intelligebatur*.

5. *Veritatis Splendor*, §41.

6. *S.t.* I-II, q. 91.2.

7. *S.t.* I-II, q. 91.1, ad 3. And in q. 91.3, ad 2: "Thus, although the human practical reason is a measure, it is not an original measure. It should be said that human reason is not itself the rule of things, but rather the principles impressed on it by nature are general rules and measures of things to be done; concerning these, the natural reason is the rule and measure, not of things that are from nature." See also *De Veritate* 1.2.

8. "Others speak, and rightly so, of theonomy, or participated theonomy, since man's free obedience to God's law effectively implies that human reason and human will participate in God's wisdom and providence" (*Veritatis Splendor*, §41).

9. *Veritatis Splendor*, §2.

10. Ibid., §§12, 46.

11. Ibid., §38.

12. Ibid., §58.

13. *Per primam Dei gratiam, id est per legem naturae*. Denzinger-Hünermann, *Symboles et définitions de la foi catholique* (Paris: Cerf, 1997), §336. See also St. Thomas, *Summa contra gentiles* III.80 (2): *per primam illuminationem divinitus*.

14. *Instit. Justin.* 2.11.

15. This is not to say that there were not many sources for the idea of a divine natural law among pagan philosophers, sources that were quickly exploited by Christian theologians. See Hermann Kleinknecht and W. Gutbrod, "Nomos in the Greek and Hellenistic World," in *Law* (1962), 1–22. For the contribution of Philo of Alexandria, see Helmut Koester, "The Concept of Natural Law in Greek Thought" in *Religions in Antiquity*, ed. Jacob Neusner (Leiden: E. J. Brill, 1968), 534–35. Koester's research indicates that the term "law of nature" occurs fewer than six times in the Greek literature of pre-Christian times. In Philo, however, over thirty occurrences of the term can be found.

16. Augustine, *De. Gen. contra Mani*. II, cap. 15, §22 (PL 34, 208).

17. "Thus, though it has all corporeal nature subject to itself, it still understands that the nature of God is above it and that it should not turn either to the right by claiming for itself what it is not, or to the left by condemning through negligence what it is. This is the tree of life planted in the middle of paradise. But the tree of the knowledge of good and evil likewise signifies the mid-rank of the soul and its ordered integrity. For the tree is planted in the middle of paradise, and it is called the tree of discernment of good and evil, because the soul ought to stretch out toward

those things which are before, that is, to God and to forget those things which are behind, that is, corporeal pleasures. But if the soul should abandon God and turn to itself and will to enjoy its own power as if without God, it swells up with pride, which is the beginning of every sin. When punishment has followed upon this sin, it will learn by experience the difference between the good which it abandoned and the evil into which it has fallen. This is what it will be for it to have tasted the fruit of the tree of the discernment of good and evil. Hence, it received the commandment to eat from every tree that is in paradise, but not to eat from the tree in which there is the discernment of good and evil. That is, it was not to enjoy it, because by eating from it would violate and corrupt the ordered integrity of its nature" (Ibid., cap. 9, §12).

18. A doctrine reiterated by St. Thomas in *S.t.* I–II, q. 91.6.

19. Ambrose, *De Parad.* I, cap. 6, §32 (PL 14, 289). See also *De Cain et Abel*, II, cap. 9 (PL 14, 355).

20. *Ergo quia per inobedientiam praerogativa naturalis legis corrupta atque interlita est. Epist.* 83 [73], §5 (PL 16, 1252).

21. For the theologians, the periodization of law cannot allow any gaps in divine governance. In *S.t.* 102.1, obj. 2, St. Thomas equates the period of natural law with the state of innocence prior to the Fall. In 102.3 ad 12, he refers to the period of the patriarchs as the state of the law of nature [*pro statu legis naturae*]. In *S.t.* I–II, q. 98.6, St. Thomas locates the Decalogue between the [time of] natural law and the law of grace [*inter legem naturae et legem gratiae*]. And in one of the more unusual, though intriguing, remarks in this vein, Aquinas expounds St. Paul's statement in Rom 5:13 ["for sin was in the world before the law was given"] to refer either to the Decalogue or to the natural law. It can refer to natural law as indicating original sin in the child prior to his ability to exercise reason. In V Rom., lect. 4 (§422).

22. Chrysostom, Hom. on Rom., Hom. XII (PG 60, 502).

23. Ibid. See also Hom. VI.

24. Chrysostom, Hom. on Acts, Hom. V. See *S.t.* I–II, q. 106.1 ad 1.

25. From St. Paul's own argument in Rom 7:1–4. On the natural law precept of one-flesh in Gn 2, see J. Duncan M. Derrett, "Romans vii.1–4: The Relationship with the Resurrected Christ," in *Law in the New Testament* (London: Darton, Longman & Todd, 1970), 461–71.

26. "Now, the life of those who are just conserves and promotes the common good, because they themselves are the principal part of the multitude. And so it is no way licit to kill the innocent" (*S.t.* II–II, q. 64.6).

27. "The sense [of the precept] therefore is 'Thou shalt not kill on thine own authority.'" *Est ergo sensus: Non occides propria auctoritat,"* *Collationes in Decem Preceptis,* V.

28. "...but to punish pertains to none but the minister of the law, by whose authority the pain is inflicted" (*S.t.* I–II, q. 92.2 ad 3).

29. *Veritatis Splendor,* §11.

30. Ibid., §13.

31. Ibid., §45.

32. See my essay, "The Problem of the State in *Centesimus Annus*," *Fordham International Law Journal* 15 (1992): 952–96.

33. With regard to muting or even evading the rigor of giving definitions, in his 1973 remarks in the "Occasion of the Tenth Anniversary of the Encyclical *Pacem in Terris*," Maurice Cardinal Roy stated that "Although the term 'nature' does in fact lend itself to serious misunderstandings, the reality intended has lost nothing of its forcefulness when it is replaced by modern synonyms. . . . Such synonyms are: man, human being, human person, dignity, the rights of man or the rights of peoples, conscience, humaneness (in conduct), the struggle for justice, and, more recently, 'the duty of being,' the 'quality of life.' Could they not all be summarized in the concept of 'values,' which is very much used today?" (April 11, 1973), sect. 128, in Joseph Gremillion, *The Gospel of Peace and Justice* (New York: Orbis Books, 1976), 557. Interestingly, on John XXIII's remark that peace is "absolute respect for the order laid down by God" (*Pacem in Terris*, §1), Roy observes: "But here again, this word jars the modern mentality, as does, even more, the idea that it summons up: a sort of complicated organic scheme or gigantic genealogical tree, in which each being and group has its predetermined place."

34. Fuchs, *Moral Demands*, 100.

35. Ibid., 40.

36. Ibid., 102.

37. "A moral judgement about right ethical conduct cannot be deduced from what is given in nature, but can be found through human, rational, evaluative reflection within human reality as a whole. Only in this way can we avoid a naturalistic fallacy and find the true meaning of the 'natural law'" (Ibid., 33).

38. Here we catch a glimpse of how natural law was at stake in the debate over contraception. Although dissenting theologians often criticized *Humanae Vitae* for reducing the natural law to biology, Fuchs suggests a quite different issue: namely, that the main point of dispute is whether natural law is a law, or in fact whether natural law is simply a shorthand way of referring to human practical reason. Fuchs writes: "The disposition over the body and life of a human person (and indeed over whether procreation occurs or not in the union of man and woman) is widely understood as the exclusive right of God and, therefore, as outside our personal control. God's sovereignty embraces not only these realities, however, but all created reality. God's universal sovereignty is transcendent, not merely in the world, and is not, therefore, in competition with human rights. . . . One cannot therefore deduce, from God's relationship to creation, what the obligation of the human person is in these areas or in the realm of creation as a whole" (Ibid., 39).

39. Suarez, *De Legibus*, II, cap. 6 (7).

40. H. L. A. Hart, *The Concept of Law* (Oxford: Clarendon Press, 1961), 92.

41. "Therefore, just as human law, in so far as it is external to the legislator, implies on the part of the subject not only active knowledge thereof, or an act of judgment, but also a permanent sign of its existence [*permanes signum*], contained in some written form which is always able to awaken knowledge of that law; even so, in the case of natural law, which exists in the lawgiver as none other than the eternal law, there is, in the subjects, not only an active judgment, or command, but also the [mental] illumination itself in which that law is (as it were) permanently written, and which the law is always capable of incorporating action" (*De Legibus* II, cap. 5 [14]).

42. Ibid., II, cap. 6 (5).
43. *S.t.* I-II, q. 90.4 ad 1.
44. *De Legibus* II, cap. 6 (24).
45. *S.t.* I-II, q. 90.3–4.
46. In II Rom., lectio 3 super 2.15 (§219).
47. This is the interpretation given in *S.t.* I-II, q. 91.2 sed contra, where Thomas cites the Glossa ordinaria: "Although they have no written law, yet they have the natural law, whereby each one knows, and is conscious of, what is good and what is evil [*qua quilibet intelligit et sibi conscius est quid sit bonum et quid malum*]" (Gloss. ordin. VI.7.E; cf. Glossa Lombardi [PL 191, 1345]).
48. See note 20, chapter 1.
49. Thus, in *Summa contra gentiles* III.38, St. Thomas states: "But the fact that a person lacks the aforesaid knowledge of God makes him appear very blameworthy [*maxime viturperabilis apparet*]." See also *S.t.* I, 2.1 ad 1 and II-II, 85.1. A point stressed in *Veritatis Splendor:* "To ask about the good, in fact, ultimately means to turn towards God…" (*Veritatis Splendor*, §10).
50. For a brief, but accurate, treatment of why natural law *as law* is reached by inferences, see Lawrence Dewan, O.P., "St. Thomas, Our Natural Lights, and the Moral Order," 67 *Angelicum* (1990). Dewan points out that although the knowledge of God is contained only virtually and implicitly in the first notions of being, and, perforce, of the good, the human intellect is nevertheless disposed "to exploit this virtuality of the notions" (Ibid., 303). Thus, in *Scg* III.38, Thomas states: "But the fact that a person lacks the aforesaid knowledge of God makes him appear very blameworthy [*maxime viturperabilis apparet*]." That the creature should quickly go on to understand the origin of the natural law, see St. Bernard of Clairvaux, *De Diligendo Deo* II.6. It is also interesting that St. Bernard followed the older tradition of interpreting Rom 2:14–15 in the context of Gn 1–2.
51. Natural law is communicated directly, without artifice, and without the mediation of subordinate legal officials. Now, in the case of natural law, additional knowledge of the legislative pedigree will prove very helpful, especially (but not only) with respect to natural law duties to God. In this context, the *lex vetus* was a system of positive law that disclosed the legislative point of origin of natural law. St. Thomas taught that the old law presupposed faith, and through faith, subjection to the lawgiver qua lawgiver. See I-II, q. 99.2 ad 2; 1-II, q. 100.5 ad 1; II-II, q. 16.1. This subjection contains principles that could be known without the positive law; for example: giving due to God by sacrifices and other signs (*S.t.* II-II, q. 85.1); loving God above all else (I-II, q. 100.3 ad I; D.v. 16.3 ad 2; 17.2).
52. Epist. 83 [73], §5 (PL 16, 1252). As the natural *civitas* unravels, so does man's knowledge of the sovereign. Thus, Chrysostom, commenting on Rom 1:24 ["He gave them up. . . ."], writes: "Hence he shows that even of the perversion of the laws it was ungodliness which was the cause, but He 'gave them up,' here is, let them alone" (Hom. on Rom., Hom. III).
53. *De Gen.* contra Mani., II cap 16 §24.
54. *De Legibus,* II, cap. 6 (7).
55. Ibid., II, cap. 6 (2).

56. Ibid., II, cap. 6 (7).

57. Mortimer Adler, "A Question about Law," in *Essays in Thomism,* ed. Robert E. Brennan, O.P. (New York: Sheed & Ward, 1942). See also John Finnis, *Natural Law and Natural Rights* (1980), 10, 20, 280, 294. Finnis states that "Natural Law . . . is only analogically law, in relation to my present focal use of the term: that is why the term has been avoided in this chapter on Law, save in relation to past thinkers who used the term" (Ibid., 280). This qualification is important because, unlike Adler, who purports to settle the issue once and for all, Finnis does not go so far as to say that natural law is not law except by analogy to positive law.

58. Adler ignores the passages where St. Thomas flatly equates natural law with the highest order of law, e.g.: *S.t.* I-II, q. 91.2 ad 1; q. 91.2 ad 3 [*proprie lex vocatur*]; q. 91.5; q. 97.1 ad 1; *Scg* III.114 (1–4). Moreover, Adler argues (220*f*) that because St. Thomas held that law is an extrinsic principle of a human act, he could not have meant that natural law, inwardly instilled, is an extrinsic principle. But St. Thomas explicitly argues that natural law is not an intrinsic principle. See *S.t.* I, q. 21.1 ad 2; I-II, q. 94.1; and Suppl. 65.1 ad 4. In fact, in *S. t.* I, q. 82.1, he contends that moral necessity, wherever there is a per se order between the end and the means, is an extrinsic principle. For St. Thomas, an intrinsic principle denotes what belongs to the quiddity, such as powers and habits. An extrinsic principle is a norm or rule that governs the quiddity. Law is always an extrinsic principle of a human act. Of the nature "human," one could predicate rational (as to a power), or just and law-abiding (as to virtues), but not "law." The term extrinsic, however, does not necessarily mean "external." A positive law is both extrinsic and external. Natural law and the New law, however, are extrinsic but internal. These two laws are called *lex non scripta* (unwritten law), or *lex indita* (instilled law). The definition of natural law, according to the notion of participation, requires one to understand how an extrinsic principle (like the ring on the wax, or the illuminating light) informs the nature of the thing being directed or normed. Adler seems to conflate extrinsic with external. On the intrinsic/extrinsic distinction, see XII Metaphys., lectio 4 (§2468); VII Metaphys., lectio 17 (§1658); V Metaphys., lectio I (§ 754, 762); De. car. a. 1. For the application of the distinction to matters of politics and law, see V Metaphys., lectio I (§757); *S.t.* I-II, prologues to qq. 49, 90.

59. Ibid.,209.

60. Ibid., 211.

61. Ibid.

62. Aristotle, *Metaphysics* IV.2 1003a33. See also St. Thomas, In IV *Metaphys.* lect. 1 (§537).

63. For a discussion of the transition from q. 90 to q. 91, see Ralph McInerny, "The Basis and Purpose of Positive Law," in *Lex et Libertas,* ed. L. J. Elders and K. Hedwig (Vatican: Libreria Editrice Vaticana, 1987).

64. But not necessarily independent of any analogical reasoning. As St. Thomas argued in *De Ver.* 5.1 c. and ad 7, we reason about and learn about divine governance by seeing how creatures are provident.

65. See also V *Metaphys.* lectio 5 (§824); *De Malo* I, a. 5 ad 19; and *Scg* I, cap. 32. In the treatise on law, St. Thomas insists that all law is derived from the eternal law. See *S.t.* I-II, q. 19.4; q. 19.5 ad 2; q. 74.7; q. 93.3; q. 93.5 ad 1; q. 96.4. Since, as he argues in

S.t. I–II, q. 91.2, the natural law is our participation in the eternal law, and is not diverse from the eternal law (q. 91.2 ad 1), it certainly seems as though the example of health, when applied to law, should lead to the opposite conclusion than the one drawn by Adler. Although positive law can be regarded as first in the order of names, in the order of being it is law only insofar as it contains and expresses the eternal law—which is to say, the natural law.

66. To assert that the intellect apprehends, and is morally bound by principles of action prior to positive law, does not settle questions about the being and source of the original principles vouchsafed to the practical intellect. Thus, so far as it goes, giving due allowance for precepts concerning duties to God, caution in the use of the words natural "law," and with some qualification regarding the scope of the words "reflectively analysed," one can say that "natural law can be understood, assented to, applied, and reflectively analysed," as John Finnis says, "without adverting to the question of the existence of God" (*Natural Law and Natural Rights,* 49). This is true, but even so one may doubt that natural law can be reflectively analyzed very thoroughly without grappling with the question whether epistemic priority implies ontological priority.

67. Specifically, to *S. t.* I, q. 22.1–2.

68. Thus, for example, H. L. A. Hart dismisses the traditional definition as "theocratic." The phrase "natural law," he contends, is "not logically dependent on that belief" (*Concept of Law,* 183). The tradition, however, never argued the point of logical dependence, but ontological dependence.

Chapter Three: Natural Law in the Positive Laws

* A version of this chapter was first published in the *Review of Politics* (winter 1993): 5–34.

1. *Summa Theologiae* II–II, 57.1 ad 1.

2. Ibid., ad 2. In his *Commentary on the Ethics,* Aquinas refers to lawmakers as *architectores in artificialibus.* VI *In Eth.,* lectio 7. And again, in *S.t.* I–II, 95.1 uses the simile of artisans hammering out *arma rationis,* the tools or weapons of reason.

3. For example, in the first distinction of the *Decretum,* Gratian proposed that "The human race is governed in two ways, by natural right and by custom. Natural right contained in [*continetur*] the Law and the Gospel, commands that each do to the other what he would wish to be done to him. Thus, Christ said 'Whatever you wish men to do to you, do also unto them. This is the Law and the Prophets.' Thus, Isidore says, 'Divine law is by nature; human law by custom'" (Gratian, *Concordantia Discordantium Canonum,* D.1, in *Corpus Juris Canonici,* ed. A. Richter and A. Friedberg [Leipzig, 1922]). Quoting Isidore of Seville, *Etymologies* v, 2, 1, d. 636. The word *continere* in this context means not only to include, but also to enclose. The positive law, whether human or divine, is said to re-present precepts of the natural law by inclusion and by fixing its boundaries in the form of writing. For Aquinas's use of the term, see *S.t.* I–II, 99.2, 100.2.

4. *S.t.* I–II, 91.2, 106.1. The contrast between *lex indita* and *lex scripta* is one of several ways that a law is said to be "natural." See the Supplementum, 65.1 and 4.

5. *S.t.* I–II, 94.5 ad 1.

6. *S.t.* I–II, 98.6.

7. Thomas Jefferson, *The Writings*, ed. Paul Leicester Ford (New York, 1898), 9:480; 18:1 ("The Batture at New Orleans"), 15:207. Cited in Donald R. Kelly, *The Human Measure: Social Thought in the Western Legal Tradition* (Cambridge, Mass.: Harvard University Press, 1990), 186.

8. Clarence Thomas, "Why Black Americans Should Look to Conservative Policies," *The Heritage Lectures* 119 (1987): 8.

9. Clarence Thomas, "The Higher Law Background of the Privileges or Immunities Clause of the Fourteenth Amendment," *Harvard Journal of Law & Public Policy* 12 (Winter 1989): 63–70.

10. Clarence Thomas, "Toward a 'Plain Reading' of the Constitution—The Declaration of Independence in Constitutional Interpretation," *Howard Law Journal* 30 (1987): 691–703.

11. Laurence Tribe asserted that Thomas is the "first Supreme Court nominee in 50 years to maintain that natural law should be readily consulted in constitutional interpretation." Natural law might be used, Tribe warned, to justify "moralistic intrusions on personal choice," especially intrusions informed by "Judeo-Christian moral standards" ("'Natural Law' and the Nominee," *New York Times,* July 15, 1991). In the most recent edition of his *American Constitutional Law,* however, Tribe not only has given a sympathetic and fair account of the role of natural law theory in our constitutional history, but also has maintained that when interpreting the Bill of Rights, the judiciary "has elaborated from the spare text an idea of the 'human' and a conception of 'being' not merely contemplated but required" (*American Constitutional Law,* 2nd ed. [Mineola, N.Y.: Foundation Press, 1988], 1309). Most scholars would regard this as not just a nod toward judicially cognizable natural law, but a summary statement of it.

12. Referring to the 1989 *Harvard* article—where Thomas wrote that "higher law is the only alternative to the willfulness of both run-amok majorities and run-amok judges" (Thomas, "The Higher Law Background," 64)—Gary McDowell warned that "Thomas is a bigger problem for conservatives than he is for liberals." It is one thing, McDowell opined, to believe that natural law might inform the legislative process; but it is quite another thing to consider natural law "in judicial interpretations" (Gary L. McDowell, "Doubting Thomas," *The New Republic,* July 29, 1991, 14). In a similar vein, the conservative pundit Bruce Fein said that if Thomas holds a natural rights doctrine (of what judges should do), "I would write a column that says he should not be confirmed because it is not consistent with an oath to uphold the Constitution." Cited by Ruth Marcus, "Thomas Doesn't Fit Conservative Mold," *Washington Post,* July 8, 1991.

13. Sen. Joseph Biden, "Law and Natural Law," *Washington Post,* September 8, 1991.

14. Plato *Gorgias* 483e.

15. See, e.g., Lon L. Fuller, *The Morality of Law,* rev. ed. with "Reply to Critics" (New Haven, Conn.: Yale University Press, 1969); H. L. A. Hart, "Lon L. Fuller: The Morality of Law," and "Positivism and the Separation of Law and Morals," in *Essays in Jurisprudence and Philosophy* (Oxford: Clarendon Press, 1983), 343–64, 49–87; Joseph Raz, *Norms and Practical Reason* (Princeton, N.J.: Princeton University Press, 1990); Neil MacCormick, "Natural Law and the Separation of Law and Morals," in *Natural*

Law Theory, ed. Robert P. George (Oxford: Clarendon Press, 1992), 130; John Finnis, *Natural Law and Natural Rights* (Oxford: Clarendon Press, 1980), ch. 1.

16. For the expression natural law as "effective law," I have relied upon Robert P. George's 1992 Goodrich Lecture at Wabash College, entitled "How Does the Natural Law Become Effective?" This lecture has been reprinted as "Natural Law and Positive Law," in *Common Truths: New Perspectives on Natural Law,* ed. Edward B. McLean (Wilmington, Del.: ISI Books, 2000).

17. E.g., the federal constitution; federal legislation; federal administrative rules and regulations; treaties entered into by the president and ratified by the Senate; federal judicial decisions; state constitutions; state legislation; state administrative rules and regulations; state judicial decisions. See P. S. Atiyah and R. S. Summers, *Form and Substance in Anglo-American Law* (Oxford: Clarendon Press, 1987), 55.

18. *S.t.* I-II, 96.4; II-II, 60.2,6.

19. In the pejorative sense, meaning that the judge acts *ultra vires.*

20. H. L. A. Hart, *The Concept of Law* (Oxford: Clarendon Press, 1961), 202–204.

21. MacCormick, "Natural Law and the Separation of Law and Morals," 130.

22. See Robert Bork, "Natural Law and the Constitution," *First Things* (March 1992), 64.

23. *S.t.* I-II, 94.5; 95.2–3; 96.4 and 2.

24. *S.t.* I-II, 91.4.

25. *S.t.* I-II, 96.3 ad 2; 100.9 ad 2; 100.11.

26. *S.t.* I-II, q. 92.

27. See *S.t.* I-II, 98.1: "Wherefore human law makes precepts only about acts of justice, and if it commands acts of other virtues, this is only insofar as they assume the nature of justice."

28. *S.t.* I-II, 96.2–3.

29. *S.t.* I-II, 95.1 ad 2.

30. *Nicomachean Ethics* 5.41132a22. On Aquinas's approach to the subject of inanimate justice, see the articles by E. A. Goerner: "On Thomistic Natural Law: The Bad Man's View of Thomistic Natural Right," *Political Theory* 7 (February 1979): 101–22; "Thomistic Natural Right: The Good Man's View of Thomistic Natural Law," *Political Theory* 11 (August 1983): 393–418.

31. *S.t.* II-II, 60.1.

32. In a recent essay on natural law, Neil MacCormick writes: "What then is the difference between practical reason as manifested in legal practice and practical reason as displayed in the moral life? The answer lies in the elements of publicity, authority, and determinacy special to law. Always the last resort moral judgement is that of an individual moral agent judging for her or himself after reflection on whatever advice, consultation, regard for convention or consensus or tradition or religious reaching is for her or him most persuasive or even authoritative. Always the last resort legal judgement, however, is that of a public tribunal acting as the responsible authority in such matters for a political community by reference to a publicly established and relatively clearly statable set of norms and standards of that community" ("Natural Law and the Separation of Law and Morals," 119). Elsewhere, I have stated that natural law is not a merely private order bereft of legal predicates. MacCormick compares moral reasoning and legal practice. Put just in this way,

however, I find nothing objectionable. For I am hesitant to call moral reasoning the natural law, since the law would consist of the antecedent premises.

33. *S.t.* II–II, 60.5 sed contra. Citing *De Vera Religione,* cap. xxxi.

34. John Locke, *The Second Treatise of Government,* ed. Peter Laslett (Cambridge: Cambridge University Press, New American Library edition, 1965), II; 7–8, 312.

35. *S.t.* I–II, 90.3; and Supplement, 60.1, ad 1. A point repeated by Vitoria, who contended that the natural law only prescribes that there be a governing power, and does not prescribe who has it. In the absence of custom, positive law, or divine decree, authority is assumed to reside in the community; in the case of international law, in the community of nations. Francisco de Vitoria, *De potestate civili* (1528), 1.4, 3.4, in *Political Writings,* ed. Anthony Pagden and Jeremy Lawrance (Cambridge: Cambridge University Press, 1991), 11, 40. An advocate of monarchical government, Vitoria held that although power (*potestas*) comes immediately from God to the king, he was very careful not to claim that jurisdictional authority (*auctoritas*) immediately arises from the divinely conferred power, but from the commonwealth (1.4–5, pp. 11, 16). Locke was to make a very different argument, that power and authority are given by God to individuals, who transfer it to the commonwealth.

36. *S.t.* I–II, q. 90.

37. *S.t.* II–II, 60.6. See, also, the relationship to the virtue of obedience, in II–II, 105.5.

38. *S.t.* II–II, 60.6, ad 4.

39. *S.t.* II–II, 67.2 sed contra. Citing Gratianum, *Decretum,* P. II, causa III, qu. 7, can. 4.

40. *S.t.* II–II, 67.2, corpus.

41. Ibid., ad 4.

42. *S.t.* II–II, 64.6 ad 3.

43. In *S.t.* I–II, 95.4, Aquinas makes passing reference to a regime in which the citizens are governed by judge-made law, under the rubric of *Ius Honorarium/Praetorium.* At least this is Thomas Gilby's interpretation. See Gilby's note 1, in vol. 28 of the Blackfriars edition of the *Summa Theologiae* (London: McGraw-Hill, 1966), 166–67. Significantly, perhaps, Aquinas places this kind of legal regime under the oligarchic rather than the aristocratic model.

44. The discipline, he is careful to note, includes the justice of procedures. *S.t.* I–II, 105.2.

45. I borrow the term "judicialization" from Gerard Bradley, "Beyond Murray's Articles of Peace and Faith," in *John Courtney Murray and American Civil Religion,* ed. Robert P. Hunt and Kenneth L. Grasso (Grand Rapids, Mich.: Eerdmans, 1992), 204.

46. Hamilton, Madison, and Jay, *The Federalist Papers,* intro. Clinton Rossiter (New York: New American Library, 1961), 467.

47. Ibid., 465.

48. For a survey of some recent cases where natural law jurisprudence is invoked against willful legislative majorities, see my article "Liberalism and the American Natural Law Tradition," *Wake Forest Law Review* 25 (1990): 429–99.

49. For a useful discussion of the sociological and institutional reasons for natural law jurisprudence in the United States, see Atiyah and Summers, *Form and Substance,* chs. 8–9.

50. Mortimer J. Adler, *Haves without Have Nots* (New York: Macmillan, 1991), 197–98.

51. Adler mentions in passing that there ought to be "judicial restraint" (Ibid., 188). But his case against Bork rests entirely upon a philosophical consideration of the moral merit of the substance of laws rather than upon the moral restraints upon the office of judges. For example, with respect to the decisions of the Warren Court on racial segregation, Adler asserts that they "were not based on the unconstitutionality of such laws, but upon their injustice" (Ibid., 209). On the judge-made privacy law of the Warren and Burger Courts, Adler asserts that it is "impossible to demarcate the proper spheres of liberty and of law without drawing a line between private and public" (Ibid., 209). Throughout Adler's essay, there is scarcely a thread of argument touching moral questions of authority and jurisdiction.

52. Which was cited approvingly by Clarence Thomas in his *Harvard* article, "The Higher Law Background."

53. Adler comes close to arguing as much. Concerning the Nuremberg Trials, he observes: "If there are no natural rights, there are no human rights; if there are no human rights, there cannot be any crimes against humanity" (*Haves without Have Nots*, 200). This confuses, however, the reason for ascertaining a crime and the jurisdictional authority under which it is prosecuted. In point of fact, the Nuremberg proceedings were not undertaken in the absence of international law. Adler's enthusiasm for the traditional doctrine of objective *iura,* inhering in humanity, moves him to all but claim that judicial deliberations are simply a concomitant of the fact that rights exist, and hence that the American judiciary is a kind of *ius gentium* court in perpetual session.

54. In virtually all modern legal systems, litigation is appropriately put under artificial limitations regarding procedures and evidentiary rules. Such rules would not be handy for the moral or legal theorist attempting to search out the meaning or scope of natural law.

55. Robert Bork, "Natural Law and the Constitution," *First Things* (March 1992): 16.

56. Citing: Hadley Arkes, *Beyond the Constitution* (Princeton, N.J.: Princeton University Press, 1991); Russell Hittinger, "Liberalism and the American Natural Law Tradition"; William Ball, "The Tempting of Robert Bork: What's a Constitution without Natural Law?" *Crisis* (June 1990). For their response, and Bork's rejoinder, see *First Things* 23 (May 1992): 45–54.

57. Robert Bork, "Neutral Principles and Some First Amendment Problems," *Indiana Law Journal* 47 (1971): 30.

58. Robert Bork, *The Tempting of America* (New York: Free Press, 1990), 258.

59. Bork's rejoinder, 52.

60. When Bork writes that "there may be a natural law, but we are not agreed upon what it is, and there is no such law that gives definite answers to a judge trying to decide a case" ("The Struggle over the Role of the Court," *National Review,* September 17, 1982, 1138), he may or may not be right. But it is not immediately relevant to his stronger argument, which does not rest upon skepticism about natural law, nor upon the issue of consensus about its content. The stronger argument is that, whatever the degree of knowledge about the natural law, the judge must judge within the bounds of the authority conferred upon his office. As I said, this is a moral requirement that was recognized by nineteenth-century federal judges. For example, sitting on circuit

in 1853, Justice McLean, wrote: "With the abstract principles of slavery, courts called to administer the law have nothing to do. It is for the people, who are sovereign, and their representatives, in making constitutions and the enactment of laws, to consider the laws of nature, and the immutable principles of right. This is a field which judges cannot explore. . . . They look to the law, and to the law only. A disregard of this by the judicial powers, would undermine and overturn the social compact" (*Miller v. McQuerry*, 17 F. Cas. 332 [No. 9,583] [C.C.D. Ohio, 1853], 339; cited in Robert M. Cover, *Justice Accused: Antislavery and the Judicial Process* [New Haven, Conn.: Yale University Press, 1975], 119–20). It was precisely this notion of how the positive law delegates authority to make natural law effective that moved Justice McLean four years later to dissent in the *Dred Scott* case, when Justice Taney, by judicial fiat, denied the national legislature any authority over the matter of slavery.

61. Bork, "Natural Law and the Constitution," 18.
62. *S.t.* II–II, 120.1 ad 1.
63. Ibid., ad 2.
64. See William Nelson, *The Fourteenth Amendment* (Cambridge, Mass.: Harvard University Press, 1988).
65. *Planned Parenthood of Southeastern Pennsylvania v. Casey*, 112 S.Ct. 2791, 2807 (1992).
66. See Arkes's examination of this issue, *Beyond the Constitution*, ch. 4.

CHAPTER FOUR: AUTHORITY TO RENDER JUDGMENT

* This essay was first published, in slightly altered form, as "Aquinas and the Rule of Law," in *The Ever-Illuminating Wisdom of St. Thomas Aquinas: The Proceedings of the Wethersfield Institute, 1994, vol. 8* (San Francisco: Ignatius Press, 1999), 99–119.
1. *Summa Theologiae* I–II, 93.2 ad 3. The word mind (*mens*) itself is taken from judging and measuring (*iudicare vel mensurare*), *S.t.* I, 79.9 ad 4.
2. *Summa contra gentiles* II, 48.
3. Thomas explains that free action depends upon this endowment of the intellect. Commentary De Anima, Bk. III, lectio 16.
4. And with the acquired virtues, speculative and practical, this competence is enhanced, extensively as to the range of objects and intensively with regard to the surety and ease of judgment.
5. *S.t.* I–II, 93.2 ad 3.
6. S.t. II–II, 58.1 ad 5.
7. *S.t.* II–II, 67.2 ad 2. See also *Scg* IV, 72. [*Alii autem indices non iudicant secundum propriam potestatem*]."
8. *S.t.* I–II, 90.1–4. Notably, Thomas does not include coercion (*vis coactiva*) in the definition. Of its essence, law is a binding directive of reason (*vis directiva*) intended to move a multitude of free and intelligent agents to a common good. The multitude is not moved by physical but by moral necessity. Eliminate any one of the four principles of law (command of reason, authority, common good, promulgation) and we have coactive rather than directive force. Coercion is an act of law, *actus legis* (*S.t.* I–II, 92.2). Coaction is said to be lawful if it flows from the four principles that constitute direction; but none of the four traits of law depend essentially upon coercion.

9. *S.t.* I-II, 90.1 obj. 1.

10. *S.t.* I-II, 90.1 ad 1.

11. *S.t.* I-II, 91.1 ad 3.

12. *S.t.* I-II, 13.1.

13. *S.t.* I-II, 91.2 ad 3.

14. *S.t.* I-II, 91.2.

15. *S.t.* I-II, 97.1 ad 1.

16. "[I]t should be said that human reason is not itself the rule of things, but rather the principles naturally instilled in it are general rules and measures of things to be done; concerning these, the natural reason is the rule and measure, not of things that are from nature" (*S.t.* I-II, 91.3 ad 2). And see *S.t.* I-II, 93.1 ad 3; 93.4.

17. *S.t.* I-II, 90.4 ad 1. *Quod promulgatio legis naturae est ex hoc ipso quod Deus eam mentibus hominum inseruit naturaliter cognoscendam.* It is worth recalling that, for Thomas, law is an extrinsic principle of action (*S.t.* I-II, 90 prol). But in saying that law is a *principium extrinsecum* he does not mean something exterior in the psychological sense of the term. As we have said, law properly exists in a mind. Law is an extrinsic principle because it is not a predicate of human nature. Man is a rational animal, but he is not a law. Therefore, the use of the word nature (*natura, naturalis, naturale, naturaliter*) in connection with law is meant to highlight how the intrinsic principles of human nature receive or hold the legal measure.

18. *S.t.* I-II, 91.2 ad 1. This is why, in answer to the objection that positing both an eternal law and a natural law is a needless reduplication of laws, Thomas answers that natural law is not diverse from the eternal law; there are not two laws. There is rather one law, the eternal law, which is God; by participation, it is in the rational creature.

19. Angels too are under the natural law (*S.t.* I, 60.5). Thomas differed from other medieval theologians in holding that angels are not a source of law. "It is for the sovereign alone to make a law by his own authority; but sometimes after making a law, he promulgates it through others. Thus God made the Law by His own authority, but He promulgated it through the angels" (*S.t.* I-II, 98.3, Reply OBJ 3). If we focus upon the mode of promulgation, there are as many species of law as there are ways to communicate it. But if we are interested in proper definitions, there are only two kinds of law that correspond to two kinds of minds. There is law that proceeds from the mind of God and law that proceeds from the mind of man who partakes of the eternal law. As Augustine said, one is eternal the other temporal (*S.t.* I-II, 91.3 sed contra). See Stephen Louis Brock, *The Legal Character of Natural Law according to St. Thomas Aquinas*, dissertation, University of Toronto (1988), ch. 2-C.

20. See Matthew Cuddeback, *Light and Form in St. Thomas Aquinas's Metaphysics of the Knower*, dissertation, The Catholic University of America (1998)

21. *S.t.* I-II, 47.15.

22. The triadic structure of first precepts in I-II, 94.2 follow this pattern. See also I-II, 19.4.

23. *S.t.* I-II, 90.3 ad 3.

24. Moreover, admonition rather than punishment is naturally suitable to the relations of a domestic society. In certain codes of ancient law, the *paterfamilias* receives from the city delegated power to make and enforce legal judgments, even those of criminal

law. In that case, however, we are not speaking simply of domestic prudence.

25. *S.t.* II–II, 50.1 ad 2.

26. *S.t.* II–II, 50.1 ad 3.

27. *S.t.* II–II, 50.2.

28. Ernst H. Kantorowicz, *The King's Two Bodies: A Study in Mediaeval Political Theology* (Princeton, N.J.: Princeton University Press, 1957), 135.

29. *S.t.* I–II, 95.1 ad 2. Emphasis added.

30. In the very next article, I–II, 95.2.

31. For a useful analysis of the traditional dictum, see Javier Hervada, *Natural Right and Natural Law: A Critical Introduction* (Pamplona: Servicio de Publicaciones de la Universidad de Navarra, 1990), 19–45.

32. Note the similarity of Thomas's position to Lon Fuller's discussion of the hapless Rex in *The Morality of Law*, rev. ed. (New Haven, Conn.: Yale University Press, 1969), ch. 2.

33. "The principle of government law," Simon notes, "is subject to such precarious conditions that, if it were not constantly reasserted, it soon would be destroyed by the opposite and complementary principle, viz., that of adequacy to contingent, changing, and unique circumstances." Yves R. Simon, *The Tradition of Natural Law: A Philosopher's Reflections,* ed. Vukan Kuic, intro. Russell Hittinger (New York: Fordham University Press, 1992 reprint, orig. 1965), 84.

34. Pontius Pilate, for example, is a *iudex inferior* under the authority of Caesar. Thus, Thomas reasons, he had no authority to lawfully remit punishment (*S.t.* II–II, 60.4).

35. *S.t.* II–II, 60.2.

36. *S.t.* II–II, 60.5.

37. *S.t.* II–II, 64.6.

38. Supra, note 34.

39. He may judge only according to what he "knows as a public person" (*S.t.* II–II, 67.2).

40. Ibid., ad 4.

41. *S.t.* I–II, 96.6.

42. *S.t.* II–II, 120.1.

43. *S.t.* I–II, 57.6 ad 3. Here, Thomas uses the expression *lex communis*, indicating the exercise of *gnome* within a legal framework; elsewhere he speaks of *communes regulas agendorum*, common rules of action (II–II, 51.4), indicating a broader scope of *gnome* in reaching a verdict about unusual facts.

44. *S.t.* II–II, 120.1 ad 1.

45. Ibid.

46. *S.t.* I–II, 96.6 ad 2.

47. *S.t.* II–II, 60.5 ad 2.

48. *S.t.* II–II, 120.1 ad 2.

49. *S.t.* I–II, 96.6. ad 2; II–II, 120.1 ad 2.

50. *S.t.* II–II, 60.5 ad 1.

51. *S.t.* I–II, 96.4.

52. *S.t.* I–II, 100.

CHAPTER FIVE: NATURAL RIGHTS, UNDER-SPECIFIED RIGHTS, AND BILLS OF RIGHTS

* This essay first appeared in the *Revue Générale de Droit* 29, no. 4 (1998): 449–64.

1. For a useful analysis of the traditional dictum, see Javier Hervada, *Natural Right and Natural Law: A Critical Introduction* (Pamplona: Servicio de publicaciones de la Universidad de Navarra), 1990, 19–45.

2. Ibid., 28*f*.

3. "Theft, murder, adultery, and all injuries, are forbidden by the laws of nature; but what is to be called *theft*, what *murder*, what *adultery*, what *injury* in a citizen, this is not to be determined by the natural, but by the civil law. For not every taking away of a thing which another possesseth, but only another man's goods, is theft: but what is ours, and what another's, is a question belonging to the civil law" (*De Cive* VI.16. Thomas Hobbes, *Man and Citizen*, ed. Bernard Gert [Indianapolis: Hackett Publishing Co., 1991], 185).

4. Thomas Aquinas summarizes this tradition when he says that the *ius* is suitably divided as (a) what arises *ex ipsa natura rei* (from the nature of the thing or case), (b) what arises *ex condicto, sive ex communi placito* (from agreement or consent); the latter ground of the *ius* is divided into what arises (c) *per aliquod privatum condictum* (from private agreement), and (d) *ex condicto publico* (from public agreement) (*S.t.* II–II, q. 57, a. 2). So, there is more than one ground of a *ius*. We might expect that in any relatively well-developed legal culture most *iura* are the creatures of human agreements at private and public law. The natural right tradition holds that there are *some* rights that follow from the very nature of the thing or the things to be considered.

5. Insofar as bills, charters, and declarations of rights also make some mention of the obligation of the state to protect the common good, as well as its obligation to eradicate manifestly unjust modes of commutation between private persons, presuppositions about natural or human rights likewise come to include notions of legal and commutative justice.

6. Heinrich Rommen, *The Natural Law: A Study in Legal and Social History and Philosophy* (Indianapolis: Liberty Press, 1998 reprint of 1947 ed.), 261.

7. *Olmstead v. United States*, 277 U.S. 438, 478 (1928) (Brandeis, J., dissenting).

8. U.N. International Covenant on Economic, Social, and Cultural Rights (1966), §11. *The Human Rights Reader*, ed. Micheline R. Ishay (New York: Routledge, 1997), 436.

9. William Blackstone, *Commentaries of the Laws of England*, facsimile of 1st ed. 1769, IV cap. 13 (Chicago: University of Chicago Press, 1979), vol. 4, p. 62.

10. James Wilson, "Opening Address at the Pennsylvania Ratifying Convention" (November 24,1787), in *The Debate on the Constitution*, 791 (New York: Library of America, 1993), 793.

11. Alexis de Toqueville, *Democracy in America*, ed. J. P. Mayer (New York: Doubleday-Anchor, 1969), 115.

12. *Federalist* 51. *The Federalist Papers* (London: Penguin Classics, 1987), 321.

13. The Fourteenth Amendment (1868) created federal supervisory and enforcement powers over some of the police powers of the state governments. Although the amendment did not make the federal government a government of general jurisdiction, it sowed the seeds for that transformation. For the power to supervise police

powers is, at least operationally, to have police powers. Since the police powers of the states are, as Madison said, "numerous and indefinable," the supervisory powers of the U.S. government will be enlarged accordingly. Once the Article III courts got into the business of incorporating the Bill of Rights against the states, it is not surprising that judges would feel compelled to introduce substantive moral principles.

14. *West Virginia State Board of Education v. Barnette,* 319 U.S. 624, 639*f*.

15. For studies on this part of the story, see R. Higgs, *Crisis and Leviathan: Critical Episodes in the Growth of American Government* (Oxford: Oxford University Press, 1989); H. Arkes, *The Return of George Sutherland* (Princeton, N.J.: Princeton University Press, 1994).

16. J. Story, *Commentaries on the Constitution,* Bk. III, ch. xliv (Durham: Carolina Academic Press, 1987), 979.

17. Federalist 84, *The Federalist Papers,* 477.

18. Ibid., 476.

19. Ibid., 475*f*.

20. These are what Wesley Hohfeld would call "liberties"; that is to say, the absence of a power or a right creates a zone in which others are free to act. W. N. Hohfeld, *Fundamental Legal Conceptions* (New Haven, Conn.: Yale University Press, 1919). So, for example, the First Amendment does not recognize a right of conscience. Rather, it declares a lack of congressional right or power over matters religious. Citizens, then, are free to exercise their religious conscience in the absence of congressional power. Now, it might be true that citizens, by the mere fact of being human, have a natural right to religious liberty. The First Amendment does not contradict that idea. But neither does it constitutionalize such a far-reaching and under-specified right as the right to free conscience.

21. *Planned Parenthood of Southeastern Pennsylvania v. Casey,* 112 S. Ct. 2791, 2807 (1992).

22. Simone Weil, "Human Personality," in *Selected Essays,* trans. Richard Rees (Oxford: Oxford University Press, 1962), 9–10.

23. Take, as another example, the recent U.N. Convention on the Rights of the Child. Article 12 asserts "that the child who is capable of forming his or her own views has the right to express those views freely in all matters affecting the child." Article 13 asserts "that the child shall have the right to seek, receive and impart information and ideas of all kinds, regardless of frontiers, either orally, in writing or in print, in the form of art, or through any other media of child's choice" (Convention on the Rights of the Child, November 20, 1989, 28 I.L.M. 1448, 1461). Moral desiderata are not the same thing as morally binding prescriptions, even if one tries to compel these desiderata into the rhetoric of moral prescriptions.

24. On the evolution of such generalized rights claims in U.S. constitutional law, see Russell Hittinger, "Liberalism and the American Natural Law Tradition," *Wake Forest Law Review* 25 (1990): 429–499.

25. Hence, the common good makes its appearance in the scheme of justice precisely at the point that the state can override rights. This is a predictable result of under-specified rights.

26. Speech at Columbus, Ohio (September 16, 1859), in *Lincoln: Speeches and Writings*

1859–1865 (New York: The Library of America, 1989), 53.

27. Address at Cooper Union (February 27, 1860), *Lincoln: Speeches and Writings*, 129.

28. Max Farrand, ed., *The Records of the Federal Convention of 1787*, rev. ed., 4 vols. (New Haven, Conn.: Yale University Press, 1937), II, 417.

29. I am indebted once again to Robert George for sharpening my understanding of this distinction.

CHAPTER SIX: PRIVATE USES OF LETHAL FORCE: THE CASE OF ASSISTED SUICIDE

* An earlier version of this chapter was first published in the *Loyola Law Review* 32 (1987): 1–28.

1. *Olmstead v. United States*, 277 U.S. 438, 478 (1928) (Brandeis, J., dissenting).

2. *Compassion in Dying v. Washington*, 49 F.3d, 586 (9th Cir. 1995), *reh'g en banc*, 79 F.3d, 790 (9th Cir.), and *cert. granted sub nom, Washington v Glucksberg*, 117 S. Ct. 37 (1996).

3. *Compassion in Dying*, 79 F.3d, 815–16 (Reinhardt, J.).

4. Wash. Rev. Code Ann. § 9A.36.060 (West 1988).

5. *Compassion in Dying v. Washington*, 850 F. Supp. 1454, 1467 (W.D. Wash. 1994).

6. 505 U.S. 833 (1992).

7. *Compassion in Dying*, 850 F. Supp., 1459–60 (quoting *Casey*, 505 U.S., 851).

8. *Casey*, 505 U.S., 851.

9. *Compassion in Dying*, 850 F. Supp., 1462–64. In *United States v. Salerno*, 481 U.S. 739 (1987), the Supreme Court defined facial challenges to the constitutionality of statutes: "A facial challenge to a [statute] is, of course, the most difficult challenge to mount successfully, since the challenger must establish that no set of circumstances exists under which the Act [or statute] would be valid. The fact that the [statute] might operate unconstitutionally under some conceivable set of circumstances is insufficient to render it wholly invalid . . ."(Ibid., 745). Whereas, when a plaintiff claims that a statute is unconstitutional "as applied": "[T]he plaintiff contends that application of the statute in the particular context in which he has acted, or in which he proposes to act, would be unconstitutional. The practical effect of holding a statute unconstitutional "as applied" is to prevent its future application in a similar context, but not to render it utterly inoperative" (*Ada v. Guam Soc'y of Obstetricians and Gynecologists*, 506 U.S. 1011, 1012 [1992], Scalia, J., dissenting from a denial of certiorari). In *Compassion in Dying*, the district court determined that the plaintiffs had brought a "facial challenge to the validity" of Washington's assisted suicide statute (850 F. Supp., 1462). However, the district court "conclude[d] that the *Casey* 'undue burden' standard, set forth by the Supreme Court five years after *Salerno*," applied in this case (Ibid.). Writing in dissent to the Ninth Circuit's *en banc* opinion, Judge Beezer questioned the application and extension of "*Casey*'s undue burden test beyond abortion cases" (*Compassion in Dying*, 79 F.3d, 843, Beezer, J., dissenting).

10. *Compassion in Dying*, 49 F.3d, 588, 594 (Noonan, J.).

11. Ibid., 590–92.

12. Ibid.

13. *Compassion in Dying*, 79 F.3d, 838.

14. Ibid., 803 (referring to *Compassion in Dying*, 49 F.3d, 594).

15. 410 U.S. 113 (1973).

16. Ibid., 153.

17. Ibid.

18. Ibid. These other enumerated harms included the stigma of unwed motherhood, the obligations of maternity, and familial economic distress (Ibid). In effect, a woman has a right not to be a mother in the sociological sense of the term. For my analysis of this point, see Russell Hittinger, "Liberalism and the American Natural Law Tradition," *Wake Forest Law Review* 25 (1990): 429, 459–65.

19. *Compassion in Dying*, 79 F.3d, 798–801.

20. Ibid., 812.

21. 330 U.S. 1 (1947).

22. Ibid., 15–18.

23. Ibid., 15

24. Ibid.

25. Ibid.

26. 370 U.S. 421 (1962).

27. Ibid., 424.

28. 403 U.S. 602 (1971).

29. Ibid., 612–13.

30. *Lee v. Weisman*, 505 U.S. 577, 589 (1992).

31. Ibid., 589–90.

32. *Compassion in Dying*, 79 F.3d, 839.

33. Ibid., 826.

34. 381 U.S. 479 (1965).

35. Ibid., 485–86.

36. 405 U.S. 438 (1972).

37. Ibid., 453.

38. 431 U.S. 678 (1977).

39. Ibid., 684 (quoting *Whalen v Roe*, 429 U.S. 589, 599–600 [1977]).

40. *Roe*, 410 U.S., 153.

41. Ibid., 159–63.

42. In his brief for respondents in *Compassion in Dying*, Laurence H. Tribe makes the interesting point that "[t]his case involves state interests of less weight than those at stake in *Casey*" (Brief for Respondents, 1996 WL 708925, ★30, *Compassion in Dying*, 79 F.3d 790 [9th Cir. 1996] [No. 96-110]). For in *Roe*, the Court did not deny that some life apart from the mother is being killed; in fact, the Court recognized some interest of the state in that life. Tribe writes: "It is the state interest in fetal life that makes the abortion cases so difficult. This case directly involves no life apart from that of the individual making the personal choice" (Ibid.).

43. 492 U. S. 490 (1989).

44. Ibid., 506–7.

45. In *Webster*, the plaintiffs challenged several provisions of a Missouri act that "amended existing state law concerning unborn children and abortions" (Ibid., 500). The act contained a preamble recognizing that "'[t]he life of each human being begins at conception,' and that 'unborn children have protectable interests in life, health, and well being'" (Ibid., 501) (quoting Mo. Rev. Stat. §1.205.1(1), (2) [West 1986]). The

Court did not invalidate this preamble for the simple reason that it was not actionable; no woman's right to choose had been restricted by the preamble (Ibid., 506–7).

46. *Casey,* 505 U.S., 876–77.
47. Ibid., 873.
48. Ibid., 846.
49. Ibid., 851.
50. *Roe,* 410 U.S., 153.
51. See supra notes 6–8 and accompanying text.
52. *Compassion in Dying,* 49 F.3d, 590–91 (citations omitted).
53. Ibid.
54. See Judge Beezer's dissent in *Compassion in Dying,* 79 F.3d, 847–57.
55. See *United States v. Seeger,* 380 U.S. 163 (1965).
56. *Compassion in Dying,* 49 F.3d, 590–91.
57. Ibid. In his brief for the United States, the Solicitor General argued that gender separates the liberty "right" in *Casey* from the liberty "interest" in *Compassion in Dying:* "The right to choose an abortion thus implicates the liberty of a woman 'in a sense unique to the human condition and so unique to the law'" (Amicus Brief for the United States, 1996 WL 663185, 15, *Compassion in Dying,* 79 F.3d 790 [9th Cir. 1996] [No. 96-110] [citing *Casey,* 505 U.S., 852]). Like Judge Noonan, the Solicitor General believed that the decisional liberty asserted in *Casey* is too broad, and that it ought to be limited to reproductive liberty (Amicus Brief, 1996 WL 663185, 15). However, he provided a specific principle of limitation on the basis of gender and equal protection:

> Terminal illness does not single out any discrete or insular minority; it potentially affects all Americans—all races, both genders, and every income group. All legislators must face the possibility that they will one day suffer from a terminal illness; there are no immunities from that fate. There is, in sum, no constitutional basis for preempting the continuing legislative reexamination of the urgent issues involved in this case (Ibid., 27).

Thus, it seems that only women—and perhaps other discrete or insular minorities—have the constitutionally protected "right to define one's own concept of existence, of meaning, of the universe, and of the mystery of human life" (*Casey,* 505 U.S., 851).

The Solicitor General's position can be questioned on two points. First, the gender analysis is prominent only in the second part of the joint opinion of *Casey,* where the Court seeks not to define the liberty right in relation to its precedents in the case law, but rather to explain the application of *stare decisis* to the case. In answer to the question of why *Roe* should not be overturned, the authors of the joint opinion in *Casey* give two reasons: the first is the meaning of constitutionally protected "liberty," the second is the reliance of women on the abortion right (*Casey,* 505 U.S., 851). In *Casey,* the Court does not say that the first depends upon the second. Second, the train of privacy cases, beginning with *Griswold* and *Eisenstadt,* does not limit decisional autonomy to reproduction or to gender. In his brief for the respondents in *Compassion in Dying,* Laurence Tribe accurately points out that the train of privacy cases never limited individual autonomy to reproduction or to gender equality:

> The Solicitor General's argument that abortion precedent is premised on principles of gender equality is inaccurate. While the Court recognized an equality component in liberty, which is also important here, the Court has always found the right of reproductive choice to be protected as a matter of human liberty, and not just as a matter of gender equality. (Respondents' Brief, 1996 WL 708925, *20 n.11)

58. *Compassion in Dying,* 79 F.3d, 799.

59. Ibid., 816.

60. Ibid., 817–20

61. On this point, consider Justice Stevens's dissenting opinion in *Cruzan,* which is cited in passing, but not exploited, by Judge Reinhardt.

> The State's unflagging determination to perpetuate Nancy Cruzan's physical existence is comprehensible only as an effort to define life's meaning, not as an attempt to preserve its sanctity.... Yet, "[a]lthough the State may properly perform a teaching function," and although that teaching may foster respect for the sanctity of life, the State may not pursue its project by infringing constitutionally protected interests for "symbolic effect." (*Cruzan,* 497 U.S., 345, 350–51 [Stevens, J., dissenting] [quoting *Carey,* 431 U.S., 715 (Stevens, J. concurring)])

In other words, the decisional liberties discovered by the Court in the sexual/abortion cases require the state to defer to the individual on the issue of the "meaning" of life. The state may declare its own view of the matter, but may not impose its view to the detriment of individual liberty, unless, of course, it shows a compelling interest. The mere declaration, as a sort of teaching function of the state, is not a compelling interest. As for the problem of homicide, Stevens writes: "The laws punishing homicide, upon which the Court relies . . . do not support a contrary inference. Obviously, such laws protect both the life *and* interests of those who would otherwise be victims" (*Cruzan,* 497 U.S. 347). The key to homicide, then, is the absence of consent.

62. *Compassion in Dying,* 79 F.3d, 828.

63. 80 F.3d 716 (2d Cir.), *cert. granted,* 117 S. Ct. 36 (1996).

64. Ibid., 731.

65. Ibid., 729.

66. Ibid., 730 (quoting *Casey,* 505 U.S., 851).

67. Ibid.

68. *Compassion in Dying,* 79 F.3d, 820.

69. Ibid., 825–26.

70. Ibid.

71. Ibid., 826.

72. Ibid., 851 (Beezer, J., dissenting) (citing *In re* Guardianship of Grant, 747 P.2d 445, 451 [Wash. 1987]; In re Colyer, 660 P.2d 738, 743 [Wash. 1983]).

73. Amicus Brief, 1996 WL 663185, *9.

74. *Compassion in Dying,* 49 F.3d, 588.

75. Ibid., 594.

76. Locke, *Second Treatise of Government.*

77. Locke stated that:

> [t]he State of Nature has a Law of Nature to govern it which obliges every one, and Reason, which is that Law, teaches all Mankind who will but consult it; That being all equal and independent, no one ought to harm another in his Life, Health, Liberty or Possessions; for Men being all the Workmanship of one Omnipotent and infinitely wise Maker; All the Servants of one Sovereign Master, sent into the World by his order and about his business, they are his Property, whose Workmanship they are, made to last during his, not one anothers Pleasure. And being furnished with like Faculties, sharing all in one Community of Nature, there cannot be supposed any such Subordination among us, that may Authorize us to destroy one another, as if we were made for one anothers uses, as the inferior ranks of Creatures are for ours, every one as he is bound to preserve himself, and not to quit his Station wilfully, so by the like reason when his own Preservation comes not in competition, ought he as much as he can to preserve the rest of Mankind, and not unless it be to do Justice on an Offender, take away, or impair the life, or what tends to the Preservation of the Life, the Liberty, Health, Limb, or Goods of another. (Locke, *Second Treatise of Government,* §6)

78. "No body can give more Power than he has himself, and he that cannot take away his own Life, cannot give another power over it." Locke, *Second Treatise of Government,* §23.

79. To understand Locke at a proper level of detail and complexity, we would not sidestep his position on suicide. However, I do not pretend here to expound Locke's philosophy for its own sake.

80. Locke expressed it this way:

> I doubt not but it will be objected That it is unreasonable for Men to be Judges in their own Cases, that Self-love will make Men *partial* to themselves and their Friends. And on the other side, Ill-Nature, Passion and Revenge will carry them too far in punishing others. And hence nothing but Confusion and Disorder will follow, and that therefore God hath certainly appointed *Government to restrain the partiality and violence* of Men. I easily grant that Civil Government is the proper Remedy for the Inconveniences of the State of Nature, which must certainly be Great where Men may be *Judges in their own Case* . . . . (Locke, *Second Treatise of Government,* §13 [emphasis added])

81. "For every one in that State being both Judge and Executioner of the Law of Nature, Men being partial to themselves, Passion and Revenge is very apt to carry them too far, and with too much heat in their own Cases, as well as negligence and unconcernedness, make them too remiss in other Mens" (Ibid., §125). The County of Milwaukee made a similar observation in its amicus brief in *Compassion,* noting that violent crimes and abuses are often perpetrated by friends and family members:

> The Milwaukee County District Attorney's Office charges about 135 homicides each year, and in about two-thirds of these the killer is related to or knows the victim. Nationally, only about 25 percent of homicide victims are known to be killed by strangers. In many cases, there are no eyewitnesses to the killing itself, a fact which makes the prospect of having to prove absence of consent in a homicide prosecution quite problematic. (Amicus Brief of Milwaukee County, 1996 WL 657807, *2 [citation omitted], *Compassion in Dying,* 79 F.3d, 790 [9th Cir. 1996] [No. 96-110])

82. Locke, *Second Treatise of Government*, §87.

83. "The Power that every individual gave the Society, when he entered into it, can never revert to the Individuals again, as long as the Society lasts, but will always remain in the Community; because without this, there can be no Community—no [commonwealth], which is contrary to the original agreement . . ." (Ibid., §243).

84. To put the matter in another way, we might say that when public powers are concerned, there can be no such thing as victimless wrongdoing. The state (the "people") are always wronged whenever a person acts *ultra vires*. Thus, when a public power is usurped, we do not have to track down injuries to private parties to make the case against the usurper.

85. This point is made in the amicus brief of Milwaukee County:

> "[A] criminal offense is a wrong affecting the general public, at least indirectly, and consequently cannot be licensed by the individual directly harmed. Thus, it is no defense to a charge of murder that the victim, upon learning of the defendant's homicidal intentions, furnished the defendant with the gun and ammunition." (Amicus Brief, 1996 WL 657807, *11 [quoting Wayne R. LaFave & Austin W. Scott Jr., Criminal Law, 687 §5.11(a) [2d ed., 1986]])

86. The reduction of legal to commutative justice is rhetorically reflected in Laurence Tribe's remark that "[t]he State has a strong interest in protecting against usurpation of the dying patient's wishes by others" (Respondents' Brief, 1996 WL 708925, *31). A "usurpation" is the unjust taking of public authority. By suggesting that it applies to commutative justice at private law, Tribe turns the concept of usurpation upside down.

87. 494 U.S. 210 (1990).

88. Ibid., 231–32.

89. Ibid., 215–16.

90. *Harper v. Washington*, 759 P.2d 358, 364–65 (Wash. 1988).

91. *Parham v. J. R.*, 442 U.S. 584 (1979). In *Parham*, the Court held that a judicial hearing was not required prior to the involuntary commitment of a child to a mental hospital (Ibid., 613). In *Parham*, however, the Court did not have to reckon with the problem of a patient competent to give or withhold consent, nor with the problem of physicians having to make judgments about interests other than those of the patient.

92. *Harper*, 494 U.S., 231 (citing *Parham*, 442 U.S., 607).

93. *Harper*, 494 U.S., 237 (Stevens, J., dissenting).

94. See supra text accompanying note 1.

95. *Harper*, 494 U.S., 250–58 (Stevens, J., dissenting).

96. *Compassion in Dying*, 79 F.3d, 820.

CHAPTER EIGHT: A CRISIS OF LEGITIMACY (INCLUDING A RESPONSE TO CRITICS)

* The first part of this chapter originally appeared in *First Things* (November 1996): 25–29. "A Response to Critics" was published in the *Loyola Law Review* 44 (spring 1998): 83–101.

1. 60 U.S. (19 How.) 393 (1856), superseded by U.S. Constitution Amendments XIII and XIV.

2. Abraham Lincoln, Speech at Columbus, Ohio (September 16, 1859), in *Lincoln: Speeches and Writings 1859–1865* (New York: The Library of America, 1989), 53.

3. Ibid.

4. David Brooks, "The Right's Anti-American Temptation," *Weekly Standard,* November 11, 1996, 26.

5. Ibid.

6. Ibid.

7. Ibid.

8. Symposium, "On the Future of Conservatism: A Symposium," *Commentary* 103 (February 1997): 14.

9. Ibid.

10. Ibid.

11. Ibid.

12. Ibid.

13. Ibid.

14. Ibid.

15. 505 U.S. 833 (1992).

16. Gerard V. Bradley, "The New Constitutional Covenant," *The World & I,* March 1994, 375.

17. See, e.g., *Cooper v. Aaron,* 358 U.S. 1 (1958); *Dred Scott v. Sandford,* 60 U.S. 393 (1857); *Marbury v. Madison,* 5 U.S. 137 (1803).

18. *Olmstead v. United States,* 277 U.S. 438, 478 (1928) (Brandeis J., dissenting).

19. In *Washington v. Glucksberg,* 117 S. Ct. 2258 (1997), Chief Justice Rehnquist refused to extend the *Casey* dictum about liberty to the issue of physician-assisted suicide. See *Casey,* 505 U.S., 851 ("At the heart of liberty is the right to define one's own concept of existence, of meaning, of the universe, and of the mystery of human life. Beliefs about these matters could not define the attributes of personhood were they formed under compulsion of the State."). With respect to the *Casey* dictum, Rehnquist stated that "Casey described, . . . in light of our prior cases, those personal activities and decisions that this Court has identified as so deeply rooted in our history and traditions, or so fundamental to our concept of constitutionally ordered liberty, that they are protected by the Fourteenth Amendment" (*Washington,* 117 S. Ct. at 2271). He concluded that "many of the rights and liberties protected by the due process clause found in personal autonomy does not warrant the sweeping conclusion that any and all important, intimate, and personal decisions are so protected" (Ibid.). Yet this is not a repudiation of the *Casey* dictum; it only puts the brakes on its application to physician-assisted suicide. And it leaves completely untouched the *Casey* dicta about the social contract.

20. Here, I rely upon the useful discussion of this matter in Paul A. Rahe, *Republics Ancient & Modern: Classical Republicanism and the American Revolution* (Chapel Hill, N.C.: University of North Carolina Press, 1992), 8–13.

21. *Casey,* 505 U.S., 853.

22. Ibid.

23. 410 U.S. 113 (1973).

24. *Casey,* 505 U.S., 865 (emphasis added).

25. Ibid., 845–46.
26. 381 U.S. 479 (1986).
27. 410 U.S., 113.
28. *Casey*, 505 U.S., 847.
29. Ibid., 851.
30. Ibid.
31. As the authors of the joint opinion wrote: "It will be recognized, of course, that *Roe* stands at an intersection of two lines of decisions, but in whichever doctrinal category one reads the case, the result for present purposes will be the same. *Roe*, however, may be seen not only as an exemplar of *Griswold* liberty but as a rule (whether or not mistaken) of personal autonomy and bodily integrity, with doctrinal affinity to cases recognizing limits on governmental power to mandate medical treatment or to bar its rejection. If so, our cases since *Roe* accord with *Roe*'s view that a State's interest in the protection of life falls short of justifying any plenary override of individual liberty claims" (Ibid., 857).
32. 163 U.S. 537 (1896).
33. 347 U.S. 483 (1954).
34. 198 U.S. 45 (1905).
35. 300 U.S. 379 (1937).
36. *Casey*, 505 U.S., 856. As the joint opinion noted:

> Abortion is customarily chosen as an unplanned response to the consequence of unplanned activity or to the failure of conventional birth control, and except on the assumption that no intercourse would have occurred but for *Roe*'s holding, such behavior may appear to justify no reliance claim . . . . To eliminate the issue of reliance that easily, however, one would need to limit cognizable reliance to specific instances of sexual activity. But to do this would be simply to refuse to face the fact that for two decades of economic and social developments, people have organized intimate relationships and made choices that define their views of themselves and their places in society, in reliance on the availability of abortion in the event that contraception should fail. The ability of women to participate equally in the economic and social life of the Nation has been facilitated by their ability to control their reproductive lives. (Ibid., 856)

37. Ibid.
38. Ibid.
39. I freely borrow the term from John Rawls, who explains that the Supreme Court is "the exemplar of public reason" John Rawls, *Political Liberalism* (New York: Columbia University Press, 1993), 236. My use of the term emphasizes the implicitly despotic character of exemplarism. Its ideological and historical precedents are Continental (Rousseauian). The traditional doctrine of participation has always emphasized the plurality of authority under the natural law.
40. *Casey*, 505 U.S., 866–87 (emphasis added).
41. Ibid., 865.
42. Bradley, "The New Constitutional Covenant," 374.
43. 5 U.S. 137 (1803).
44. 358 U.S. 1 (1958).

45. *Marbury*, 5 U.S., 137.
46. *Cooper*, 358 U.S., 1.
47. *Marbury*, 5 U.S., 177–78.
48. Lincoln, First Inaugural Address (March 4, 1861), in *Lincoln: Speeches and Writings*, 220–21 (emphasis added).
49. *Cooper*, 358 U.S., 18.
50. Ibid., 23.
51. *Casey*, 505 U.S., 868 (emphasis added).
52. *Casey*, 505 U.S., 833. Rawls maintains that "[t]he constitution is not what the Court says it is. Rather, it is what the people acting constitutionally through the other branches eventually allow the Court to say it is" (Rawls, *Political Liberalism*, 237). On its face, this seems very close to the *Casey* doctrine. He goes on to suggest that the people, acting through Article V, could not amend the First Amendment, without revolution (Ibid., 238–39). Would the same be true if the people amended the Constitution to remediate a judicial mistake?
53. *Casey*, 505 U.S., 864. "In constitutional adjudication as elsewhere in life, changed circumstances may impose new obligations, and the thoughtful part of the Nation could accept each decision to overrule a prior case as a response to the Court's constitutional duty" (Ibid.).
54. 117 S. Ct., 2157 (1997).
55. 42 U.S.C. §2000(b) (1994).
56. *Boerne*, 117 S. Ct., 2157.
57. 494 U.S. 872 (1990).
58. Ibid., 877–82.
59. See *Boerne*, 117 S. Ct., 2158.
60. *Boerne*, 117 S. Ct., 2172.
61. Brooks, "The Right's Anti-American Temptation," 26.
62. See ibid.
63. *Casey*, 505 U.S., 864.

Chapter Nine: *Dignitatis Humanae*, Religious Liberty, and Ecclesiastical Self-Government

* This chapter appeared in the *George Washington University Law Journal* (July/Sept. 2000): 1035–58.
1. Throughout this essay, I use the upper case for the word Church because I shall be speaking specifically of the Roman Catholic Church.
2. "[B]y divine ordinance, the Roman church possesses a pre-eminence of ordinary power over every other church, and this jurisdictional power of the Roman pontiff is both episcopal and immediate." *Pastor Aeternus* (1870), §3. See also Robert A. Graham, *Vatican Diplomacy: A Study of Church and State on the International Plane* (Princeton, N.J.: Princeton University Press, 1959), 215.
3. It is worth bearing in mind that religions and churches fared differently in post-Napoleonic Europe. Jews, for example, were liberated from the political and legal vestiges of the older Christendom. While it is dangerous to generalize, it can be said that Protestants were not so affected by the move to national churches, for this was

their experience before the revolutions. Catholicism, however, was hit hard—not only in the material sense of having lost properties and monasteries; nor only in the political sense of having ecclesiastical government interrupted or suppressed; but also in the spiritual and theological sense, for the doctrines of state supremacy contradicted the Church's understanding of its own origin, nature, and mission.

4. Pius IX, *Quanta Cura* (1864). Two propositions relating to broad cosmological questions (nos. 1, 2); nineteen relating to authority of human reason and Indifferentism in its moral mode (nos. 3, 4, 6–12, 14–18, 56–60); six on progress and culture (nos. 5, 12, 13, 32, 40, 80); fifty-nine relating to specific church-state issues and political morality (nos. 15, 19, 20, 23–38, 39–55, 57–71, 73–80); and five on ecclesiology (nos. 21, 22, 35, 38, 72). By my count, only seven of the propositions are *not* related to the issue of Church and state.

5. Augsburg *Allgemeine Zeitung* (January 21, 1870). Leaked by Döllinger. See also Émile Ollivier, *L'Église et l'État au Concile du Vatican*, 3rd ed., vol. 2 (Paris: Garnier Frères, 1877), 46–48.

6. Mansi (Ioannes Dominicus), Sacrorum Conciliorum (Nova et Amplissima Collectio). Tom. 51. Arnhem (Pays-Bas) and Leipzig (1926). Primum Schema Constitutionis *De Ecclesia Christi*, 539–554. Chaps. X–XV, 543–551; canons I–XXI, 551–553.

7. The one untroubled relation was with the United States. In 1783, the Apostolic Nuncio in France, via Benjamin Franklin, asked the Second Continental Congress for permission to establish a Vicar apostolate and to reorganize dioceses in America. In effect, he was asking Congress to exercise the ancient privilege of the *placet*. Congress wrote back:

> That Dr. Franklin be desired to notify to the Apostolical Nuncio at Versailles that Congress will always be pleased to testify their respect to his sovereign and State; but that the subject of his application to Dr. Franklin, being purely spiritual, is without the jurisdiction and powers of Congress, who have no authority to permit or refuse it, these powers being reserved to the several states individually. (Robert Graham, *Vatican Diplomacy*, 336.)

8. See ibid., 228. See generally *Quod Apostolici muneris* (1878); *Diuturnum* (1881); *Immortale Dei* (1885); *Officio Sanctissimo* (1887); *Libertas* (1888); *Praeclara gratulationis* (1894).

9. A concordat is a public treaty between the Church and state regulating relations in some area of mutual concern. Most likely, the first concordat was the Concordat of Worms (1122), which tried to settle the Investiture Controversy. For a reliable study of the concordats, see generally Graham, *Vatican Diplomacy*. The 1801 Concordat was the model for the nineteenth-century concordat policy. See William Roberts, "Napoleon, the Concordat of 1801, and Its Consequences," in *Controversial Concordats*, ed. Frank J. Coppa (Washington, D.C.: The Catholic University of America Press, 1999), 34–80.

10. In the 1944 address, the following lines were particularly important:

> Moreover [and this is perhaps the most important point] beneath the sinister lightning of the war that encompasses them, in the blazing heat of the furnace that imprisons them, the peoples have, as it were, awakened from a long torpor. They have assumed, in relation to the state and those who govern, a new atti-

tude—one that questions, criticizes, distrusts. Taught by bitter experience, they are more aggressive in opposing the concentration of dictatorial power that cannot be censured or touched, and call for a system of government more in keeping with the dignity and liberty of the citizens . . . to avoid for the future the repetition of such a catastrophe, we must vest efficient guarantees in the people itself . . . . If, then, we consider the extent and nature of the sacrifices demanded of all the citizens, especially in our day when the activity of the state is so vast and decisive, the democratic form of government appears to many as a postulate of nature imposed by reason itself. (Pius XII, Christmas Address, True and False Democracy [*Benignitas et humanitas*] (1944), AAS/37 (1945), 13.)

This address is cited at the outset of *Dignitatis Humanae* §1 n.1.

11. Pius XII is cited no less than seven times in *Dignitatis Humanae*.

12. The final tally: *Placet* 2308, *Non placet* 70.

13. See generally Michael Davies, *The Second Vatican Council and Religious Liberty* (Long Prairie, Minn.: Neumann Press, 1992) (presenting a sympathetic survey of objections, both on the Left and the Right). See also Brian Harrison, *Religious Liberty and Contraception* (Melbourne, Australia: John XXIII Fellowship Co-op, Ltd., 1988) (creating a more critical survey of the same range of opinions). The most complete account of the history and doctrine of *Dignitatis* is the six-volume study by Fr. Basile, O.S.B., *La liberté religieuse et la tradition catholique. Un cas de développement homogène dans le magistère authentique*, 6 vols. (Abbaye Sainte-Madeleine du Barroux, 1998).

14. See generally Richard J. Regan, *Conflict and Consensus: Religious Freedom and the Second Vatican Council* (New York: Macmillan, 1967), 147 (presenting an earlier work by a disciple of John Courtney Murray). See also John T. Noonan Jr., "Development in Moral Doctrine," in *Theological Studies* 54 (1993): 662–77.

15. *Dignitatis Humanae* is a *declaratio*, which differs from a *constitutio* and a *decretum*. Constitutions and decrees have binding force upon the whole Church. A declaration, on the other hand, is reserved for matters and persons who are not under the public law of the Church. Hence, the document on non-Christian religions (*Nostra Aetate*, 1965) is also called a *declaratio*.

16. See generally Ernst H. Kantorowicz, *The King's Two Bodies: A Study in Mediaeval Political Theology* (Princeton, N.J.: Princeton University Press, 1957).

17. See generally David Nicholls, *Deity and Domination: Images of God and the State in the Nineteenth and Twentieth Centuries* (London; New York: Routledge, 1989). See also Frances A. Yates, *Astraea: The Imperial Theme in the Sixteenth Century* (London; Boston: Routledge & K. Paul, 1975) (examining the evolving doctrines of political theology in modernity).

18. See *Immortale Dei* (1885), §21

There was once a time when States were governed by the philosophy of the Gospel. Then it was that the power and divine virtue of Christian wisdom had diffused itself throughout the laws, institutions, and morals of the people, permeating all ranks and relations of civil society. Then, too, the religion instituted by Jesus Christ, established firmly in befitting dignity, flourished everywhere, by the favor of princes and the legitimate protection of magistrates; and Church and State were happily united in concord and friendly interchange of good offices. The State, constituted in this wise, bore fruits important beyond all expectation.

19. Translation of conciliar documents from *Sacrosantum Oecumenicum Conclium Vaticanum II: Constitutiones, Decreta, Declarationes* (1993) [hereinafter *CDD*].

20. *Catechism of the Catholic Church* §2105. In the material quoted, the *Catechism* notes *Dignitatis Humanae* §1, *Immortale Dei,* and *Quas Primas.* Undoubtedly, the three are cited together to emphasize their continuity.

21. The second part of *Dignitatis Humanae* (§§ 9–15), under the heading *Libertas religiosa sub luce Revelationis,* focuses specifically on the liberty of the Church. In §12 of his first encyclical, *Redemptoris Hominis* (1979), John Paul II contended that the two parts be read together. The civil right is grounded in human dignity, not only as it is understood at the historical and philosophical plane, but also in the light of what the Church understands about herself.

> By Christ's institution the Church is its guardian and teacher, having been endowed with a unique assistance of the Holy Spirit in order to guard and teach it in its most exact integrity. In fulfilling this mission, we look towards Christ himself, the first evangelizer, and also towards his Apostles, martyrs and confessors. The *Declaration on Religious Freedom* shows us convincingly that, when Christ and, after him, his Apostles proclaimed the truth that comes not from men but from God ('My teaching is not mine, but his who sent me', that is the Father's), they preserved, while acting with their full force of spirit, a deep esteem for man, for his intellect, his will, his conscience and his freedom. Thus the human person's dignity itself becomes part of the content of that proclamation, being included not necessarily in words but by an attitude towards it. This attitude seems to fit the special needs of our times. Since man's true freedom is not found in everything that the various systems and individuals see and propagate as freedom, the Church, because of her divine mission, becomes all the more the guardian of this freedom, which is the condition and basis for the human person's true dignity. (§34)

22. See *Planned Parenthood v. Casey,* 505 U.S. 833 (1992). ("At the heart of liberty is the right to define one's own concept of existence, of meaning, of the universe and of the mystery of human life. Beliefs about these matters could not define the attributes of personhood were they formed under compulsion of the State.")

23. James Madison, "Memorial and Remonstrance against Religious Assessments" (1785), reprinted in *Church and State in the Modern Age: A Documentary History,* ed. J. F. Maclear (New York: Oxford University Press, 1995), 60. The Memorial and Remonstrance, directed against a pending bill in the Virginia General Assembly, formed no part of the U.S. Constitution or the Bill of Rights (Ibid., 59). It was only after the Second World War that the Supreme Court made Madison's Remonstrance an interpretive key to First Amendment jurisprudence. See *Everson v Board of Education,* 330 U.S. 1, 12 (1947).

24. Of the many uses of Wisdom 8.1 by Thomas, see *Summa contra gentiles* III.97; *Summa Theologiae* I 22.2, and 103.8; I-II, 110.2; II-II, 23.2, and 161.1.

25. Here, *Dignitatis Humanae* §2 cites §7 of Pius XI's encyclical against the Nazis, *Mit Brennender Sorge:* "Whoever follows that so-called pre-Christian Germanic conception of substituting a dark and impersonal destiny for the personal God, denies thereby the Wisdom and Providence of God who reacheth from end to end mightily, and ordereth all things sweetly."

26. It is the same position argued in *Gaudium et Spes* §16, where conscience is said to be a *sacrarium*, a holy place: "For man has in his heart a law inscribed by God. His dignity lies in observing this law, and by it he will be judged. His conscience is man's most secret core, and his sanctuary. There he is alone with God whose voice echoes in his depths." This teaching is reiterated by John Paul II in *Veritatis Splendor*:

> Saint Bonaventure teaches that 'conscience is like God's herald and messenger; it does not command things on its own authority, but commands them as coming from God's authority, like a herald when he proclaims the edict of the king. This is why conscience has binding force.' Thus it can be said that conscience bears witness to man's own rectitude or iniquity to man himself but, together with this and indeed even beforehand, conscience is *the witness of God himself*, whose voice and judgment penetrate the depths of man's soul, calling him *fortiter et suaviter* to obedience. (§58)

27. Still, critics complain that *Dignitatis Humanae* adopts an emaciated liberal notion of public order. To set things absolutely clear, the *Catechism of the Catholic Church*, at §2109, states:

> The right to religious liberty can of itself be neither unlimited nor limited only by a 'public order' conceived in a positivist or naturalist manner. The 'due limits' which are inherent in it must be determined for each social situation by political prudence, according to the requirements of the common good . . . .

To emphasize continuity with previous teachings, the *Catechism* cites Pius VI, *Quod aliquantum* (1791) and Pius IX, *Quanta Cura* (1864).

28. The issue of public order, or what American jurisprudence would call "compelling state interest," has a long and troubled history in Catholic relations with modern states. The first article of the 1801 Concordat with Napoleon reads: "The Catholic, Apostolic, and Roman religion shall be freely practi[c]ed in France; its worship shall be public, in conformity with police regulations which the Government shall judge to be necessary for public tranquility." *Church and State through the Centuries: A Collection of Historic Documents with Commentaries,* ed. and trans. Sidney Z. Ehler and John B. Morall (Westminster, Md.: Newman Press, 1954), 252. From the outset, the Vatican argued that Article 1 was an all-purpose instrument for governmental regulation of the Church.

29. 343 U.S. 306 (1952).

30. 406 U.S. 205 (1972).

31. See ibid., 234–35 n.22; *Zorach,* 343 U.S., 314. The better comparison is to the Champaign program, which was ruled unconstitutional in *McCollum v. Board of Education,* 333 U.S. 203, 210–11 (1948).

32. 330 U.S. 1 (1947).

33. 403 U.S. 602 (1971).

34. See ibid., 612–13.

35. This problem was noted by Justice Potter Stewart in his concurring opinion in *Sherbert v. Verner,* 374 U.S. 398, 413–18 (1963) (Stewart, J., concurring). In *Sherbert,* a Sabbatarian was denied unemployment benefits because she was unable to work on Saturdays for religious reasons (Ibid., 399). The majority agreed that the free exercise

clause required the state to accommodate her religious beliefs, but the problem of a conflict between the two clauses was apparent. See ibid., 409–10 (Stewart, J., concurring). The separationist logic enjoins government from favoring, aiding, promoting, or cognizing religion, while the free exercise clause commands government to accommodate religious belief, even in the instance of a law or policy that the state is otherwise entitled to make. See ibid., 414–15. Justice Stewart noted: "And the result is that there are many situations where legitimate claims under the Free Exercise Clause will run into head-on collision with the Court's insensitive and sterile construction of the establishment clause" (Ibid., 414).

36. See, e.g., *City of Boerne v. Flores,* 521 U.S. 507, 536–37 (1997) (Stevens, J. concurring). In response to Congress's bid to codify a broader interpretation of the free exercise clause, requiring government to show compelling state interest when its otherwise valid laws impair free exercise of religion, Justice Stevens said:

> In my opinion, the Religious Freedom Restoration Act of 1993 (RFRA) is a "law respecting an establishment of religion" that violates the First Amendment to the Constitution. . . . Whether the Church would actually prevail under the statute or not, the statute has provided the Church with a legal weapon that no atheist or agnostic can obtain. This governmental preference for religion, as opposed to irreligion, is forbidden by the First Amendment. (Ibid.)

The free exercise clause does suggest that religious liberty enjoys special constitutional favor and protection. U.S. Constitution Amendment I.

37. See, e.g., *Rosenberger v. Rector,* 515 U.S. 819 (1995); *Capital Square Review Bd. v. Pinette,* 515 U.S. 753 (1995); *Lamb's Chapel v. Center,* 508 U.S. 384 (1993); *Widmar v. Vincent,* 454 U.S. 263 (1981); see also *Chandler v. James,* 180 F.3d 1254, 1265 (11th Cir. 1999) (noting that "government violates the First Amendment when it denies access to a speaker solely to suppress the point of view he espouses. Suppression of religious speech constitutes viewpoint discrimination, the most egregious form of content-based censorship."). Significantly, the court in *Chandler* held that while the First Amendment protects free speech against content discrimination, the Constitution forbids religiously proselytizing speech by private parties in public schools (Ibid. Hence, the specifically and substantively "religious" aspect of speech is still intercepted by the separationist logic.

38. Fr. Basile's study has best covered the reason for and implications of dropping the phrase *ineptam esse*. See *La liberté religieuse et la tradition catholique,* particularly vol. I/B, 613*ff*, and 584, where he correctly concludes that the state's limit is "*une incompétence juridictionnelle en aval, non une incompétence gnoséologique en amont*" (a jurisdictional incompetence as to the source, not an epistemological incompetence downstream from the source"). This is classic higher law doctrine. For to say that there is an authority higher than the state implies a jurisdictional limit, but not necessarily an epistemological deficit.

39. Wilhelm Emmanuel von Ketteler, "Freedom, Authority, and the Church," in *The Social Teachings of Wilhelm Emmanuel von Ketteler: Bishop of Mainz,* trans. Rupert J. Ederer (Washington, D.C.: University Press of America, 1981), 145.

40. Ibid.

41. Lucius Annaeus Seneca, *Moral Essays,* trans. John W. Bacone (William Heinenmann,

Ltd., 1928), 357.

42. Von Ketteler, "Freedom, Authority, and the Church," 141.

43. The long background referred to is the *cuius regio* doctrine that the church is established in the state. Closer to the historical foreground is a variant of this position. The French Separation Law (9 December 1905) unilaterally abrogated the 1801 Concordat. See "Separation of Church and State in France: Law of December 9, 1905," in Ehler and Morall, eds., *Church and State through the Centuries*, 355–71. The most important and controversial portions of the Law (§§18–24) transferred practical administration of the Church into the hands of associations of laymen. See ibid. §§18–24, 366–68. In his encyclical *Vehementer Nos*, Pius X objected that the Law "despoils the Church of the internal regulation of the churches in order to invest the State with this function . . . " (Pius X, *Vehementer Nos* §9). Despite the language of "Separation," the Law tried to effect the same result as the older *cuius regio* regimes without a formal state "confession."

44. Graham, *Vatican Diplomacy*, 278. In Bavaria, for example, Maximilian taught: "The doctrine of the two powers is a monstrosity of priestly ambition. The church is in the state and not the state in the church" (Ibid., 278).

45. *Officio Sanctissimo* (1887), §13.

46. John Courtney Murray, "The Issue of Church and State at Vatican II," *Theological Studies* 27 (1966): 580–606, reprinted in *Religious Liberty: Catholic Struggles with Pluralism*, ed. J. Leon Hooper (Louisville, Ky.: Westminster/John Knox Press, 1993), 207.

47. See Graham, *Vatican Diplomacy*, 228–32, for a discussion of Cardinal Tarquini's influence upon canon law.

48. Complaining that the title to freedom is reduced to that of other associations, Leo XIII noted in *Immortale Dei* §27 that "the Catholic religion is allowed a standing in civil society equal only, or inferior, to societies alien from it; no regard is paid to the laws of the Church, and she who, by the order and commission of Jesus Christ . . . ."

49. See Pius XII, "Allocution, Juridical Jurisdiction of the Church: Its Origin and Nature," in *The Canon Law Digest: Officially Published Documents Affecting the Code of Canon Law 1942–1953, vol. 3*, trans. T. Lincoln Bouscaren (1954), 587–93. See also Pius XII, "Allocution, Juridical Power of the Church Compared with that of the State," in *Canon Law Digest, vol. 3*, 593–99.

50. As late as the papal conclave of 1903, three states asserted the right to veto papal elections. Indeed, at that conclave, Franz Josef of Austria, via Cardinal Puzyna, Bishop of Krakow, exercised the veto to prevent the election of Cardinal Rampolla.

51. 1983 *Code of Canon Law*, canon 377, §5. The exact words *societas perfecta* are used neither in the 1917 nor 1983 codes. The concept is indisputably operative, however. In the 1983 Code, canon 113, §1 asserts: "The Catholic Church and the Apostolic See have the status of a moral person by divine disposition." This means two things: (1) that the church is a bearer or rights and obligations beyond what might be ascribed by positive law; (2) that the church is something that transcends the individuals who comprise her. Canon 1254, §1 asserts: "The Catholic Church has an inherent right, independently of any secular power, to acquire, retain, administer and alienate

temporal goods, in pursuit of its proper objective." Canon 1311 also states: "The Church has its own inherent right to constrain with penal sanctions Christ's faithful who commit offenses."

52. Davies, *The Second Vatican Council and Religious Liberty*, 183.

53. Ibid., 184.

54. Murray, "The Issue of Church and State at Vatican II," 212.

55. Ibid.

56. Ibid., 209. Murray contended (p. 210) that the autonomy of the state is violated if the Church claims liberty on anything but secular grounds.

57. *CDD*, 1086.

58. Consider, too, Paul VI's homily at the last general session of the Council, the day before his message *Aux Gouvernants*. "The theocentric and theological concept of man and the universe, almost in defiance of the charge of anachronism and irrelevance, has been given a new prominence by the council, through claims which the world will at first judge to be foolish, but which, we hope, it will later come to recognize as being truly human, wise and salutary" (Paul VI, *Homily* [December 7, 1965]).

59. See, e.g., John Paul II, "Freedom Cannot Be Suppressed," address to the U.N. General Assembly (October 5, 1995), in 41 *Pope Speaks* 32, 36 (1996) (discussing the rights of nations as distinct from the state).

CHAPTER TEN: TECHNOLOGY AND THE DEMISE OF LIBERALISM

★ A version of this chapter was first published in *Christianity and Western Civilization: Christopher Dawson's Insights: Can a Culture Survive the Loss of Its Religious Roots, Proceedings of the Wethersfield Institute, 1993, vol. 7* (San Francisco: Ignatius Press, 1995), 73–95.

1. Christopher Dawson, *America and the Secularization of Modern Culture* (Houston: University of St. Thomas, 1960), 12.

2. Ibid., 21.

3. Ibid., 18–19.

4. Ibid., 25.

5. Pius IX, *Syllabus of Errors* (1854), §69.

6. John Stuart Mill, *On Liberty* (Indianapolis: Hackett Publishing Company, 1978), 61–62.

7. Ibid., 67.

8. Ibid., 69.

9. Adam Smith, *The Theory of Moral Sentiments*, vol. 6.

10. Christopher Dawson, *Enquiries into Religion and Culture* (New York: Sheed & Ward, 1933), 62.

11. Christopher Dawson, *Religion and the Rise of Western Culture* (New York: Doubleday, 1958), 21.

12. "It is obvious that there is a profound difference between the old dualism of the Christian way of life and unregenerate human nature, on the one hand, and the new dualism between the revolutionary ideas of liberalism . . .but there is a certain relation between the two, so that it is possible to maintain that the whole revolutionary tradition is a post-Christian phenomenon that transposes a pre-existent psycho-

logical pattern to a different sociological tradition." Christopher Dawson, *Understanding Europe* (New York: Sheed & Ward, 1952), 28.

13. Christopher Dawson, *The Dynamics of World History* (LaSalle, Ill.: Sherwood Sugden, 1978), 355.

14. Christopher Dawson, *The Judgement of the Nations* (New York: Sheed & Ward, 1942), 31–32.

15. Dawson, *America and the Secularization of Modern Culture*, 20.

16. Dawson, *The Judgement of the Nations*, 105.

17. Christopher Dawson, *Progress and Religion* (Peru, Ill.: Sherwood Sugden & Co., 1992), 207.

18. Dawson, *America and the Secularization of Modern Culture*, 17.

19. Dawson, *Progress and Religion*, 206.

20. Dawson, *The Judgement of the Nations*, 31–32.

21. Dawson, *Progress and Religion*, 97.

22. Dawson, *The Judgement of the Nations*, 113.

23. Dawson, *America and the Secularization of Modern Culture*, 10.

24. That is to say, *techne* is a substitute for *praxis*.

25. Cited in Michael Adas, *Machines as the Measure of Men* (Ithaca, N.Y.: Cornell University Press, 1989), 226.

26. "Liberal culture sought to avoid the danger of complete secularization by insisting on the preservation of a margin of individual freedom, which was immune from State control and to which, in theory at least, economic life was subordinated. And within the zone of individual freedom, religious freedom was the ultimate stronghold which defended the human personality. But the progress of mechanization and the social organization which it entails has steadily reduced this margin of freedom, until today in the totalitarian states, and only to a slightly less degree in the democratic ones, social control extends to the whole life and consciousness. And since this control is exercised in a utilitarian spirit for political, economic and military ends, the complete secularization of culture seems inevitable." Dawson, *The Judgement of the Nations*, 107.

27. Dawson, *The Judgement of the Nations*, 106.

28. Dawson, "The Patriarchal Family in History," *The Dynamics of World History*, 165.

29. Ibid., 159.

30. Edmund Burke, *Thoughts on the Present Discontents* (1770).

31. Dawson, "The Patriarchal Family in History," *The Dynamics of World History*, 163–64.

32. George Grant, *Technology and Justice* (Notre Dame: University of Notre Dame Press, 1986), 32.

33. Christopher Dawson, *Christianity and the New Age* (Manchester, N.H.: Sophia Institute Press, 1985), 3.

34. Dawson, *The Judgement of the Nations*, 10.

35. John Paul II, Encyclical Letter *Veritatis Splendor* (August 6, 1993), §88.

36. Grant, *Technology and Justice*, 32.

CHAPTER ELEVEN: REASONS FOR CIVIL SOCIETY

★ An earlier version of this chapter appeared in *Reassessing the Liberal State: Reading Maritain's* Man and the State, ed. Timothy Fuller and John P. Hittinger (Washington, D.C.: American Maritain Association and The Catholic University of America Press, 2001), 11–23.

1. Jacques Maritain, *Man and the State* (Chicago: The University of Chicago Press, 1951), 14; 16, n.11.

2. Ibid., 52. Maritain deploys the older papal criticism that the modern state rests upon a "fiction." "Since there is no such thing as the general popular will," von Ketteler argued, "one has to rely on a fiction." "The Labor Problem and Christianity" (1864), in *The Social Teachings of Wilhelm Emmanuel von Ketteler,* trans. Rupert J. Ederer (Lanham, Md.: University Press of America, 1981), 363. Von Ketteler's critique of the modern state as a "fiction" was adopted by Leo XIII twenty years later. "It is plain, moreover, that the pact which they allege is openly a falsehood and a fiction." *Diuturnum,* §§11–12.

3. Maritain, *Man and the State,* 53.

4. Ibid., 23.

5. Ibid., 95.

6. This is what John Courtney Murray quite accurately called the "juridical state." For this discussion, see Murray's essays: "The Problem of Religious Freedom," *Theological Studies* 25 (December 1964): 503–75; and "The Issue of Church and State at Vatican Council II," *Theological Studies* 27 (December 1966): 580–606.

7. "1944 Christmas Message of His Holiness Pope Pius XII: Addressed to the People of the Entire World on the Subject of Democracy and a Lasting Peace," §19. He says that the world would not have been "dragged into the vortex of a disastrous war" had there been "efficient guarantees in the people themselves" (§12).

8. *Gaudium et Spes,* §59.

9. Ibid., §74.

10. Pius XI inaugurated the Feast of Christ the King in the encyclical *Quas Primas,* issued on 11 December 1925. Participation in Christ's kingship is no longer exemplified in the temporal king.

11. "The Labor Problem and Christianity," in *The Social Teachings of Wilhelm Emmanuel von Ketteler,* 408–9. The next sentence reads: "Whatever future it may have, therefore, the cooperative idea belongs to Christendom."

12. Ernest Gellner, *Conditions of Liberty: Civil Society and Its Rivals* (New York: The Penguin Press, 1994), 32.

13. Ibid., 5.

14. Montesquieu, *The Spirit of the Laws,* trans. Anne M. Cohler, Basia Carolyn Miller, and Harold Samuel Stone (Cambridge: Cambridge University Press, 1989), 11.4.

15. "The morals and intelligence of a democratic people would be in as much danger as its commerce and industry if ever a government wholly usurped the place of private associations. Feelings and ideas are renewed, the heart enlarged, and the understanding developed only by the reciprocal action of men one upon another" (Alexis de Tocqueville, *Democracy in America,* trans. George Lawrence [Garden City, N.Y.: Doubleday & Co., 1969], II.2.5).

16. Gellner, *Conditions of Liberty*, 212.

17. John R. Lott, *More Guns, Less Crime* (Chicago: The University of Chicago Press, 1998).

18. Nancy L. Rosenblum, *Membership and Morals: The Personal Uses of Pluralism in America* (Princeton, N.J.: Princeton University Press, 1998).

19. Thomas Aquinas, *Contra impugnantes Dei cultum et religionem* (Rome: Marietti, 1954) *Opuscula Theol.*, vol. 2, 5–110; *An Apology for the Religious Orders*, trans. J. Proctor (Westminster, Md.: Newman, 1950). See discussion by James A. Weisheipl, *Friar Thomas D'Aquino: His Life, Thought, and Works* (Garden City, N.Y.: Doubleday, 1974), 88–91, 383–84.

20. *Contra impugnantes*, II.7.

21. Ibid., I.3.

22. Ibid., I.5.

23. Ibid., I.3.

24. Ibid., I.4.

25. Ibid.

26. Ibid., I.7.

27. See Leo XIII, "On the Rights and Duties of Capital and Labor," in *The Church Speaks to the Modern World: The Social Teachings of Leo XIII*, ed. Étienne Gilson (Garden City, N.Y.: Image, 1954), 200–44.

28. Ernest I. Fortin. "'Sacred and Inviolable': *Rerum Novarum* and Natural Rights," *Theological Studies* 53 (1992): 202–33.

29. John Paul II, *Centesimus Annus* (1991), §49.

30. Ibid., §41.

31. Isaiah Berlin, "John Stuart Mill and the Ends of Life," in *Four Essays on Liberty* (Oxford: Oxford University Press, 1969), 173–206.

32. "In this way what we nowadays call the principle of solidarity, the validity of which both in the internal order of each nation and in the international order I have discussed in the encyclical *Sollicitudo Rei Socialis*, is clearly seen to be one of the fundamental principles of the Christian view of social and political organization. This principle is frequently stated by Pope Leo XIII, who uses the term 'friendship,' a concept already found in Greek philosophy. Pope Pius XI refers to it with the equally meaningful term 'social charity.' Pope Paul VI, expanding the concept to cover the many modern aspects of the social question, speaks of a 'civilization of love.'" (*Centesimus Annus*, §10)

33. John Paul II, *On Social Concerns (Sollicitudo Rei Socialis)* (Washington, D.C.: United States Catholic Conference, 1987), §38.

34. John Paul II, *The Gospel of Life (Evangelium Vitae)* (New York: Times Book/Random House, 1995), §8.

35. John XXIII, *Peace on Earth (Pacem in Terris)* (Boston: Daughters of St. Paul, 1963), §7.

36. *Gaudium et Spes*, §4.

37. Thomas Aquinas argued that the ontological perfection of being human is common according to what reason understands (*secundum rationem*), or common by predication (*commune in praedicando*). The same can be said for health, temperance, and knowledge, which are in individuals, but "take on a universal character in the intellect." Useful goods are not necessarily public, indeed such things as food and money are

usually the things privately exchanged in commutative justice. They can be made common, however, to ensure their distribution to the welfare of the community. If "common" is exhausted by the aforesaid notions, we face the problem of a conflict between the good of the individual and the public good. This is why St. Thomas argues that the common good immediately relevant to social order is not the good common by community of genus or species, but rather the good "common by the community of final cause" (*non quidem communitate generis vel specici, sed communitate causae finalis*), (*Summa Theologiae* I-II, 90.2).

38. *Centesimus Annus*, §43.
39. Ibid., §46.
40. Ibid., §13. See also *Sollicitudo Rei Socialis*, §15.
41. *Sollicitudo Rei Socialis*, §40.
42. *Reynolds v United States* (1878) 98 U.S. 145 (1878), 165*f*.
43. *Sollicitudo Rei Socialis*, §31.
44. Tocqueville, *Democracy in America*, II.4.2.
45. Gellner (p. 88) makes this point very crisply: "political pluralism in terms of independent or autonomous coercive units is out. Local units simply lack adequate weight. Liberty, on the other hand, is impossible without pluralism, without a balance of power. As it cannot be political, it must be economic."
46. Gellner, *Conditions of Liberty*, 100.
47. Pierre Manent, "The Contest for Command," *New French Thought*, ed. Mark Lilla (Princeton, N.J.: Princeton University Press, 1994), 185.

Index